DATE DUE

Seven Famous Trials in History

Seven Famous Trials in History

BY ROBIN McKOWN

illustrations by William Sharp

THE VANGUARD PRESS, INC., NEW YORK

Fourth Printing

In Memory of

WILLIAM SHARP

Other Books by Robin McKown

Fiction:

JANINE
THE ORDEAL OF ANNE DEVLIN
PUBLICITY GIRL
FOREIGN SERVICE GIRL
AUTHOR'S AGENT

Non-Fiction:

MARIE CURIE
SHE LIVED FOR SCIENCE, Irène Joliot-Curie
GIANT OF THE ATOM, Ernest Rutherford
THE FABULOUS ISOTOPES
WASHINGTON'S AMERICA
THOMAS PAINE
BENJAMIN FRANKLIN
ROOSEVELT'S AMERICA
PAINTER OF THE WILD WEST, Frederic Remington
PIONEERS IN MENTAL HEALTH

ACKNOWLEDGMENTS

The minutes of actual court proceedings are followed in all the trials herein, with the exception of that of Socrates, where no official recording clerk was present. In this case we have depended on the account given by Plato in his *Dialogues*, as translated by Benjamin Jowett, which, if not literally exact, has the figurative and spiritual truth of all great literature.

The excerpts from Joan of Arc's testimony are from the translations of Sven Stolpe and W. S. Scott, and the recantation of Galileo is quoted from the Giorgio de Santillana translation.

I should like to express my appreciation to Helen Landreth, for permission to use the version of Robert Emmet's last speech that appears in her biography of Emmet, and to Matthew Josephson for his permission to quote his translation from the French of Emile Zola's *J'Accuse.*

My gratitude also to Abraham L. Pomerantz, chief deputy counsel at Nuremberg in the Trial of Nazi Industrialists, who generously supplied me with material and gave me firsthand impressions of the Nuremberg trial. My thanks too to Captain Robert Granville Burke and to Clyde B. Clason for advice on matters of law and of Galileo's science.

R McK

FOREWORD

It is the essence of justice that no man may be condemned without a chance to defend himself. In legal terminology, the *defendant* is the person on trial. Since ancient times, laws have granted to the defendant the right to speak for himself, or to permit others to speak for him. In the seven trials of this book the judges all recognized this fundamental principle of justice.

The defendants in six of these trials—a philosopher, a saint, a scientist, a printer, a revolutionist, and a soldier —were all of uncommon courage and high moral character. That five of them were found guilty is not an indictment of legal procedure. They were the victims of superstition, ignorance, prejudice, and tyranny. Yet because they were granted a public hearing by the due process of law, history is enabled to reappraise the verdicts.

In the seventh trial, not one but twenty-one defendants were tried. These twenty-one did not consider themselves criminals but important personages in a powerful state that had suffered the reverses of war. Many of their fellow citizens, and others, had been persuaded to agree with them. Without the Nuremberg trial, there might have lurked some latent suspicion that the political creed known as Nazism had some justification in being. The trial, with its mighty weight of evidence, produced incontestable proof of dastardly crimes against people and against nations.

These seven trials are set in Greece, France, Italy, Ireland, America, and Germany. They range in time from four centuries before the birth of Christ to post World War II. They show legal procedures in different epochs and different countries.

If there is one truth to be learned from them, it is that laws are as just as the society that makes them and the men who enforce them.

CONTENTS

Seven Famous Trials in History

SOCRATES

"You are charged, Socrates, son of Sophroniscus, with not worshiping the gods whom the State worships. You are further charged with corrupting the young. The death penalty has been demanded by your accusers."

These words were spoken by the archon at the trial of the philosopher Socrates held in ancient Athens in the year 399 B.C. The archon was responsible for seeing that the trial was conducted according to the laws of Athens. He was not a judge. The jurors would be the judges. There were five hundred of them, chosen by lot. They alone would decide whether the defendant was guilty of the crimes with which he was charged.

It was early in the morning. Socrates would have that day, and that day only, to offer his defense. Before nightfall the jury would give its verdict.

Who would miss such a drama? It promised more excitement than the Olympian games, than the great

plays of Aeschylus and Euripides. Practically all Athens was there, everyone except women and slaves, who were not admitted to public trials. The spectators sat along stone benches or stood leaning against the marble columns of the open court, some sympathetic, some hostile, some merely curious.

On a small stool at one side of the raised platform was the defendant. He was a bearded old man with a pug nose, bulging brow, and round, bright, quizzical eyes. He wore a patched and ragged tunic, and he was barefoot. His expression was tranquil. Slowly he rose and walked to the center of the platform in a curious waddling gait that endeared him to his friends and gave his enemies another reason to mock him. As he faced his audience, he leaned forward slightly, balancing on the balls of his feet.

At the far end of the platform stood the three men who had brought the indictment against him. They looked worried, and with good reason. If less than one-fifth of the jury voted to dismiss the charges, they would receive either a lashing or a fine of a thousand drachmas, the penalty for making false charges.

Close by the platform were gathered a small group of Socrates' friends and disciples. (Among them was a youth named Plato, who would serve as court reporter, writing down what was said as best he could remember, certainly with some literary embellishments not permitted in a later age.) Their faces were anxious and troubled. They loved Socrates and feared for him. He cast them a reassuring glance—as though he wanted to tell them how unimportant it was whether he lived or died; as though he must make them understand that the way he had lived, the way he accepted death, were all that mattered.

"O men of Athens," he began, addressing himself not only to the jury but to everyone present. "O men of Athens, I cannot tell how you have been affected by my accusers, but I know they almost made me forget who I was—so persuasively did they speak. . . ."

He had begun by giving a compliment to his opponents, which was typical of him. It was typical of him as well to destroy at once the effect of that compliment. He continued with a guileless air: ". . . And yet they have hardly uttered a word of truth. . . ."

The spectators must have gasped with delight. They had come to be entertained and they were not going to be disappointed. The old man who, for more years than most of them had lived, had been heaping scorn on the smug and hypocritical, was not beaten yet. A hush fell over the assembly.

In Athens the name of Socrates was familiar to all. There was hardly a citizen who did not know who he was, what he did, and the legends that had grown around him. The modern reader, to understand the meaning and reason of his trial, has need of this same intimate acquaintance with the man and the times in which he lived. The difficulty is that he left no written works, either memoirs or philosophy. Much of what we know comes from Plato, though Plato in his writings often used the character of Socrates to express his own ideas. The historian Xenophon, also a disciple of Socrates, left an idealized portrait of him in his *Memorabilia*. Other contemporary accounts are inconsistent and often contradictory. There are periods of his life about which nothing is known. Yet in spite of the fragmentary quality of the information concerning him, Socrates emerges as one of history's unique personalities.

He was born just outside Athens in 469 B.C. His mother was a midwife. Sophroniscus, his father, was a stonecutter and minor sculptor, and as such was considered little better than a slave. Even such superb sculptors as Phidias and Polyclitus were regarded slightingly, since they worked with their hands instead of with their brains.

There is no description of the house in which the boy spent his childhood. Probably it was like other lower-class Athenian homes—a small, two-story dwelling of stucco or sun-baked brick; the side facing the street a blank wall except for a narrow door; the rooms built around a central courtyard where the family lived and worked. It would have been furnished simply—a few chairs, chests, tables, beds, reed mats for floor covering, and a brazier to supply heat during the cold months.

Children's games in those days were not too different from those of today. The boy Socrates would have fought battles with clay soldiers, rolled hoops, flown kites, and played on seesaws and swings. He may have shot marbles with dried beans or small smooth stones. Since public schools were unknown, he probably attended the classes of a private schoolmaster, where the children sat on benches and held on their knees a roll of parchment from which they read or on which they wrote.

All sons of free citizens received intensive athletic training. Teen-agers were taught to run, leap, wrestle, hunt, throw a javelin, and sometimes to drive a chariot.

At eighteen the boys were officially enrolled in Athens' soldier youth, where they lived and ate together and practiced a form of self-government modeled after the democracy of Athens. In addition to strenuous drilling, they attended lectures on literature, music, geometry, and rhetoric. At nineteen they were sent to guard the frontier. At twenty-one they were freed of parental authority and made full citizens.

From childhood Socrates must have witnessed the elaborate religious festivals that were part of the daily life of the ancient Greeks. Their gods were many. The mighty Zeus (whom the Romans would call Jupiter); his tempestuous wife Hera (Juno); the warlike Ares (Mars); beautiful Aphrodite (Venus); Poseidon (Neptune), god of the sea; Hermes (Mercury), messenger of the gods; Demeter (Ceres), goddess of fertility and of the harvest; the little lame Hephaestus (Vulcan); the noble Apollo; the martial Athena (Minerva), for whom Athens had been named—these and others were believed to control the destinies of mortal man.

The gods were endowed with human faults and failings and to the contemporaries of Socrates they were very real indeed. Temples and statues were erected in their honor. Their favor was sought or their wrath appeased by prayer, processions, symbolic tableaux, chants, and gifts. In earlier times, human sacrifices to the gods had been frequent, but this practice was dying out.

By Socrates' time there existed also a concept of a supreme and benevolent deity, strangely akin to the Christian God, Plato, for example, in his *Republic*, written after the death of Socrates, criticizes the poets who called the Trojan War and other warlike actions of men "the works of God." "Let this then be one of our rules and principles concerning the gods," he wrote, "to which our poets and reciters will be expected to conform—that God is not the author of all things, but of good only."

For the most part, Greek religion was a matter of ceremony and ritual, having little connection with moral behavior or spiritual improvement. Any man might act or believe as he chose, provided he did not commit the unforgivable sin of "blaspheming the gods."

Athens in this period was a stimulating place for those with intellectual curiosity. Athenians loved to talk, and they talked about anything and everything wherever two or more of them came together. Since heavy labor was done by slaves, free citizens had plenty of leisure in which to develop philosophical ideas. No man was required to produce experimental proof of a scientific theory. If he was eloquent enough to make his theory sound plausible, he was sure of a following. Athens did not give birth to all the varied schools of thought that arose in this astounding age, but they were all discussed there.

Although Socrates mastered his father's trade, he found the pursuit of knowledge far more enticing than the cutting of stone or the making of lifeless statues. "When I was young," Plato quotes him in the *Phaedo*, "I had a prodigious desire to know that department of philosophy which is called the investigation of nature; to know the causes of things and why a thing is and is created or destroyed . . . and I rejoiced to think that I had found in Anaxagoras a teacher of the causes of existence. . . ."

Anaxagoras, Socrates' first teacher, was concerned

with "the investigation of sun, moon, and heavens." He taught that the universe was originally a chaos of various kinds of seeds pervaded by a Mind. The Mind set these seeds to gyrating in a whirlpool, or *vortex*, guiding them to develop organic forms and to divide into the four elements: fire, air, water, and earth. Nobody disputed this imaginative concept—indeed, there was no way of disproving it—but strong objections were raised when Anaxagoras, making a remarkable guess, stated that the sun was "a mass of stone on fire . . . larger than the Peloponnesian Peninsula."

The sun, so the Greeks believed, was the god Helios. It was blasphemy to call it "a mass of stone on fire." The Athenian Assembly accused Anaxagoras of heresy and condemned him to death. By fleeing Athens, he escaped execution of the sentence.

After the abrupt departure of Anaxagoras, Socrates studied with Archelaus, who was responsible for an early version of the theory of evolution: "As regards living creatures, when the earth grew warm, at first in its lower portion, wherever the warm and cold mingled, man appeared and many other living creatures, all having the same mode of life, nurtured as they were from slime. . . ."

In later years Archelaus changed from a physicist to a student of ethics. He may have influenced Socrates to a similar transfer of interests.

Another who had a role in the early education of Socrates was Protagoras, who called him the ablest man of his years that he ever met. Protagoras was a Sophist, which originally meant a teacher of wisdom. He taught that there were no absolute truths, but only such truths as hold for given men under given conditions. Of the gods, he rashly said, "I know not whether they exist or not, or what they are like. Many things prevent our knowing: the subject is obscure and brief is the span of our mortal life." To the Athenian Assembly this was blasphemy; they banished Protagoras and burned his books.

Socrates may have known Gorgias, another Sophist, who carried the skepticism of Protagoras further, seeking to prove, first, that nothing exists; second, that if anything does exist it would be unknowable; third, that if anything were knowable, the knowledge of it could not be communicated from one person to another. The Sophists gradually became known for this type of subtly deceptive reasoning.

The Sophists of Socrates' time wandered from town to town, giving lectures in rhetoric and logic and other subjects. Their fees were often high. Gorgias and Protagoras charged pupils as much as 10,000 drachmas for their education. One reason Socrates deserted the Sophist school of thought was that he believed knowledge should be given freely, not sold.

Another contemporary philosopher was Parmenides, who contended that all things are one and never change. "One thing are Thinking and Being . . . Beginning and end, birth and death . . . are of forms only." The one reality "never begins and never ends." Plato, in the *Parmenides*, shows young Socrates, puzzled, trying to understand what Parmenides means by his "the one" and "the many."

Parmenides had a disciple, Zeno of Elea, who became celebrated for his paradoxes. One of these stated that "swift-footed Achilles" can never pass the slow-moving tortoise—since as often as Achilles reaches the tortoise, the tortoise has moved beyond that point! Socrates was nineteen when Zeno came to Athens to confuse citizens with such conundrums.

How much was the mind of Socrates formed by the theoretical scientists Anaxagoras and Archelaus, by the Sophists Protagoras and Gorgias, and by Parmenides and Zeno of Elea? No one can say exactly. It is fairly certain that he explored all existing philosophies before his own ideas crystallized.

Somewhere in his late twenties or early thirties, he stopped being a student and began to gather his own group of disciples. In the beginning they were artisans and craftsmen, young men as poor as he. At least one, according to Diogenes, was a cobbler, who took notes on his leather stock. Socrates may at first have discussed astronomy and other matters of science with these young men, but he soon abandoned all else to examine the qualities of the human mind. "He discoursed," wrote Xenophon, "always of human affairs."

What is justice and what is injustice? What is absolute good, or truth, or beauty? What is piety and impiety? What is courage, and is it not true that courageous men face death because they are afraid of yet greater evils? And, that being the case, what a strange thing that a man should be courageous through fear!

The Socratic method was not to give speeches but to ask questions. It was his habit to rise early and set out for the marketplace or the Lyceum or the gymnasium or the workshops—wherever men gathered together. Innocently, he would start the conversation with a question, of which these lines from Plato's *Phaedo* are typical:

"Is it not true that anything that becomes greater must become greater after being less?"

"True."

"And that which becomes less must have been once greater and then have become less?"

"Yes."

"And the weaker is generated from the stronger, and the swifter from the slower?"

"Very true."

"And the worse is from the better, and the more just is from the more unjust?"

"Of course."

Socrates believed that only through such questioning could one find truth. Knowledge to him was the highest virtue, whereas evil grew from ignorance. Without proper knowledge right action was impossible. The highest good was happiness; the highest means to happiness was knowledge or intelligence.

His young disciples were convinced that Socrates was the wisest man in the world, and one of them, a youth named Chaerephon, decided he would prove that he was. Chaerephon made a pilgrimage to the Temple of Delphi, high on the barren slopes of Mount Parnassus, to consult the priestesses of the oracle. The gleaming marble temple had been built in honor of the god Apollo. Anyone with a perplexing question could address the oracle, and it was said that Apollo himself, speaking through the priestesses, would give the correct answer.

"Is anyone wiser than Socrates of Athens?" Chaerephon asked the oracle.

Sometimes the replies of the oracle were confusing and difficult to interpret, but not in this case. "No one is wiser," the oracle informed Chaerephon.

Chaerephon hurried back to Athens to report what he had learned. Inevitably the story was repeated to Socrates. Though Socrates would not dispute the oracle, he took the verdict humbly. His only claim to wisdom, he said, was that he admitted he knew nothing. Whereas others pretended they knew everything.

It was possibly the decision of the oracle that brought Socrates his first enemies. Certain pompous citizens, who believed themselves much cleverer and better informed than the son of the stonecutter Sophroniscus, were highly indignant that Socrates' protestation of ignorance should be considered wisdom. They began to watch him carefully, hoping to get something against him, some "dangerous" statement uttered by him that could be used to discredit him. Eventually they found what they wanted.

Socrates loved Athens and would not have felt at home anywhere else, but he lamented the bitterness of political factions. What the city needed, he once said, was government by "knowledge and ability." It was not difficult to construe this remark as an attack on democracy. Thus the rumor was started that Socrates favored an oligarchy, a form of government in which power is in the hands of the few.

Although Socrates faithfully observed the city's religious ceremonies, he was reported as saying: "Of the gods we know nothing." Why, he was as bad as Protagoras! Those whom he had offended began to whisper that Socrates lacked respect for the gods.

His enemies also claimed that he tore down but never built, that in many cases his clarification of an idea made it more obscure than it had been before. Someone accused him of being unwilling to state an opinion himself. To which he answered calmly that the reproach was just. He was a midwife, as his mother had been. Only he helped give birth to ideas instead of babies.

Sometime in his young manhood—the date is not known—he married Xanthippe, a woman of his own class. Xanthippe has become a symbol of a nagging wife. She scolded him incessantly—for not providing for his family, for not dressing himself properly, for spending all his time in interminable philosophical arguments. Socrates loyally defended her to his friends, saying she was perfectly right. Many years later he had another wife named Myrto, a woman of a noble family. History does not say whether she was more patient with him than Xanthippe had been.

The years between 445 and 431 B.C. (the twenty-fourth to the thirty-eighth years of Socrates' life) were a splendid period for Athens. This was "the Golden Age of Pericles," which the poet Shelley called "the most memorable in the history of the world." The city-state of Athens was at peace after a long and intermittent war with the Persians. An uneasy truce had been signed with their ancient enemies, the Spartans, citizens of a city-state like Athens on the Peloponnesian peninsula. Pericles, at once general, statesman, and partron of culture and the arts, was in power.

Pericles revered Athens with a single-minded devotion and set out to make it the most beautiful city of the ancient world. A wealthy aristocrat himself, he "invited" other rich citizens to fit out ships and to subsidize games, musical contests, and plays. He also exacted tribute from less powerful Greek city-states that, with Athens, formed the Delian Confederacy, using the money collected to beautify his city.

During this time the Parthenon, a temple to Athena, was erected on the fortified hill known as the Acropolis. The Parthenon was a rectangular building with Doric columns, of a beauty and simplicity of design that has never been surpassed. The sculptor Phidias and his pupils carved the incredibly lovely ivory and gold statue of Athena and the hundreds of lifelike figures that adorned the building.

Other temples were built on the Acropolis, and it is said that Socrates worked on some of them, perhaps with his father. He is personally credited with a statue of Hermes and the three Graces for one temple. If this is so, it was before he became a full-time philosopher.

As his reputation spread, many rich and well-born young men joined the ranks of his disciples. Most prominent of them was a brilliant, spoiled, willful, and exceedingly handsome youth named Alcibiades. He and Socrates differed widely in appearance, background, and character. For Socrates, the ugliest of men, fame and wealth were meaningless. He wore the same ragged tunic throughout the years and went barefoot oftener than he wore sandals or shoes. "How many things there are that I do not want!" he once exclaimed, on seeing the clutter of merchandise on sale in the market. "You seem to think that happiness consists in luxury and extravagance," he reproached one of his pupils, "but I think that to want nothing is to resemble the gods, and that to want as little as possible is to make the nearest approach to the gods."

As for young Alcibiades, he craved all the worldly pleasures life had to offer. His wild escapades and his drunken revels with the lowest of companions were the scandal of Athens. Yet in spite of his frivolity he adored Socrates more than he did any other human being. "He is the only person who ever made me ashamed," he once admitted.

The peace of Athens had lasted fourteen years when, in 432 B.C., Potidaea, a tiny peninsula in northern Greece, declared its independence of Athenian power. Socrates was called back into military service and stationed there with the army Pericles sent to suppress the uprising. There was a cruel frost that winter. Most of the soldiers bundled themselves up in warm garments and swathed their feet in felt and fleece. Socrates wore his ordinary tunic and went barefoot, even on ice. He had kept healthy by wrestling and other sports and, according to his comrades, knew neither fatigue nor hunger.

Alcibiades was an officer in the same division in which Socrates served as a private. In one skirmish Alcibiades was severely wounded. Socrates risked his life to carry him to safety. Their general wanted to give Socrates a prize for valor, but he insisted it be given to Alcibiades.

The year after the Potidaea campaign began, the Spartans declared war on Athens. Sparta was a formidable opponent. The military training of Athenian youths was soft compared to that of young Spartans. Spartan boys were taken from their families at the age of seven and brought up by the state. They were taught to endure pain without flinching; once a year the bravest boys were beaten until their blood stained the stones on which they stood. Winter and summer they slept in the open on beds of rushes, and until they were thirty they lived with their companions of the barracks. They were unschooled in art and culture and the free exchange of ideas, but they were excellent soldiers.

The Spartans, joined by certain city-states that resented paying tribute to Pericles, laid siege to Attica, the province in which Athens was situated. Pericles, foreseeing the siege would be long, called the farmers of

Attica within the walls of Athens. A plague broke out
in the crowded city; in the three years it lasted it killed
a fourth of the soldiers and unnumbered civilians. In
their misery the Athenians denounced Pericles as the
cause of both the war and the plague and he was de-
posed from office. Though he was soon forgiven and recalled to power, it was too late. He was ill of the plague
himself and died in 429 B.C. With him ended Athens'
"Golden Age."

There is no record of how Socrates spent the years of
the plague, but in 424 B.C. when the war had been under-
way six years, he was fighting at Delium. Alcibiades,
who had become a general and a brilliant military strate-
gist, was again in the same campaign. Plato, in his *Symposium*, quotes a vivid account by Alcibiades of Socrates the soldier during the retreat after the battle of
Delium:

"He and Laches [a companion] were retreating, for
the troops were in flight, and I met them and told them
not to be discouraged, and promised to remain with
them . . . you might see him [Socrates] . . . just as
he is in the streets of Athens, stalking like a pelican, and
rolling his eyes, calmly contemplating enemies as well
as friends, and making very intelligible to anybody, even
from a distance, that whoever attacked him would be
likely to meet with a stout resistance; and in this way he
and his companion escaped—for this is the sort of man
who is never touched in war; those only are pursued
who are running away headlong. I particularly observed
how superior he was to Laches in presence of
mind. . . ."

The year after the battle of Delium, Socrates was
home again, attending the opening of a new play by the

popular comic dramatist, Aristophanes. It was called
The Clouds, and Socrates was lampooned in it.

The setting of *The Clouds* was the "Thinking Shop,"
a school where one could learn to prove anything, even
if it was false. Aristophanes obviously had the Sophists
in mind, though Socrates had long since deserted sophis-
try.

In the play, an old man named Strepsiades bangs on
the gate of the Thinking Shop, crying, "Take me to
Socrates." He wants to learn how to prove that he
need not pay his debts. A student appears and tells him:

> *"The master is busy.*
> *He is asking Chaerephon*
> *How many times its length a flea can jump."*

(This must have delighted members of the audience
who had been trapped by Socrates' endless questions.)

Inside the Thinking Shop, Strepsiades finds the stage
Socrates seated in a basket suspended in mid-air. His
pupils are beneath him, staring downward. The guide
explains that they are studying what is below the
ground, while their backs are studying astronomy.

Strepsiades approaches Socrates, pleading:

> *"Teach me one of your lessons in haste—*
> *The way by which one never pays . . .*
> *You shall have the proper fee:*
> *Ye gods bear witness that I speak the truth."*

"By what gods do you swear?" demands the stage
Socrates. "The gods are not a current coin with us." (It
is true, then, some of the audience may have whispered,
that Socrates does not worship the gods whom the State

worships.) Socrates then announces that the clouds are the real gods. They make the rain. "For have you ever seen rain without clouds?" The clouds are responsible for thunder, too. "When they are full of water and are driven along, they fall heavily upon one another, and burst with a clap." It is not Zeus who drives them, as everyone thinks, but Vortex. (Vortex was the "Mind" that Anaxagoras invented in the least scientific part of his theory; there is no evidence that Socrates ever believed in it.)

Strepsiades next persuades his good-for-nothing son, Phidippides, to attend the Thinking Shop. (Since Phidippides speaks with a lisp, the audience quickly guesses that he is supposed to be Socrates' pupil Alcibiades, who also lisps.) In the shop, Phidippides meets Just Argument, who pompously advises him to imitate the just and the virtuous, and Unjust Argument, who wants to know what good men have ever gained by justice or virtue. Are there not among the leaders ten dishonest men to one honest man? Do not the gods themselves lie, steal, murder, commit other sins?

Phidippides is easily swayed by Unjust Argument, and immediately begins to beat his father. Strepsiades begs him for mercy in the name of Zeus, but Phidippides, continuing his beating, informs him that Zeus no longer exists, having been replaced by Vortex. (It is thus that youth is corrupted, the spectators may have murmured, and it is certainly Socrates who does the corrupting.)

In the last scene the enraged father runs out into the streets, calling upon all good citizens to destroy this new philosophy. Thereupon the people burn down the Thinking Shop, leaving the stage Socrates to perish in the flames.

It is said that no one laughed more heartily at the first performance of Aristophanes' *The Clouds* than Socrates himself, and that when the play was over he stood up, so that all present could compare him with his stage double. Xanthippe, who reportedly was at his side, was probably not amused at all; no woman likes to see her husband made a laughingstock. It is even possible that she realized this caricature might one day cause Socrates serious harm.

The next year Socrates resumed military service, this time fighting at Amphipolis. At forty-seven he still displayed remarkable endurance and fortitude. So far as is known, this was his last campaign. When it was over, he could return to Athens to resume his role of making people think for themselves, of instilling in them to the best of his ability the love of good, of knowledge, and of all the higher virtues that are man's heritage.

He was at the height of his fame now. The most important persons in Athens sought his company. In 416 B.C., he attended a banquet given by the poet Agathon, who was celebrating the winning of a prize for a tragic drama. We know of this banquet from Plato's account of it in the *Symposium*. Plato was only thirteen at the time and was not present, but he reconstructed it from the reminiscences of one of the guests.

The guests reclining around the banquet table were the intellectual elite of Athens, among them Aristophanes, against whom Socrates bore no grudge. After dining they sent away the hired flute girl in order to devote themselves to conversation. The subject was love. Socrates, when his turn came to speak, described love as something that was in itself poor and needy but that raised man from earthly passions to a vision of the absolute beauty of God. Typically, he took no credit for his ideas, attributing them to a mysterious woman of great wisdom.

The discussion was interrupted by the arrival of Alcibiades, drunk and crowned with ribbons and violets. Ignoring the other guests, he burst into ecstatic praise of Socrates:

"When we hear any other speaker, even a very good one, he produces absolutely no effect upon us, or not much, whereas the mere fragments of . . . your words, Socrates, even at second hand, and however imperfectly repeated, amaze and possess the souls of every man, woman, and child who comes within hearing of them."

In this vein he continued to extol the greatness of Socrates until some uninvited merrymakers dragged him away with them. One by one the guests departed. When the crowing of the cock marked the dawn, only three were left: Agathon, the host; Aristophanes, and Socrates. Socrates talked on, wisely and profoundly, until his two exhausted companions were asleep. Then he covered them up gently and departed to the Lyceum for his bath, from there going to the marketplace to find new listeners for the rest of the day.

At the time of this banquet, Alcibiades, because of his military victories, was the idol of Athens. The Athenian Assembly appointed him commander of a fleet with which Alcibiades planned to attack and conquer Syracuse, in Sicily, thus cutting off Sparta's imports from this city and giving Athens a new source of grain, manpower, and tribute. It was an ambitious project but he was not permitted to carry it out. Just before the fleet was to sail, the Athenians discovered that during the night certain statues of the god Hermes had been mutilated. It was rumored that Alcibiades and his drunken friends were responsible, though Alcibiades denied the charge and there was no proof. His fleet was already at sea when another charge was brought against him: that he had mocked the sacred religious rites known as the Eleusinian mysteries. A fast ship was sent to bring him back to Athens for trial. Alcibiades escaped to a nearby island, but was tried *in absentia* and condemned to death. Indignant at such treatment, he turned traitor, serving first the Spartans and later the Persians.

He was forgiven and invited home three years later and in an effort to redeem himself led the Athenians in a series of naval victories, but again he found himself in trouble. He had taken off for Athens, to enjoy the fruits of his successes, leaving his fleet in charge of an incompetent commander who promptly lost it to the Spartans. Alcibiades, blamed for the loss and censured by the Athenian Assembly, fled to take refuge in Bithynia (in present-day Turkey).

Even after this, he attempted to help his countrymen, coming down out of the hills at the risk of his life to warn an Athenian commander that his fleet was in danger. The commander disregarded his warning and the next day all but eight of the 208 Athenian ships of the fleet were sunk by the Spartans.

Alcibiades continued to get into scrapes, even with those who gave him refuge. He was assassinated by the Spartans at the age of forty-six.

Alcibiades was the most spectacular of Socrates' pupils. His good qualities were eclipsed by the fact that he had turned traitor, however sporadically, and those who did not like Socrates held him up as the prime example of the philosopher's "corruption of youth."

The war with the Spartans had proved costly and the coffers of Athens were empty. In desperation the citizens voted to melt down the gold and silver from their statues to raise money for a new and powerful fleet. Slaves were offered their freedom and aliens were promised citizenship if they would join the crews. This armada demolished the Spartan fleet in 406 B.C., losing only twenty-five ships in battle. But there was no victory celebration.

The crews of the twenty-five lost ships had perished in a storm without proper burial, which, according to the belief of the time, meant that the souls of the dead would wander forever around the universe, blaming Athens for their fate. Hastily, the Athenian Assembly held a trial to judge the eight generals in charge of the expedition. Socrates attended as a senator, the only public office he ever held. When a motion was made to execute the generals, on the grounds that this would appease the souls of those who had drowned, Socrates protested the action as illegal. He stood alone. The others threatened to impeach or arrest him for not agreeing with them.

"I would rather run the risk, having law and justice with me," said Socrates, "than take part in your injustice from fear of imprisonment and death."

The motion was passed, even without Socrates' vote, and the eight generals were promptly put to death. Socrates was not punished. The fickle Assembly soon decided they had made a mistake—and imposed the death penalty on the orators who had "bewitched" them into killing their generals.

One by one the cities on the Aegean coast had fallen to the Spartans. Lysander, the ruler of the Spartans, ordered a siege of Athens. The Athenians held out bravely, but in three months their food was gone and their streets were full of the dead and dying. In 404 B.C., after a war of twenty-seven years, Athens surrendered.

The surrender terms were considered lenient, for although Lysander ordered the walls around Athens leveled and demanded the support of Athens in future wars, he did not destroy the city nor make slaves of its citizens. A Council of Thirty was set up to establish an oligarchy in this city that had been so proudly democratic. This Council of Thirty quickly became unpopular with rich and poor alike. It seized the property of wealthy merchants, plundered the temples, exiled some five thousand prominent democrats, and condemned fifteen hundred others to death. It put an end to freedom of assembly, of teaching, and of speech.

Socrates was not at first affected by these rulings, apparently because Critias, one of the leaders of the Council of Thirty, had once briefly been among his disciples. Critias had heard Socrates criticize certain weaknesses of Athenian democracy and mistakenly believed he could count on him to support the oligarchy. But when the council ordered five citizens, including Socrates, to arrest the democrat Leon of Salamis, Socrates, unlike the other four, went quietly home to bed, ignoring the order. In reprisal, Critias forbade him ever again to teach or speak in public places.

This punishment, which must have been as cruel as a flogging to one as garrulous as Socrates, did not last long. The Council of Thirty had been in power hardly a year when it was overthrown by the democrats. Critias was killed, along with his general, Charmides, also a former pupil of Socrates. Democracy was restored to Athens in 403 B.C. The new government set out to bring prosperity back to their city and to right the wrongs of the oligarchy. But Socrates, because of his doubtful relationship to Critias, was not fully restored to favor. Toward this old man who had never taken an active part in politics, the restored democracy of Athens, so generous to most of its enemies, would commit a monstrous act.

It so happened that one of the democratic leaders, Antyus, held a bitter grudge against Socrates. While Antyus had been in exile, his son had stayed in Athens, supposedly to study under the philosopher but actually to spend his days in drinking and reckless living. Antyus, a reasonable man in other respects, convinced himself that Socrates alone was responsible for his son's turning into a drunkard and became obsessed with the desire to have him punished.

He enlisted the support of a mediocre poet named Meletus and an orator named Lycon. Meletus was a man of little intelligence and great conceit who had on occasion been exposed to Socrates' wit and who thirsted for revenge. Lycon was a *rhētōr*, the predecessor of the lawyer. Antyus, Meletus, and Lycon were the three men who brought Socrates to trial for his life on that long-ago day in 399 B.C. The full script of their indictment against him does not exist. Though Lycon, as *rhētōr*, was supposedly better qualified to present the case than the other two, it would seem that Meletus did most of the talking, since Socrates, in his defense (as reported by young Plato), addressed most of his remarks to the poet.

"O men of Athens," he began—after the archon had summarized the indictment accusing him of not worshiping the gods the State worshiped and of "corrupting

the young"—"O men of Athens, I cannot tell how you
have been affected by my accusers, but I know they almost made me forget who I was—so persuasively did
they speak . . ."

The old man with the white beard, pug nose, and
high, bulging, furrowed brow, stood on the platform of
the vast open court, leaning forward slightly and balancing on the balls of his feet. Before him he could see,
seated on stone benches, the five hundred jurors, stern
and serious with the responsibility of deciding whether
a man should live or die, and beyond them the crowd
of spectators, some hostile, some sympathetic, and some
merely curious.

Close by, just beneath him, were gathered his most
intimate friends—Chaerephon, who had asked the Del-
phic oracle if there was anyone wiser than he; the elderly and wealthy Crito; Adeimantus, and his younger
brother Plato, who would serve as court reporter. To
them Socrates cast a reassuring glance. We can imagine
that the sky above the marble pillars was deep blue and
cloudless and that the air was dry and warm and the sun
bright.

" . . . and yet they have scarcely spoken the truth at
all," Socrates continued, "but from me you shall hear
the whole truth: not, however, delivered after their
manner in a set oration duly ornamented with words and
phrases. No, by heaven! But I shall use the words and
arguments which occur to me at the moment; for I am
confident in the justice of my cause . . . I am more
than seventy years of age, and appearing now for the
first time in a court of law. I am quite a stranger to the
language of the place, and therefore I would have you
regard me as if I were really a stranger, whom you

would excuse if he spoke in his native tongue, and after
the fashion of his country . . ."

It was true. With all the talking Socrates had done, he
had never been an orator nor had he pretended to be
one. This was the first time he had been called upon to
make a long and almost uninterrupted address. He had
to make that clear. He proceeded:

"I will begin at the beginning, and ask what is the
accusation which has given rise to the slander of me, and
in fact has encouraged Meletus to prefer this charge
against me. Well, what do the slanderers say? They
shall be my prosecutors, and I will sum up their words
in an affidavit:

" 'Socrates is an evildoer, and a curious person, who
searches into things under the earth and in heaven, and
he makes the worse appear the better cause; and he
teaches the aforesaid doctrines to others.'

"Such is the nature of the accusation: it is just what
you have yourself seen in the comedy of Aristophanes
[he was referring to *The Clouds*], who has introduced
a man whom he calls Socrates, going about and saying
that he walks in air, and talking a deal of nonsense concerning matters of which I do not pretend to know
either much or little—not that I mean to speak disparag-
ingly of anyone who is a student of natural philosophy. . . ."

Was he not rambling? When would he get to the
specific charges of the indictment? But Socrates took
his time. He must first rehearse all the slanders that had
arisen about him over the years, and explain the reason
for them. Then, suddenly, he lashed out:

"Meletus says that I am a doer of evil, and corrupt the
youth, but I say, O men of Athens, that Meletus is a

doer of evil, in that he pretends to be in earnest when he is only in jest, and is so eager to bring men to trial from a pretended zeal and interest about matters in which he really never had the smallest interest. And the truth of this I will endeavor to prove to you. Come hither, Meletus. Let me ask a question of you. You think a great deal about the improvement of youth?"

The poet must have stepped forward reluctantly. In his heart he knew he was no match for Socrates. Nonetheless he spoke out defiantly:

"Yes, I do."

"Tell the judges, then, who is their improver; for you must know, as you have taken the pains to discover their corrupter, and are citing and accusing me before them. Speak, then, and tell the judges who their improver is."

Meletus was silent, fearing a trick.

"Speak, my friend," Socrates insisted. "Tell us who is the improver of youth."

"The laws," Meletus blurted out.

"But that, my good sir, is not my meaning. I want to know who the person is, who, in the first place, knows the laws."

"The judges, Socrates," he said finally, "who are present in court."

"What? Do you mean to say, Meletus, that they are able to instruct and improve youth?"

"Certainly they are."

"All of them, or some only and not others?" Socrates asked next.

"All of them."

"By the goddess Hera, that is good news!" Socrates said sweetly. "There are plenty of improvers, then. And what do you say of the audience? Do they improve them?"

"Yes, they do."

"And the senators?"

"Yes, the senators improve them." Meletus must have realized he was being forced into an awkward position, but he could not back down.

"But perhaps the members of the assembly corrupt them? Or do they improve them?"

"They improve them."

"Then every Athenian improves and elevates youth; all with the exception of myself; and I alone am their corrupter? Is that what you affirm?"

"That is what I stoutly affirm."

He had said exactly what Socrates wanted him to say.

"Happy indeed would be the condition of youth if they had one corrupter only, and all the rest of the world were their improvers." He turned to the poet, his voice rising, "But you, Meletus, have sufficiently shown that you never had a thought about the young; your carelessness is seen in your not caring about the very things which you bring against me. And now, Meletus, I will ask you another question. By Zeus, I will.

"Which is better, to live among bad citizens, or among good ones? The question is one which may be easily answered. Do not the good do their neighbors good, and the bad do them evil?"

"Certainly." What else could Meletus say?

"And is there anyone who would rather be injured than benefited by those who live with him? Does anyone like to be injured?"

"Certainly not." This, too, was obvious.

"And when you accuse me of corrupting and deteriorating the youth, do you allege that I corrupt them intentionally or unintentionally?"

"Intentionally, I say." Again Meletus had fallen into a trap.

"But you have just admitted that the good do their neighbors good, and the evil do them evil." Socrates continued triumphantly. "Now, is that a truth which your superior wisdom has recognized thus early in life, and am I, at my age, in such darkness and ignorance as not to know that if a man with whom I have to live is corrupted by me, I am very likely to be harmed by him; and yet I corrupt him, and intentionally, too—so you say, although neither I nor any other human being is ever likely to be convinced by you. But either I do not corrupt them, or I corrupt them unintentionally; and on either view of the case, you lie. . . ."

So far Socrates had won the argument. His friends could have no doubt about it. He was ready for the next round.

"But I still should like to know, Meletus, in which ways I am affirmed to corrupt the young. I suppose you mean . . . that I teach them not to acknowledge the gods which the State acknowledges, but some other new divinities or spiritual agencies in their stead. These are the lessons by which I corrupt the youth, as you say?"

"Yes, that I say emphatically," Meletus admitted.

"Then, by the gods of whom we are speaking, tell me and the court, in somewhat plainer terms, what you mean! For I do not as yet understand whether you affirm that I teach other men to acknowledge some gods, and therefore that I do believe in gods, and am not an entire atheist . . . or do you mean that I am an atheist simply, and a teacher of atheism?"

"I mean the latter—that you are a complete atheist," Meletus shouted.

"What an extraordinary statement! Do you mean that I do not believe in the gods of the sun or moon, like other men?"

Meletus turned to the jury. "I assure you that he does not. He says the sun is stone and the moon earth."

Ah, Socrates explained, Meletus had made a grave mistake here. He had confused him with Anaxagoras, who had indeed advanced such a doctrine. The jury would have to concede this point. All knew by now that Socrates was no longer concerned with the substance of the sun and moon, but with the good and evil in man.

Now, as to the charge of the indictment that Socrates worshiped gods other than those the State worshiped: Here Meletus had made a "factious contradiction," Socrates told the jury.

He faced Meletus. "Did ever man believe in the existence of human things and not of human beings? Did ever any man believe in horsemanship and not in horses? Or in flute playing and not in flute players? No, my friend. . . .Now, please answer the next question. Can a man believe in spiritual and divine agencies and not in spirits or demigods?"

"He cannot," Meletus conceded.

"What are spirits or demigods? Are they not either gods or the sons of gods?"

"Certainly they are."

Once more the poet had been routed by the logic of Socrates. It was absurd to claim that the philosopher believed in spirits and demigods—in the sons of gods, that is—and not in the gods themselves.

"You might as well affirm the existence of mules,"

Socrates pointed out, "and deny that of horses and asses. Such nonsense, Meletus. . . . You have put this into the indictment because you had nothing real of which to accuse me."

He had said enough to answer the indictment. There was much more he wanted to tell his fellow citizens on this one day he was granted to defend himself.

"Someone will say: And are you not ashamed, Socrates, of a course of life which is likely to bring you to an untimely end? To him I may fairly answer: There you are mistaken. A man who is good for anything ought not to calculate the chance of living or dying; he ought only to consider whether in doing anything he is doing right or wrong—acting the part of a good man or of a bad. . . ."

He spoke of heroes of the past who had time and time again preferred death to dishonor or disgrace. Should a philosopher behave differently? "Strange, indeed, would be my conduct, O men of Athens, if I, who, when I was ordered by the generals whom you chose to command me at Potidaea and Amphipolis and Delium, remained where they placed me, like any other man, facing death —if now, when, as I conceive and imagine, God orders me to fulfill the philosopher's mission of searching into myself and other men, I were to desert my post through fear of death, or any other fears. . . ."

Were he to be granted his life on the condition of silence, he would refuse: ". . .while I have life and strength I shall never cease from the practice and teaching of philosophy, exhorting anyone whom I meet and saying to him after my manner: You, my friend, a citizen of the great and mighty and wise city of Athens, are you not ashamed of heaping up the greatest amount of money and honor and reputation, and caring so little about wisdom and truth and the greatest improvement of the soul, which you never regard or heed at all. . . . I tell you that virtue is not given by money. . . ."

Some of his judges—the wealthier ones—must have winced. Ragged as a beggar he was, and yet he dared sneer at them because they loved money. And by his own admission he was not going to change his ways.

"And now, Athenians," he continued, "I am not going to argue for my own sake, as you may think, but for yours, that you may not sin against God by condemning me, who am his gift to you. For if you kill me you will not easily find a successor to me, who, if I may use such a ludicrous figure of speech, am a sort of gadfly, given to the State of God; and the State is a great and noble steed who is tardy in his motions owing to his very size, and requires to be stirred into life. I am that gadfly which God has attached to the State, and all day long and in all places am always fastening upon you, arousing and persuading and reproaching you. You will not easily find another like me, and therefore I would advise you to spare me."

Socrates comparing himself to a gadfly! In spite of the solemnity of the occasion, his friends must have chuckled. But the jurors who had been "stung" by that gadfly could only have considered the comparison as unbridled insolence.

The sun was low on the horizon and still Socrates talked on: about his life's work, his teaching, about what he believed and why. He must have been tired, but there was one more thought he had to express to those assembled to listen to him:

"There seems to be something wrong in asking a favor of a judge, and thus procuring an acquittal, instead of informing and convincing him. For his duty is, not to make a present of justice, but to give judgment; and he has sworn that he will judge according to the laws, and not according to his own good pleasure; and we ought not to encourage you, nor should you allow yourselves to be encouraged, in this habit of perjury—there can be no piety in that. Do not, then, require me to do what I consider dishonorable and impious and wrong, especially now, when I am being tried for impiety on the indictment of Meletus. For if, O men of Athens, by force of persuasion and entreaty I could overpower your oaths, then I should be teaching you to believe that there are no gods, and in defending myself should simply convict myself of the charge of not believing in them. But that is not so—far otherwise. For I do believe that there are gods, and in a sense higher than that in which any of my accusers believe in them. And to you and to God I commit my cause to be determined by you as is best for you and me."

He had said it all. It was over and he returned to his place to await the vote. He had spoken as he never had before and his friends were weeping. But the jurors saw him neither as a philosopher nor as a poor old man worthy of mercy and pity. For the majority of them, Socrates was someone they would be well rid of because he was not like them, because he made them uncomfortable, or because, as they no doubt reasoned loftily, he was really a danger to the democratic State of Athens.

When their ballots were counted, it was found that 280 had voted against him and only 220 for him. Socrates had lost. Meletus and Antyus and Lycon would not have to face a lashing, nor would they be fined. There remained the sentencing.

The three accusers had asked for death, but the prisoner was allowed to suggest an alternative. Socrates obliged them by saying that though he was a poor man he might offer one mina (about ten dollars) in exchange for his life. In the startled lull that followed this absurd proposal, four of his friends, Plato, Crito, Critobulus, and Apollodorus, approached the platform and whispered something to him. "My friends here bid me say thirty minae," Socrates said. "Let thirty minae be the penalty; for which sum they will be ample security to you."

The jury refused the offer. They hoped, and there is reason to believe that his accusers hoped, too, that Socrates would plead for exile from Athens. But for Socrates exile would have been a disgrace he did not deserve. He spoke instead of his pity for those who had condemned him and who would henceforth have to live with his murder on their consciences.

We are told that Socrates spent a month chained in his prison cell waiting for the execution of the death sentence. A ship had been sent to Delos on a sacred mission, and until its return capital punishment was forbidden. In that month his friends worked out a plan for his escape. One morning Crito visited him in his cell to try to convince Socrates to let them carry out their plan. Socrates refused. The State had given him an unjust sentence, but it had been made lawfully. To break the law would be to bring injury to the State. That he was unwilling to do. Reluctantly, Crito left.

The day the ship returned from Delos—the day his friends knew would be Socrates' last—they gathered in his prison cell. They found his wife there, with her youngest son in her arms. (Plato says it was Xanthippe. Modern scholars have pointed out that it must have been his second wife, Myrto.)

"O Socrates," she cried, "this is the last time that either you will converse with your friends or they with you."

Socrates turned to the aged Crito: "Let someone take her home."

She was led away, weeping.

The jailer had taken off Socrates' chains, and he sat on his couch rubbing his legs. "How singular is the thing called pleasure," he said, "and how curiously related to pain, which might be thought to be the opposite of it; for they are never present to a man at the same instant, and yet he who pursues either is generally compelled to take the other; their bodies are two, but they are joined by a single head."

He talked to his friends of many things after that: of the reason why he had been composing poetry in prison, although he had never done so before; of why no philosopher should fear death but still should never try to take his own life; and of how the physical senses mislead the soul in its search for truth.

Crito interrupted at one point to say that the jailer had warned him not to let Socrates talk too much, for talking would excite him and interfere with the action of the poison he was to take.

"Let him mind his business and be prepared to give the poison twice or even thrice if necessary; that is all," said Socrates. He continued to discourse with his friends on life and death and the harmony of the spirit, on the immortality of the soul, on why the greatness in people can drive out the smallness, and other such matters that had concerned him in the past.

As sunset approached, he left his friends to bathe and prepare himself for his final departure. Then his wife was admitted again with all three of his sons and the other women of his family. He spoke with them briefly, giving them advice for their future, but soon dismissed them and returned to his friends.

The jailer brought in the cup of hemlock, saying, "You have only to walk about until your legs are heavy, and then to lie down and the poison will act."

As Socrates raised the cup to his lips, his friends were unable to control their emotions and their tears flowed openly. "What is this strange outcry?" he reproached them. "I sent away the women so they might not misbehave in this way, for I have been told that a man should die in peace. Be quiet then, and have patience."

As the jailer had instructed, he paced the cell, and when his legs began to fail him, he lay down on his couch. After a while the jailer pressed his foot and then his leg, and asked him if he could feel anything.

"No," said Socrates. "When the poison reaches the heart, that will be the end."

He looked up at his oldest friend. "Crito, I owe a cock to Asclepius; will you remember to pay the debt?"

"The debt shall be paid," Crito assured him. "Is there anything else?"

There was no answer. The soul of Socrates had quit its earthly body and was now free to explore the realm beyond man's knowledge.

JOAN OF ARC

The preparatory trial opened at eight o'clock, the morning of February 21, 1431. It was held in the royal chapel of the castle of Rouen, which is in Normandy, France, at this time occupied by English soldiers.

Tall wax candles lit the chapel's dim interior and cast shadows on the features of the judges and the assessors (who acted as jury), some sixty in all. They were high Church officials from the Rouen Cathedral, abbots, heads of big Norman monasteries, theological faculty members from the University of Paris, doctors of law and of medicine.

In charge of the trial was the haughty Pierre Cauchon, former Bishop of Beauvais, a traitor to France who had sold his services to the English. At his side was Jean LeMaître, deputy inquisitor, present as representative of the Inquisition, that body of men appointed by the Holy Church to seek out and punish heretics. He was there unwillingly, had agreed to come only to make sure that the trial was conducted in accordance with Church law. Also present was the chief prosecutor, Jean d'Estivet, a bitter, cynical man with an evil disposition.

The prisoner was brought before them—a young girl with shoulder-length hair worn in the style of a court page, said to be attractive although no accurate description of her exists. To the common people of France she was known as the Maid of Orléans.

She was accused of heresy, of sorcery, of practicing the "diabolic arts."

There were red marks on her wrists where prison fetters had bitten into her flesh. Her ragged and shabby clothes were of the sort worn by a youth—a short girdled tunic and long hose. Her eyes were unafraid and she held herself proudly before the imposing gentlemen in their stately robes who had come to judge her.

How shocking, they whispered to one another, how unspeakably shocking that a woman would dare appear in the garb of a man! An Augustinian hermit covered his eyes with his hands to hide the shameful sight.

No formal charges had been made against her. These would be formulated on the basis of her replies to the questions asked during the preparatory trial, and she would then be permitted to try to refute them. In contrast to Anglo-Saxon legal practice, she would be found guilty unless she could prove her innocence.

Bishop Cauchon opened the proceedings.

"Put your hand on the Bible, Joan," he said. "Swear to tell the truth to all the questions you are asked."

"I cannot take such an oath." Her voice rang out clear and firm. "There are questions to which I have no right to reply. Not even if you cut off my head. The revela-

WS.

tions that have come to me from God—I have no right to speak of them to any human being."

The Bishop frowned. It was a bad beginning, a humiliating thing to be defied at the very outset by this ignorant country girl. He had a personal grievance against her. It was her fault that the English had been driven from Beauvais, where he had been bishop. To escape the wrath of the people, Cauchon had been forced to flee. He hoped that his successful handling of this trial would lead to his appointment as archbishop of Rouen—a dream that would never be realized.

England and France had been fighting intermittently since 1337, with the English scoring many victories on French soil. In 1420, when Joan was ten, Charles VI of France, a madman, signed the Treaty of Troyes, by which he bequeathed the French crown to Henry V of England, thus disowning his own son, the Dauphin Charles. Henry V died two years before Charles VI. The ruthless Duke of Bedford became acting regent for one-year-old Henry VI. The Duke of Burgundy and his followers, who were French, claimed that this baby was King of both France and England. Other Frenchmen staunchly maintained that the French crown belonged only to the Dauphin.

The Dauphin, ineffective weakling though he seemed, had sufficient courage to repudiate the Treaty of Troyes, and from Chinon in southwest France organized an army from Gascony and Armagnac, pawning his jewels and, it was said, even the clothes on his back, to pay his soldiers. It seemed a futile gesture. The Dauphin was unskilled in the arts of war; his generals and ministers, who should have advised him, did nothing but quarrel among themselves.

The English occupied the greater part of France north of the Loire River. Early in 1429, two years before Joan's trial, they sent an army to besiege Orléans, on a bend in the Loire. If Orléans fell—and it then seemed inevitable that it would—all France would soon be an English colony.

It was at this moment of crisis that the peasant girl Joan arrived at Chinon, demanding boldly that she be taken to the Dauphin. She had traveled some four hundred miles across war-torn France with an escort of men supplied by Robert de Baudricourt of Vaucouleurs, the Dauphin's representative in the Vosges. She was sent by God, she said. St. Catherine, St. Margaret, and the Archangel Michael had spoken to her in His name. They had told her she was to raise the siege of Orléans and have the Dauphin crowned the true King of France.

The Dauphin, who had reasonable doubts that a seventeen-year-old girl could accomplish these miracles, avoided seeing her as long as he could. When she was finally admitted to the palace, he had a knight take his place on the throne and disguised himself as one of his courtiers. She had recognized him at once. Sensible and matter-of-fact and confident, she convinced him of her sincerity. For an ecclesiastical opinion as to her divine mission, he sent her to the Archbishop of Reims, at Poitiers, who, following a lengthy examination, gave Joan his blessing and told her to do as she must. After that the Dauphin made her head of the French armies, providing her with a black horse and a suit of white armor.

Joan proved to be the equal of the most experienced generals. The soldiers, tough and undisciplined, vowed to follow her to the death, and, just as surprising, gave up swearing and carousing for her sake. One after another, the English fortresses around Orléans fell, and on May 8, 1429, the besieged city was saved.

With the Maid of Orléans at their head, the French armies won more battles in the next weeks, liberating town after town. There had never been a military leader like her. She took no credit for victory. She wept bitterly at the sight of the English dead. Once she leaped from her horse to comfort a dying prisoner, holding his head in her arms until the priest arrived. Everywhere people claimed her as their savior, crowded around her, trying to touch her horse, gazing at her "as if they were beholding God." On July 9, she captured Troyes, the site of the infamous Treaty of Troyes. On July 15, French armies entered Reims where, in a beautiful ceremony, the Dauphin was crowned Charles VI of France —just as the Maid had prophesied.

Following the coronation there were reverses. In an unsuccessful attempt to take Paris, the French suffered some fifteen hundred casualties. The Maid herself was wounded in the thigh by an arrow. Her comrades were surprised to find that she felt pain, like anyone else. This was on September 8, the feast day of the Virgin's birth, and some claimed that the defeat came because they fought on a holy day. The winter passed in a stalemate.

On May 23, 1430, Joan led a sally from Compiègne against the Burgundians, who were allies of the English. Though her armies were forced to retreat, Joan stayed behind with the rear guard. The gates of the town closed before she could enter. An archer dragged her from her horse and the noble, Jean de Luxembourg, took her prisoner. Her splendid days as a soldier were over.

That was eight months before she was brought to trial. During her lonely prison life at Luxembourg's chateau of Beaurevoir, she must have wondered why the former Dauphin made no effort to secure her release. It may have seemed strange to her too that her close companions in battle, the valiant La Hire, the brave Jean Dunois, the gallant Duc d'Alençon, handsome Gilles de Rais, did not come to rescue her. Nor could she guess the joy with which the English learned of her capture, or the large ransom they offered to have her transferred to them, only so they could give her to the Church—and to the Bishop of Cauchon—to be tried as a heretic and sorceress.

Not all Church authorities approved the proceedings. In fact, during the preliminary discussions, Bishop Cauchon had thrown into prison a Rouen priest named Nicolas de Houppeville for pointing out that the Archbishop of Reims, who outranked Cauchon, had vouched for Joan's saintliness, thus casting a doubt over the legality of the trial. Other churchmen were forced to appear under the threat of losing their freedom or their posts.

To Joan, on that first day of the preparatory trial, it may have seemed that she had not a friend in the world. If so, she did not let herself betray distress or sorrow. An inner strength sustained her, and from the beginning she displayed a firmness and a resolution that astounded everyone.

She would not promise Cauchon to answer all the questions that were put her. "As for the revelations sent me from God, never will I reveal them save to Charles, my King." He had to be content with her vow "to tell everything about which I shall be questioned about the Faith."

The opening interrogation had to do with her child-hood in the village of Domrémy, in the province of Lorraine. She answered freely.

She was baptized Jeanne, though at home her family called her Jeannette, she told Cauchon. Her father, a farmer, was Jacques Darc.* Her mother was named Ysabeau. She gave him the names of her godparents and of her priest. She had three brothers and two sisters. She was nineteen years old, she thought. And she wished they would not keep her in irons. "Ever since I was brought here my hands and feet have been fettered with iron manacles that hurt terribly."

Cauchon informed her that he had ordered the fetters because she had several times tried to escape.

"I would like to escape, as is lawful for every pris-oner," Joan said.

He asked her to say the Pater Noster and the Ave Maria.

She would do so, she said, if he would hear her con-fession, a privilege denied her since her capture. He in-sisted she should say the Pater Noster and Ave Maria to "two notable persons of this company." She shook her head. "I will not say them at all, if they do not hear my confession."

The first session was over. She was taken back to her cell, a dismal chamber in one of the seven towers of the castle held by the Earl of Warwick, the English-ap-pointed Governor of Rouen. Her feet were put in fet-ters. A chain, secured to an overhead beam, was fas-tened around her waist. Though theoretically she was a

---

* More than a century later a poet of Orléans renamed Jeanne Darc, calling her "Jeanne d'Arc," implying she came of noble birth, which was not so. In English, this was translated as "Joan of Arc."

prisoner of the Church, English soldiers guarded her. Two of them were stationed outside her door. Three others stayed in her cell night and day. Rough and uncouth, they took advantage of her helplessness to curse and mistreat her.

The preparatory trial continued the next day, February 22, not in the chapel but in a smaller hall. Again Cauchon ordered her to take a vow to tell the truth.

"I did so yesterday. That will suffice."

He asked more questions about her childhood.

Had she as a child been taught any profession?

She answered proudly that she could sew and spin and could challenge any woman of Rouen in these crafts.

He asked next about the voices that she claimed guided her in all her actions. She answered fully and frankly.

She was thirteen when she had first heard one of them and she had been greatly afraid. It was noon on a summer's day in her parents' garden. The voice had come from the right, from the direction of the church, and it had been accompanied by a light. After she had heard it three times she knew it was the voice of the Archangel Michael. Later, St. Catherine and St. Margaret spoke to her. They came two or three times a week, sometimes in the garden, sometimes in the forest, usually after the church bells sounded. Both St. Catherine and St. Margaret wore crowns on their heads and were robed in beautiful garments. In their first visits they simply told her to take care of herself and attend church frequently.

From her mother she learned the story of these saints. Both had taken a vow of chastity, swearing they would never marry but would devote themselves to God's will. Joan, too, took a vow of chastity. It was after this that her saints told her of her unique destiny: "Daughter of God, you must go into France and raise the siege of Orléans."

She asked them how she, a young girl without money, could cross France alone. They gave her specific instructions. "Daughter of God, you will go to the captain, Robert De Baudricourt, in the town of Vaucouleurs. He will provide you with soldiers who will take you to the Dauphin."

Vaucouleurs was not far distant. Joan coaxed an uncle to take her there. Somehow she obtained an audience with de Baudricourt. How the captain laughed when this peasant lass, clad in a patched red dress, announced that *she* was sent by the King of Heaven to raise the siege of Orléans!

"Take the wench back to her father and tell him to give her a good spanking," he roared.

There was nothing she could do but go home. A few months later the English attacked their valley and pillaged Domrémy. With the enemy at their doorstep, Joan came again to see De Baudricourt, telling him, almost ordering him, to send her to the Dauphin quickly. Her voices had now instructed her to have him crowned King of France. Perhaps from desperation, since all other succor had failed, De Baudricourt decided to comply with her wishes. Joan was provided with a horse and six of De Baudricourt's men to take her to Chinon.

"On whose authority do you wear men's clothing, Joan?" This question came from Jean Beaupère, a pro-English priest whom Cauchon had assigned to examine her that day.

"I charge nobody," she said, though later, in answer

to the same question, she claimed that her voices had instructed her to cut her hair and dress as she did. If so, it was practical advice. No woman in womanly garb would have been safe on that long cold trip across France, sleeping in the open, traveling unfrequented roads to avoid thieving bands, with the hoofs of their horses wrapped in cloth so they would make no sound. Nor would it have been feasible to lead the Dauphin's armies in a woman's gown and fichu.

"How did you recognize the Dauphin?" Beaupère asked her. How had she known that the handsome knight in royal robes seated on the throne was not he? How was she able to go directly to where the real Dauphin stood, in ordinary clothes, among his courtiers?

She recognized him among many others by the advice of her voices, she replied. In truth, it could not have been difficult. Everyone had heard what the Dauphin looked like—a meek, homely man with thick lips, a long nose, watery eyes, no eyelashes, spindly bowed legs.

"Was there a light about him?" Beaupère demanded.

"Go on to the next question," Joan said.

She confided later that the King and several members of his council heard and saw her voices.

Beaupère asked her what revelations they made to the Dauphin.

If the judges wished to know, she demanded, why did they not send a message to the King and ask him?

Baffled, Beaupère changed the subject. "About what do you question your voices?"

He wanted her to admit she asked favors of them, but Joan disappointed him:

"I have never asked for any reward other than the salvation of my soul."

He asked if the attack she had led on Paris had taken place on a Church feast day. She told him she believed it had.

"Was that a good thing?"

She refused to answer. Perhaps she thought it absurd to do so. After all, the English never showed any scruples about fighting on feast days.

The second session was adjourned.

Afterward, Cauchon summoned the recording clerk, Manchon, to suggest that he amend certain of Joan's statements in the minutes. Manchon made some excuse not to obey. It is said that Cauchon made five separate attempts during the preparatory trial to alter Joan's testimony, but due to Manchon's stubborn and courageous refusal, he never succeeded.

A third examination took place on February 24. Once more Cauchon told Joan she must tell the whole truth without reservation. She did not reply. He repeated this order three times over, then burst out wrathfully, assuring Joan she was exposing herself to great perils. She told him she accepted the perils and to stop bothering her about them.

Cauchon again turned over the investigation to Beaupère. This learned man was far more subtle than Cauchon. His voice was gentle and he gave the impression of being Joan's friend, which he was not.

"When did you eat and drink last?" he asked her.

"I have neither eaten nor drunk since yesterday at noon."

He continued with questions about her voices.

"At which hour did you hear the voice yesterday?"

"I heard it three times yesterday," Joan said, "in the morning, at the time of Vespers, and when Ave Maria was said in the evening. Often I hear it more times than I can say."

"When the voice came to you yesterday morning—what were you doing?"

"I slept. The voice woke me."

"Did he touch your arm?"

"It woke me without touching me."

"Was the voice in your room?"

"Not so far as I know. But it was in the castle."

"Has the voice ever changed its meaning?"

"I have never noticed that it contradicts itself. Last night it only told me to answer bravely," she said.

He asked if her voice had a face and eyes, but Joan would not answer.

Then he demanded abruptly, "Do you know if you are in a state of grace?"

"If I am not," Joan said deliberately, "I pray to God to make me so. If I am, may God keep me so."

The examiners, some against their will, were impressed with the beautiful simplicity of her response to this difficult question. Beaupère, embarrassed, started asking her about the political beliefs of her childhood playmates.

There was only one boy in the village whose sympathies were with Burgundy, the English ally, Joan said. She added with the disdain of any patriot for a traitor, "I would have wished that they had cut off his head—of course, if it were the will of God."

Casually, Beaupère asked if her voices had told her to hate the Burgundians. But he did not succeed, as he hoped he would, in leading Joan to say that God could inspire one human being to hate another.

"When I realized my voices were for the King of

France, I could not greatly love the Burgundians," she answered him. "They will get war if they do not act as they should. That I know from the voices."

Then Beaupère asked her a most dangerous question, aimed to make her admit an alliance with unholy forces. "What do you know about a certain tree near your village?"

Joan understood at once what he meant. Not far from her home in Domrémy, surrounded by the most brilliant flowers of the countryside, was an enormous beech tree whose mighty branches touched the ground. Sometimes, with other girls of the village, Joan had danced beneath the tree and hung garlands on its branches. People believed that fairies and other spirits lived there. It was claimed that the nearby spring had magic powers and that the sick could be cured by drinking its water.

She knew of the legends about the tree and the spring. How could she not know? She denied that she believed them. She did not know what to think of such matters. She had never seen any fairies herself, and after her voices began to speak to her she no longer wished to dance beneath the tree with her playmates.

That night Joan fell violently ill, apparently as a result of eating a fish Cauchon had sent for her dinner. The prosecutor, Jean d'Estivet, ironically nicknamed "the blessed," came to her cell and cursed her for her greediness. But the English, terrified lest she die before the end of her trial, sent doctors to examine her. Cauchon, too, was upset and for the first time allowed her to have a confessor, a priest named Nicolas Loiseleur. Joan could not guess that he was a spy, in the pay of the English, and that everything she told him was repeated to her captors.

About this time, Cauchon discussed the progress of the trial with a visiting Norman priest, Jean Lohier, who was an authority on Church law. He wanted Lohier to give his approval, but instead the Norman claimed the trial was invalid. He gave several reasons for his opinion. No information had been made public to support the accusations against Joan. The honor of the King of France, whom Joan supported, was involved. Moreover, Joan was a simple and uneducated girl who could not be expected to answer questions on theological matters.

"One can easily see on which foot he limps," Cauchon muttered angrily, meaning that Lohier was a loyal Frenchman.

For his own safety, Lohier promptly left for Rome. Later he said that Joan's judges were motivated by revenge and that "they wanted her killed."

By February 27, Joan, though still weak, was well enough in the opinion of her doctors for the trial to resume. During this, the fourth session, she was questioned about the sword she carried at Orléans and in her other battles.

After the Dauphin had given her a horse and armor, she had sent a messenger to a church dedicated to St. Catherine de Fierbois, some nineteen miles from Chinon. From ancient times knights had left their swords on the altar of this church. Joan instructed her messenger to look in the ground behind the altar for the sword she wished; it was rusted but he would know it by the five crosses that adorned it. He did as she asked and brought the sword back to her. (According to some, Joan's sword had once belonged to Charles Martel, the grand-father of Charlemagne.)

"What blessing did you read or cause to be read over the sword?" Beaupère asked her. He wanted her to confess that she had cast a spell over it so it would be a more deadly weapon than any ordinary sword.

"I have never read, or caused to be read, any blessing of any kind over the sword," she said. "As far as I know, nobody has done so. . . . I only loved that sword because it was found in the church of St. Catherine. I have always loved her greatly."

Beaupère next asked her about the white banner she carried in battle, an embroidered pennant showing God with one hand raised in blessing and the other clasping the globe of the world, and with angels kneeling at His side.

Joan explained: "When I attacked the enemy I always carried my banner so as not to kill anyone. I have never killed anyone."

The grueling and cruelly insinuating questions went on and on, but Joan did not falter. "Answer bravely," her voices told her. To the best of her ability she did so.

When the questions struck her as irrelevant, repetitious, or merely stupid, she would say, "Pass on to the next one," or "I will think this over and then answer you." Frequently she said, "You have already been answered as to this and you will have no further reply," and "I will not give you any other answer at present."

It was small wonder that Cauchon became increasingly exasperated. As for the assessors, many of them were beginning to sympathize with her. A number of them dropped out of the trial and left Rouen, disgusted at the way Joan was being treated.

Father Massieu, the priest assigned to take her to and from her cell, found only "goodness and honesty in her." He permitted her to pray before the closed chapel door that they passed on the way to the examination hall, until Prosecutor d'Estivet happened to see her there. Furious, he shouted at Father Massieu that he would be thrown in prison if he ever again let "that sinful woman" approach the chapel. Henceforth Joan had no respite between the bitter strain of the long examinations and the horror of her nights in her cell.

Her fifth examination, on March 1, began with more questions about her voices.

"Do they speak in English or in French?"

"How could they speak English when they are not on the side of the English?" she asked guilelessly.

There were more attempts to make her admit she indulged in magic.

"What have you done with your mandrake?" Superstitious people attributed supernatural qualities to the root of the mandrake plant.

"I do not have a mandrake and never had one," Joan said. "I was told that they are dangerous things but I do not know why."

"What have you been told about the use of the mandrake?"

"I have heard people say it could produce money, but I do not believe that in the least. My voices have never spoken of it."

She was asked about the appearance of the Archangel Michael.

"Was he naked?"

"Do you imagine God could not afford to dress him?" Her voice was disdainful.

"Did he carry scales?"

"I know nothing about all that. I only know that when I see him I am always very happy and have a feeling that I am not in a state of sin."

At her sixth examination, on March 3, the judges made a frenzied attempt to prove her guilty of witchcraft. Had she not performed magic by pretending to sprinkle holy water on her arms? Did she not let herself be worshiped by the common people as though she were of divine origin? What about the story that she had conjured up a glove that a knight had lost during the coronation at Reims?

Such tales were nonsense, Joan said.

Did she not believe she had resurrected a dead child at Lagny?

"I know nothing of it."

The child to which they referred was born almost lifeless. When it was three days old, the mother brought it to church to have prayers said for it. Joan joined in those prayers. The baby stirred a little and the priest baptized it before it died. The rumor spread that Joan had brought it back to life, however briefly, but she made no such claim herself.

Then her judges made another damning charge: Joan had sinned by trying to take her own life. Had she not, while still imprisoned at Beaurevoir, thrown herself from the tower where she was kept prisoner?

It was true that she had leaped from the window of her cell some sixty feet to the ground. As a result she lost consciousness but luckily escaped serious injury. She hid in the castle three days with nothing to eat before she was captured again. She insisted she had not tried to kill herself. Word had reached her that everyone over seven years of age in Compiègne was to be murdered. She had made this desperate attempt to escape only because she wanted to go to the aid of her people.

Had she not said, her judge asked next, that she would rather die than fall into the hands of the English?

"I said that I would sooner commit my soul to God than fall into the hands of the English," she corrected him.

"Have you not lost your temper and cursed the name of God?"

"I have never cursed any saint and I have never used bad language," Joan said wearily.

At the end of the first six sessions of the preparatory trial, Cauchon decided that further examinations would be limited to a small group of men he could trust, and that they should take place in Joan's cell. From March 10 to March 17, he and several other examiners questioned her there, sometimes both morning and afternoon. They arrived in their fine clothes, well-fed, elegant, haughty, patronizing—and without pity for the ragged and wretched prisoner.

"Joan," they demanded, "do you or do you not wish to submit to the Church and recognize its authority?"

"I submit to God," she said. "I cannot understand otherwise than that it is the same thing, God and the Church. . . .Why do you complicate it?"

"Does God hate the English?" they persisted.

"I know nothing about the love or the hate that God can feel toward the English or how He deals with their souls," she answered this disturbing question. "I do know that they will be thrown out of France."

Did she not agree that she had behaved shamelessly by leaving her parents without permission?

"Even had I a hundred fathers and a hundred mothers," she said, "and even if I had been the daughter of the King, I would have gone when God ordered it."

Over and over, they pressed her as to why she dressed in men's clothes. Would she be willing to change to woman's attire if they allowed her to go to Holy Communion?

She might be willing to do so, she said, if she could change back to her own clothes afterward. She still refused to admit it a sin to wear the garb that God had told her was suitable for her mission.

There were ten of these meetings in Joan's cell, making a total of sixteen sessions in all for the long preparatory trial. From the "evidence" thus gathered, Prosecutor d'Estivet prepared the accusation, a massive sheaf of papers with seventy separate articles. The accusation was presented at the trial proper, which opened on March 27.

Joan was sumoned once more to the examination hall. Cauchon, d'Estivet, and the deputy inquisitor, Jean LeMaître, were present, along with some thirty theologians, priests, and doctors—only about half the number who had attended the opening of the preparatory trial. Two Dominican monks, Jean Duval and Ysambard de la Pierre, and a lawyer, Jean de la Fontaine, sat near to where Joan stood. Their glances were friendly.

Cauchon rose to open the trial. His hands were folded over his Episcopal cross. His expression was benign. These learned and pious men had assembled there because of her great sins, he told Joan. They were not against her. They wanted to help her to attain salvation.

The long accusation was read by Thomas de Courcelles. Since it was in Latin, Joan understood nothing.

He translated the articles into French, one by one. Joan was given a chance to reply to each in turn.

Article One stated that the full authority to punish heresy rested in this court—the court of Pierre Cauchon. Joan commented that she was aware that the Holy Father, the Pope of Rome, and other ecclesiastical persons had the right to protect the Christian faith, but for herself and her deed, she would submit them only to the Church in Heaven. She added that she firmly believed she had not failed in Christian faith.

The Dominican monk, Ysambard de la Pierre, whispered to her that she should ask that her case be submitted to the General Church Council in Basle, Switzerland. She did so, but Cauchon angrily signaled to the recording clerk, Manchon, to ignore her request. The translation continued.

Article Two said that Joan was guilty of magic and witchcraft, that she had evoked demons and evil spirits, and that she had allowed herself to be worshiped as an idol.

Article Three said she had uttered heresy.

The next three articles expanded the accusations about witchcraft, and flagrantly asserted she had danced and chanted spells beneath the beech tree at Domrémy.

Article Seven said she had attempted to acquire wealth by means of the mandrake plant.

Article Eight said she had left her home against the will of her parents. (They had not wanted her to go but they had not interfered, since both her father and mother believed in her divine mission.) And that she had lived with an innkeeper of evil repute. (While Domrémy was being invaded by the English, Joan and some other women of the village had fled to Neuchâtel several miles away, staying at an inn for a few days. This was the sole basis for that charge.)

The rest of the thirty articles read to her on this day accused her in turn of preferring to abstain from the sacraments rather than giving up her male attire; of refusing to live the simple life of a woman; of predicting important military events by means of witchcraft; of finding her sword with the help of demons; of bewitching her ring, her banner, and her sword; of misusing the names of Jesus and Mary; of saying that she had shed blood by the order of God.

Indeed, it was as though every word she had spoken during the interminable preparatory trial had been wiped from the record. Her judges had put in the accusation only what they wanted to believe. She offered denials of one article after another but it was futile—all the articles were lies.

"Why do you put down that which is against me but not that which is for me?" she cried out.

That evening, the two Dominican monks, Jean Duval and Ysambard de la Pierre, and the lawyer, Jean de la Fontaine, came to her cell. They assured her that Pierre Cauchon's tribunal did not represent the Church Militant, in spite of his claims. The Pope, they said, was the only one who had the right to judge her, and they told her again that she should appeal to the General Church Council. They were interrupted by the arrival of the Earl of Warwick, the English Governor of Rouen, who had evidently been warned of the visit. In a rage, he threatened to throw Ysambard de La Pierre in the Seine River unless he stopped meddling, and he ordered them all to leave.

The last forty articles of the accusation were translated for Joan on March 28. They were as distorted as the first ones: She had the presumption to claim she could distinguish angels and saints. She had insolently asserted that she was in a state of grace. She had attempted suicide. She had said that her voices had human bodies, spoke French, and hated the English. She had worshiped evil spirits. She had been in alliance with demons, calling them angels. She had refused to submit herself to the Church Militant.

That was not true, Joan burst out at this latter charge. "My heart is filled with veneration and reverence for the Church Militant. I appeal to our Holy Father, the Pope, and to the Holy Church Council."

The Pope could help her. The lawyer, La Fontaine, and the two good Dominican monks had told her that. But the Pope was far away and her appeal was again ignored.

Article Sixty-six summed up the preceding accusations.

"Have you anything to say, Joan?"

What was there to say about this mountain of misstatement?

"I am a good Christian. I will answer all these accusations before God."

The next three articles stated that Joan had ignored all the kindly advice given her. The last, Article Seventy, said that the accused had admitted the truth of the other articles. One final falsehood to add to the others.

On the next day, Good Friday, Joan's judges and examiners attended a special mass held at the beautiful Cathedral of Rouen. No one can say what their thoughts were as they shared in the holy ceremonies. Joan spent the day in her dark cell, chained and fettered as always. Her English guards, taking the occasion to torment her more viciously than usual, struck her face, shouted curses at her, tore at her clothes.

She was saved from further indignities by a visit from Father Loiseleur. Unable to control herself, she burst into tears and moaned out her sorrow. In kindly fashion he consoled her. She still did not know he was sent to spy on her. From that one disillusion she was spared.

On April 18, Cauchon had her brought before the judges to hear a long and tedious "public admonition" of her sins. Unmoved, she insisted she had done nothing but follow the instructions of the King of Heaven. Cauchon warned her that unless she submitted to the Church, she would be in danger "both of body and soul."

She was ill and so weak her voice could hardly be heard, but she replied boldly: "*You* will not do as you say against me without suffering evil, both of body and soul."

With all his airs of assurance, Cauchon found himself in an unpleasant situation. He dared not release the minutes so accurately kept by the clerk Manchon and his assistant Bois-Guillaume, lest they arouse public sympathy for Joan. Her refusal to admit to any truth in the seventy articles also made things awkward for him. He had to find some way of breaking her spirit. Otherwise the Church authorities would surely censure him for his handling of her trial.

In the dungeon of the castle of Rouen, he had his executioner prepare instruments of torture. Then Joan was brought in. She shuddered.

"If you do not tell the truth you shall be tortured so

you can be brought back to the path of truth," Cauchon told her.

"Even if you were to tear me limb from limb, I would not tell you more than I have," she said stubbornly. "And even if I should say something, I would always insist later that you forced me to do so."

He had her taken away. That afternoon he invited twelve of his colleagues to his home to get their official sanction of the use of torture.

"It might spoil the effect of this admirably conducted trial," one of them objected. One after another they found some excuse to vote against this drastic measure. Father Loiseleur said pompously, "For the sake of her soul I think it would be beneficial if she were tortured." He added, "I bow before that which has already been said."

Reluctantly, Cauchon abandoned this method of procuring Joan's confession. Ah, well, there were other ways of getting the results he wished.

The seventy articles of the accusation were condensed to twelve articles and sent to the theologians at the University of Paris for consideration. Since Paris was in effect an English town, their opinion was foreseen. On May 23, Pierre Maurice, doctor in theology, read the twelve articles to Joan, giving the University's verdict on each.

"You, Joan, have said that from the age of thirteen you have had revelations and apparitions of angels. . . . The clergy of the University of Paris . . . have said that all the afore-mentioned things are lies, untrue, pernicious, and evil. . . ."

"You have said that you recognized the angels and the saints by the good advice and the comfort and teaching they gave you. And you also believe that it was St. Michael who appeared to you. . . . The clergy say that . . . you err in faith. . . ."

"You have said that, by God's command, you have continually worn man's dress . . . that you have also worn your hair short. . . . As for these points, the clergy say that you blaspheme God in His sacraments . . . you boast vainly; you are suspect of idolatry. . . ."

"You have said . . . that ever since you learned that the voices were on your King's side, you have not loved the Burgundians. . . . The clergy say that this is . . . blasphemy against the saints and transgression of God's commandment to love one's neighbor. . . ."

His voice droned on until he had recited the entire list of "charges" contained in the twelve articles—along with the condemnation by the University of Paris clergy. When he had finished he called the prisoner before him:

"Joan, my dear friend, it is now time, at the end of your trial, to think carefully of what you have said and done."

He continued to admonish her at length, in a gentle and fatherly manner, pleading with her to put aside her "arrogance" and submit herself to the judgment of the Church.

Listening to him, Cauchon must have beamed with pleasure. Surely the Church had shown infinite patience with this recalcitrant sinner. No one could now say that everything possible had not been done to lead her to repentance.

"I will maintain what I have always said at my trial," Joan stated when the Paris theologian finished his admonition.

The next day, May 24, guards escorted her from her cell and outside the castle gates. A cart was waiting to take her to the town of Saint-Ouen. She was not told the purpose of the journey, nor did she care. Momentarily her spirits soared. It was wonderful to breathe fresh air once more, to gaze at the countryside in its spring greenery.

The driver stopped at the Saint-Ouen cemetery. A group of dignitaries were waiting for her. "Get out, Joan." Jean Beaupère helped her down. Father Loiseleur joined her. If she would do what the priests told her to do, he whispered, she would be released from the English guards and surrendered to the Church.

Mystified, she followed him through the gate of the churchyard. It was crowded with notables—Church officials and English officers.

A French priest named Guillaume Erard delivered a sermon. It was based on the parable from St. John about the branch that cannot bear fruit of itself "except it abide in the vine," and he compared Joan to the branch broken from its vine. At the end he spoke to her directly: "Joan, I say to you that your King is a heretic."

How could a French priest utter such slander?

"Speak of me, not of the King," Joan called out clearly. "I dare swear that my King is the most noble Christian of all Christians!" No matter that the former Dauphin had not raised a hand to relieve her sufferings. He was still her King and she was faithful to him.

"Silence her," shouted Cauchon.

He then prepared to read her sentence. The Church would give her, he said, one more chance to recant— that is, to admit she had sinned. Otherwise she would be burned at a stake.

"You are going to burn me?" she cried out in terror.

"Unless you recant . . ."

"I do not know what is meant by 'recant,'" she said dully.

Someone attempted to explain the meaning of the word. She still did not understand. Her impression was that her life would be spared if she would promise not to bear arms, dress as a man, or wear her hair short. That if she would so oblige them, she would, as Father Loiseleur had whispered, be taken from her brutish English guards and turned over to the Church.

"I will do what you will have me do," she agreed.

Far longer than anyone could have expected, she had held out against her judges—those erudite men who knew how to twist everything she said to their own aims. Her voices, so she believed, had given her the strength to do so. But her voices had never warned her that she might be burned. They had only told her to have no fear. It seemed to her they had deceived her and she felt betrayed and defeated. The thought of dying in such a cruel manner was more than she could bear, and so, at last, she yielded.

The deputy inquisitor, LeMaître, handed her a short document. It read:

I, Joan, called The Maid, a miserable sinner, after I recognized the snare of error in which I was held; and now that I have, by God's grace, returned to our mother Holy Church; in order that it may be apparent that not feignedly but with good heart and will I have returned to her; I do confess that I have grievously sinned, in falsely pretending that I have had revelations from God and His angels, St. Catherine and St. Margaret, etc.

And all my words and deeds which are contrary to the Church, I do revoke; and I desire to live in unity with the Church, nevermore departing therefrom.

"Sign, Joan. Recant."

A pen was put in her hand. She did not know how to read or write, but she obediently made a cross for her signature. Someone guided her hand to write her name.

Cauchon read the amended sentence. It was still a severe one: "Joan, we condemn you to pass the rest of your days in prison, on the bread of grief and water of anguish, and so to mourn your sins."

Dazedly, she replied only that she wanted to be surrendered to the Church and freed from her English guards.

The Earl of Warwick called Cauchon aside in great indignation. Joan must die as a heretic, he said. To the blazes with all this nonsense of a recantation. Only if people saw her burned would they renounce her. For the glory of England this must be done. The French bishop told him in effect to be patient. Warwick would have his wish—eventually. But it must be done in the proper manner and at the proper time.

Joan was taken back to her old cell and once more put in chains. The same English soldiers guarded her. A tailor brought her a dress. Her male attire was stuffed in a sack and thrown in a corner.

"Let me now have women around me and send me to the Church prison so I can be guarded by priests," she pleaded.

In answer, her guards beat her until her blood flowed.

When Cauchon next visited her she had exchanged

her dress for her old tunic and long hose. Some say that the English guards forced her to do this.

"Did you not recant and promise to dress as a woman?" Cauchon reproached her piously.

"I shall do what the Church asks," Joan said, "if I am allowed to attend Mass, released from fetters, and given a woman to look after me."

Craftily, Cauchon asked her if she had heard from her voices.

"Yes, I have. God told me by St. Catherine and St. Margaret that I had committed a serious act of treachery in agreeing to recant so as to save my life."

This was all Cauchon needed to hear. He paid a visit to the Earl of Warwick. "Have no fear," he said. "She is ours."

To his colleagues he reported that Joan, after recanting her heresies, again claimed to hear her demon voices and was again wearing male clothes. In so doing, she had committed the worst of all sins. She had repented and fallen from grace. No mercy could be shown her now. Her execution was set for May 31, 1431.

They came for her at eight in the morning, released her chains, and clad her in a long linen gown. She was placed in a cart. Father Massieu, her friend, was permitted to sit at her side. Eight hundred armed English troops preceded and followed her cart as it drove down the street.

Her confessor, Father Loiseleur, watched the procession. There is a legend that suddenly he pushed his way through the crowd, ran up to the cart, and, weeping, begged Joan to forgive him.

At the town square, three stands had been erected. One was for the men of the Church—Pierre Cauchon, the deputy inquisitor, the English cardinal. The second stand was for the city counsellors and lawyers, and in the third stood notables from the University of Paris.

In front of the stands was the stake, built unusually high so that all could have a clear view. Joan was led up to it. She was praying, and asked for a crucifix. An English soldier made a cross from two twigs and handed it to her. She pressed it close.

She made one other request: "I beg of you to bring me a crucifix from the Church and hold it just before my eyes until I die."

Father Massieu granted this, her last wish. Others of the priests left, unable to watch any longer. The executioner lashed her to the stake and set his torch to the faggots at her feet.

"St. Catherine! St. Margaret! St. Michael!" Joan called in her agony.

Slowly the flames climbed higher.

There is a story that the executioner came sobbing to the door of the Dominican monastery the next morning. In spite of the oil and sulphur he had thrown into the flames, he said, Joan's heart had refused to burn. "I have burned a saint!" he lamented.

An English soldier claimed that he saw a white dove rise from the flames.

The rumor spread that all who had a hand in Joan's death would be punished. In many cases this proved true. The war dragged on for another twenty-odd years, with constant losses for the English. Finally they gave up their conquests in France. The struggle that history would call the "Hundred Years' War" ended officially in 1453 when Charles VII, the former Dauphin, took Bordeaux.

Three years later he made tardy recognition to the peasant girl who had insisted he be crowned King of France. At Nôtre Dame, in Paris, her "Rehabilitation Trial" was held. All evidence was re-examined, as were the judges and assessors who were still living. Among these were Ysambard de la Pierre, the Dominican monk; Manchon, the recording clerk; Father Massieu; and the examiner, Jean Beaupère. Pierre Cauchon had died thirteen years before, in 1442.

The testimony revealed that the trial of Joan of Arc had not been conducted with impartiality and that she had been treated brutally and unjustly. Her own conduct was proved to have been irreproachable. On July 7, 1456, after seven months of deliberation, she was pronounced innocent of witchcraft and heresy.

A cross was placed on the spot where she had been burned. There were festivities all over France, but the biggest and gayest celebration was in Orléans, where she had known her first victory. Charles VII defrayed all costs.

In 1920, nearly five centuries after her death, Joan of Arc was canonized as a saint by the Catholic Church.

Over the years many learned persons have attempted to explain Joan's "voices" from a rational viewpoint. No scientific interpretation can alter the beauty and tragedy of her story. Her trial and execution brought none of the results her enemies intended. They succeeded only in making her a martyr, whose ordeal would be told and retold the world over—in painting, pageantry, sculpture, poetry, drama, literature. For millions everywhere she remains the symbol of their aspirations and dreams.

GALILEO

Galileo was the first man on earth to view the heavens through a telescope. He located new stars and nebulae and discovered many hitherto unknown truths about the sun and planets. Because of his studies on the laws of motion and gravity, he is known as the founder of modern physics. He was at once scientist, engineer, inventor, and a brilliant writer.

On April 22, 1633, when he was nearly seventy, he was brought before the Roman Inquisition, charged with "holding, defending, and teaching" the theory of Nicolaus Copernicus that the earth moves around the sun. This was some two thousand years after Anaxagoras, the first teacher of Socrates, had been condemned to death for calling the sun "a mass of stone on fire."

Like Anaxagoras so many years before, Galileo was on trial for extolling scientific theories deemed contradictory to religious teaching. He was nearly the same

age as Socrates when his trial took place and, as in the case of Socrates, the real crime against Galileo was that he had dared to say what he thought.

His full name was Galileo Galilei. Like many older sons of his time, his first name was derived from the family name. He was born on February 15, 1564, the year of Shakespeare's birth and of the death of the sculptor, Michelangelo. The glorious Renaissance, an age of cultural achievement rivaled only by that of Athens in the time of Pericles, was drawing to a close. Seventy-two years before, Columbus had discovered a new world. More than a century had passed since Johann Gutenberg perfected his invention of printing from movable type.

The birthplace of Galileo was Pisa on the banks of the Arno River, a lovely town of many white marble buildings, among them the famous Leaning Tower. Pisa, like its sister city Florence, was part of the Duchy of Tuscany, an independent state ruled by a grand duke of the Medici family.

Vincenzio Galilei, Galileo's father, was a Florentine nobleman who because of family reverses had come to Pisa to work as a cloth merchant. He was a liberal thinker, a man of unusual intelligence and of many talents, especially in music. The man that Galileo became was due in no small part to his father's influence.

From his father he learned to play the lute and he also mastered sketching and drawing at an early age. The monks of Vallombroso, who gave him his first schooling, instilled in him a lasting religious piety. When he was ten the Galilei family moved back to Florence. He was sixteen when his father, seeing how quickly he learned, arranged for him to study medicine at the University of Pisa. During his stay there, he lived with relatives.

As a university student he listened to lectures based on the works of Aristotle (384-322 B.C.), whose numerous treatises covered anatomy, zoology, botany, astronomy, logic, and a host of other sciences, often with great intuitive brilliance and inevitably with innumerable errors. For medicine, he was taught to rely on Galen, who had lived in the second century A.D. According to the orthodox scholars, Aristotle and Galen were indisputable authorities on all scientific or philosophical subjects; there was nothing new to be learned. Before long, Galileo rebelled at this smug attitude and turned from medicine to the more precise studies of mathematics and physics.

One day, inside the Pisa Cathedral, he noted that some workmen had set a lamp swinging from the ceiling. He timed the swings, or oscillations, by his pulse beats, finding that each oscillation took the same length of time, even as the arc of the swings decreased. In his room, he verified his observations by swinging balls from a piece of string. Moreover, when one ball was of cork and another of lead, their oscillations were almost the same, provided that the strings were of the same length. The invention of the pendulum clock resulted later from this discovery of Galileo of the uniformity of pendulum vibration.

When he was nineteen and in his third year of the university, he attended a class on Euclid's geometry, given by Ostilio Ricci, the court mathematician of the Grand Duke of Tuscany. Geometry so fascinated him that he decided to abandon medicine altogether. Very probably his father was disappointed. A physician had more chance of acquiring wealth than a mathematician. Galileo's sisters were growing up and needed dowries if they were to make good marriages. Whatever his objections, Vincenzio did not press them, perhaps because he knew by personal experience that it is sad for a man to spend his life in a distasteful profession.

Galileo left the University of Pisa in 1586, when he was twenty-two, but continued his studies at home in Florence. In Archimedes (287?-212 B.C.), the genius of ancient Syracuse in the field of mechanics, he found a mind kindred to his own. Archimedes' observations on the center of gravity in planes inspired him to prepare a work in Latin on the center of gravity in solid bodies, which he circulated in manuscript form and which won him some recognition in scientific circles. Also under the influence of Archimedes, he invented a water balance, or hydrostatic scales, by which could be determined the proportion of weight in double alloys, such as a mixture of gold and copper. This invention he described in a treatise, written in Italian, called *The Little Balance*.

To help pay his expenses, this young university graduate also did some private tutoring and gave a few public lectures, not only in mathematics but in literature. (He once, in a lecture on Dante's *The Divine Comedy*, calculated mathematically the size of hell as Dante described it.) Not until he was twenty-five did he at last succeed in getting himself a steady position, as professor of mathematics at the University of Pisa. His salary was small but in compensation he was given time to pursue his own experiments.

The speed of falling bodies was one of his interests. According to Aristotle, objects fall in ratio to their weight: a five-pound object would fall five times as fast as an object weighing one pound. Galileo's own investigation indicated that objects fall at practically the same speed, no matter what their weight. It is said that he proved this dramatically when, according to his biographer and student, Viviani, he stood at the top of the Leaning Tower and dropped simultaneously a hundred-pound weight and a one-pound weight; observers reportedly were thunderstruck to see both hit the ground at the same instant. Galileo himself, however, never referred to this experiment in his own writings.

He went on to other experiments, proving that the path of a projectile is a parabola, and finding a new curve that he called a cycloid—the curve made by the path of a dot on a rolling cylinder, such as a wheel. His cycloid had been overlooked even by Euclid.

Gradually he gained a certain assurance, acquired the art of expressing himself freely in lively discussions with his colleagues, found time for amusements and distractions, and once wrote a poem ridiculing a regulation that professors must wear togas even outside their classrooms.

One day Giovanni de Medici, a member of Tuscany's ruling family, sent for him to ask his opinion on a dredging machine he had invented. From the model, Galileo decided that the contraption was worthless and said so. Giovanni dismissed him angrily and had the expensive machine built anyway. That it did not work and that Galileo was proved right did not improve his temper.

Giovanni's hostility was one of the reasons for Galileo's decision to quit the University of Pisa after three years. Moreover, he was irritated by the conservative attitude of the university authorities, who were continually being shocked at Galileo's effrontery in daring to contradict the great Aristotle. On a trip to Venice, he made such an excellent impression on the officials of the Republic of Venice that they offered him the chair of mathematics at the University of Padua, with three times his former salary. He accepted with alacrity, holding this post for eighteen years.

The Republic of Venice was the most progressive and enlightened state in Italy, and in Padua there was an academic freedom unknown at Pisa. Galileo found himself appreciated as he had never been in his beloved Tuscany. Students flocked to his classes, attracted by his engaging personality and original thinking. Many of them were rich sons of nobles and arrived clad in brocades and velvets, carrying their swords, and with servants to tend their needs. To those who could afford it, Galileo gave private lessons; he later took some of his students into his home as boarders.

Rich and cultured Venetians sought his companionship; among them was one who became his closest friend, Giovanni Francesco Sagredo, a young Venetian nobleman with a boundless curiosity about science and a receptive mind. Galileo and Sagredo talked endlessly about a variety of matters, they shared private jokes, and on more than one occasion they participated in amusing escapades.

During one of his first summers at Padua, Galileo and two other young men spent a few days at a friend's villa outside the city. Their host had installed a primitive air conditioner—a tunnel that brought cool, moist air from a nearby cavern. At the hot noon hour the three guests took a nap by the tunnel opening. The refreshing draft had a terrible and unforeseen effect. They awoke racked with pain, and all fell ill with a fever. One of them died as a result. Galileo survived but suffered with arthritis to the end of his life.

In 1597, he invented a "geometric compass," by means of which a variety of mathematical problems could be solved quickly and easily. Since logarithms were still unknown, the compasses were soon in much demand by engineers and military men; Galileo had to hire a craftsman to produce them in quantity. The extra money from their sale vanished as quickly as it appeared, for his father had died, leaving him a heavy debt for the dowry of one of his sisters.

His own tastes had grown more extravagant and he needed all he could earn for his house, his servants, the sumptuous garments his position required, and the lavish table at which his friends and students were always welcomed. His responsibilities increased when he fell in love with a young woman named Marina Gamba, of whom little is known except that she was "a lady of quality." He never married her, although she lived with him as his wife and bore him three children, two girls and a boy, for whom he provided until they reached maturity. He and Marina were close for many years but eventually she left him to marry someone else.

As professor of mathematics he taught not only geometry but military engineering and fortifications (valuable knowledge in an Italy divided into many warring states) and astronomy. At first he is said to have been only mildly interested in astronomy, and did not bother to question the stand of the Church of Rome that the earth was the fixed center of the universe, with the sun and planets circling around it. This was what Aristotle had believed. So had Claudius Ptolemy of Alexandria, born in the second century A.D., who was still considered the greatest of all astronomers.

Ptolemy had applied observation and mathematics to his study of the heavens and had duly noted that the planets appear from time to time to slow down, stop, and temporarily reverse their motion among the fixed stars. To account for this phenomenon, he devised an elaborate explanation. The planets moved around the earth, according to his theory, in what he called *eccentric* orbits; these orbits had their centers at some distance from the earth. Within their large eccentric orbits, however, he theorized that the planets also moved in small circular orbits, which he called *epicycles*.

Galileo was much too rational to go on forever ignoring the discrepancies in the complicated Ptolemaic system with its eccentric and epicycle orbits. Sometime before 1597—the exact date is not known—he came across a book called *The Revolution of the Heavenly Bodies* by a Polish scientist named Nicolaus Copernicus, which had been published in 1543.

Copernicus advanced the unorthodox theory that the earth revolved around the sun! He estimated that the rotation took 365 days, six hours, nine minutes, and forty seconds. (This is just thirty seconds more than the figure accepted by modern science.) He further claimed that the earth revolved on its axis in twenty-four hours and that it was a planet, as were Saturn, Jupiter, Mars, Venus, and Mercury, which all revolved not around the earth but around the sun. (Like Ptolemy, however, Copernicus believed that the planets moved in perfect circles.)

How did it happen that a book with such revolutionary contentions had been almost ignored by the scholastic world? In part, it was because of a preface that advised readers its theories were "hypothetical" and not to be taken literally. Copernicus had waited many years to publish his book, fearing it would create controversy. He was on his deathbed when the first copy was placed in his hands, and never saw this preface, written by an anonymous clergyman.

There is no doubt that Galileo found the Copernican theory extremely enticing, but he waited some time before he said anything about it. Then, in 1597, a German colleague, Johannes Kepler (1571-1630), published a book called *Mysterium*, in which he presented pure mathematical support of the Copernican theory. Galileo sent him a letter of congratulations.

"Many years ago I became a convert to the opinions of Copernicus . . . ," he wrote Kepler in part. "I have arranged many arguments . . . which, however, I have not yet dared to publish, fearing the fate of our master Copernicus, who has earned immortal fame among few, yet by an infinite number (for such is the number of fools) is held in contempt and derision."

Kepler promptly wrote back, saying how delighted he was to find someone to share his beliefs, and urging Galileo to "persevere on the road to truth." It was the beginning of a long friendship-by-correspondence. Kepler was at this time an obscure professor at the University of Graz, a sickly young man weighed down with family and financial troubles. Four years later he was appointed "Imperial Mathematician" to assist the Danish nobleman Tycho Brahe (1546-1601) who had, under the patronage of Rudolph II of Bohemia, set up a splendid observatory on the island of Hven. Brahe, who never accepted the Copernican theory, was the best-known astronomer of the time. Galileo once wrote him to praise some phase of his work but Brahe did not deign to reply. Eventually he would be eclipsed by both Kepler and Galileo.

The caution observed by Galileo in not openly sponsoring Copernicus in his own country was well warranted. Since 1592, a former Dominican monk named Giordano Bruno had languished in the dungeon of the Roman Inquisition. Bruno was not an astronomer nor even a mathematician; he was a dreamer, able intuitively to divine scientific truths. Not only had he accepted the Copernican theory; he had stated that some stars appeared dim only because they were farther away than others, that space was infinite, and that even this solar system might not be the center of the universe.

Forced to leave the Dominican order because of his unorthodox views, he had lived for years in exile, teaching his theories in France and England, but finally because of homesickness returning to Venice. Agents of the Inquisition promptly arrested him and brought him to Rome. Eight years in prison failed to break his spirit. He held to his own beliefs, renouncing the teachings of the Church. On February 16, 1600 (when Galileo was thirty-six and had taught eight years at Padua), Giordano Bruno was burned at the stake.

His terrible fate struck horror among scholars and scientists everywhere. Galileo's friends warned him to be careful. He assured them that he would. He was a devout Catholic and would not act contrary to the wishes of the Church. But the Copernican theory continued to attract him like an elusive will-o'-the-wisp.

He could understand Bruno's desperate wish to return to Italy, for even in Padua, where his many friends spoke his own language, he yearned for his native Tuscany. In 1605 he was granted a much-coveted appointment, as mathematics tutor during the summer months to Cosimo, the heir of the Medici family. In contrast to his relative Giovanni, of the dredging machine failure, young Cosimo adored Galileo. His esteem continued after he became Cosimo II, Grand Duke of Tuscany, and lasted the rest of his life.

To please his royal pupil, Galileo dedicated to him, in 1606, his first published work, a handbook of instructions on his "geometric compass," written in the Tuscan dialect. The next year a Padua student named Baldassar Capra published a very similar work, but written in Latin, and boldly declared himself the inventor of the compass. Galileo brought charges against him for plagiarism, as a result of which the Capra handbook was withdrawn, and in a further effort to clear his own name and reputation wrote a pamphlet titled *Defense Against the Calumnies and Impostures of Baldassar Capra*. It was readable, entertaining, and devastating. Galileo's special gift for polemics—the art of disputation or argument— was first evident in this pamphlet. In time his enemies acquired a healthy fear of his literary abilities and developed more undercover ways of working against him.

For several years Galileo was too busy with his classes at Padua, his social life, his writing, and with tutoring young Cosimo to give much thought to astronomy. In the meantime Johannes Kepler, more single-minded, wrote a massive volume called *New Astronomy*, which was published in 1609 and which for the first time advanced the theory that planets do not move in perfect circles, as even Copernicus had thought, but in elliptical orbits.

This discovery, so vital to the development of astronomy, created little sensation, mainly because Kepler's book, written in Latin, was so obscure in style, so mystical in tone, and so filled with digressions that almost everyone missed its significance. Galileo, so far as anyone knows, never read it through, nor did he ever grasp the importance of the theory of elliptical orbits. As a matter of fact, at the time Kepler's book was published, he was deeply absorbed in what seemed at first no more than an amusing scientific diversion.

It had come to his attention that a Dutch optician named Hans Lippershey had, from the same lenses he used for spectacles, constructed a curious toy by which far objects could be made to appear quite near. For instance, if one looked through it at the weathercock of a distant church spire, the weathercock loomed mysteriously close.

Curious as to how this trick was accomplished, Galileo purchased lenses of various types, experimented with them, discovered Lippershey's secret, and improved on it. The contraption he devised consisted of a piece of lead pipe with a concave lens in one end and a convex lens in the other. When he stared through it, he saw "objects satisfactorily large and near," as he wrote later, "for they appeared one-third of the distance off and nine times larger than when they are seen with the natural eye alone."

In modern terms, his "eyeglass" magnified an object to three times its diameter. He did not call it a telescope; that word was not invented until two years later.

Soon he made a better instrument that magnified objects eight diameters, with which he could see ships at sea two hours before they were visible to the naked eye. This he presented to the officials of the Republic of Venice in a splendid ceremony. They were so vastly pleased with him that they doubled his university salary and told him the position was his for life.

Subsequently he undertook making an even larger telescope. Finding that the eyeglass makers did not know how to grind the lenses he needed for it, he mastered their trade and ground his own lenses. His third telescope caused objects to appear "more than thirty times nearer than if viewed by the natural powers of sight alone." Today it is preserved at the Galileo Museum in Florence—a paper tube four feet long, with lenses about two inches in diameter.

One cloudless night in Padua, Galileo went out into his garden, turned his crude telescope toward the stars, and saw sights that no man had ever seen before. Night after night the mysteries of the starry skies unraveled one by one. He forgot to eat and neglected to sleep. For months he lived in a state of exaltation, feeling himself both humble and proud that he had been chosen to witness these marvels.

In 1610 he wrote *Message from the Stars* (commonly known in English more poetically and less accurately as *The Starry Messenger*), in which he shared his discoveries with the world.

Through his telescope the moon was no longer a golden ball hanging like a lamp in the sky, but a world like our own. "The moon certainly does not possess a smooth and polished surface," he wrote, "but one rough and uneven, and, just like the face of the earth itself, is everywhere full of vast heights, deep chasms, and shadowed curves."

His telescope revealed a marked difference between planets and fixed stars: "The planets show their globes perfectly round and definitely bounded, looking like little moons, spherical and flooded all over with light; the fixed stars are never seen to be bounded by a circular periphery, but have rather the aspect of blazes whose rays vibrate about them and scintillate a great deal."

The telescope made stars of the fifth or sixth magnitude (Ptolemy had first classified them in degrees of brightness, or "magnitude") as bright as Sirius, the brightest of all stars. It showed "a host of other stars, which escape the unassisted sight, so numerous as to be almost beyond belief. . . ." The Milky Way, which had baffled astronomers for centuries, was not a frothy stuff; it was "nothing else but a mass of innumerable stars planted together in clusters."

One of his incredible and innumerable discoveries pleased him perhaps more than all the rest. This was that the giant planet Jupiter had four moons—he called them planets—revolving around it. (Jupiter has twelve moons, but his telescope was not strong enough to see them all.) Ironically, nothing in *Message from the Stars* caused more controversy than the four "planets" of Jupiter.

One critic stated that Galileo must be wrong because there could not possibly be more than seven planets: "There are seven windows in the head, two nostrils, two eyes, two ears and a mouth. . . . From which and many other similar phenomena of nature, such as the seven metals, etc., which it were tedious to enumerate, we gather that the number of planets is necessarily seven. Moreover, the satellites are invisible to the naked eye, and therefore can have no influence on the earth, and therefore would be useless, and therefore do not exist."

An invitation from Galileo to look through his telescope was promptly refused. The critic had no desire to see the planets that were not there. There were others like him, both churchmen and scholars, who felt it beneath their dignity to squint an eye and stare into Galileo's fantastic little instrument. One academician loftily announced that the telescope had been invented by Aristotle—who had later discarded it since only with unaided sight should one look at the stars.

"Oh, my dear Kepler," Galileo wrote his fellow astronomer, "how I wish that we could have one hearty laugh together! Here, at Padua, is the principal professor of philosophy whom I have repeatedly and urgently requested to look at the moon and planets through my glass, which he obstinately refuses to do. Why are you not here? What shouts of laughter we should have at this glorious folly!"

He must have felt like laughing at everything in those days. The sneers of the jealous, the ignorant, and the prejudiced were like drops in the great ocean of homage and praise. A first printing of five hundred copies of *Message from the Stars* was sold out at once and orders for more streamed in. Kepler had a special edition printed at Frankfurt. Galileo was flooded with orders for telescopes. News of his discoveries spread throughout the world. Five years later an edition of the book came out in Chinese.

Message from the Stars, like his handbook on the compass, he dedicated to his former pupil, now Cosimo II,

Grand Duke of Tuscany. He called the four moons of Jupiter "the Medician stars," after the Medici family. These signs of allegiance helped him to attain what he had long wanted. He was appointed Chief Mathematician and Philosopher to the Grand Duke, as well as Head Mathematician of the University of Pisa, where he had been both student and professor, an honorary position requiring no lectures or other responsibilities. At last he could go home.

The authorities of the Republic of Venice accused him, with some justification, of ingratitude. For eighteen years they had permitted him to work, write, and think as he wished. They had given him a secure post for life. Was this the way to repay them? And from his dear and close friend, Sagredo, who was away at the time he left, came a prophetic letter:

"Where will you find freedom and sovereignty of yourself as in Venice? . . . At present you serve your natural Prince, a great, virtuous man of singular promise; but here you had command over those who command and govern others, and you had to serve only yourself. You were as the ruler of the universe. . . . Who knows what the infinite and incomprehensible events of the world may cause if aided by the impostures of evil and envious men? . . . I am very much worried by your being in a place where the authority of the friends of the Jesuits counts heavily."

It was true that the Medici of Florence accepted unquestioningly the dictates of the Holy City, whereas Venice refused to tolerate interference in its affairs, even from the Church. Galileo was aware of the situation and knew there was reason for Sagredo's fears. Optimistically, he hoped that whenever and however he decided openly to sponsor Copernicus, he would be able to sway the Church to his way of thinking.

One of the arguments against the Copernican theory then current was that Venus and Mercury could not be planets since they did not show phases; that is, they did not, like the moon, appear in turn in the crescent, quarter, and gibbous (three-quarter) stages. Thus, the anti-Copernicans reasoned, these bodies could not possibly revolve around the sun. (In ancient Babylon, a dry country where, unlike Europe, clouds and mist rarely obscured the heavens, astronomers had claimed that they saw the crescent of Venus, but this was either forgotten or ignored.)

There came a time when Galileo turned his telescope on Venus and saw clearly her successive phases. For him, here was the factual proof he wanted that Ptolemy was wrong and Copernicus was right. He communicated his findings to Kepler and a few other scholars but he did not yet publish them. Shrewdly, he decided he must first go to Rome and make as many friends there as he could.

His visit to the Holy City took place in the spring of 1611 and was a great success. A full day of ceremonies to honor "the great Galileo" was arranged by Father Clavius, a Jesuit and head mathematician of the Roman College. Pope Paul V granted him an audience and treated him with benevolence and kindness. He was made a member of the Lincean Academy (named after the sharp-eyed lynx), a group of scholars dedicated to the development of the arts and sciences without interference from the pedantic universities, and became intimate friends with the academy's founder, a cultured young prince named Federico Ceso.

"I have been received and feted by many illustrious cardinals, prelates, and princes of this city," he wrote to his friend, the Florentine nobleman Filippo Salviati, "who wanted to see the things I have observed [through his telescope] and were much pleased, as I was too on my part in viewing the marvels of their statuary, paintings, frescoed rooms, palaces, gardens, etc."

One of the dignitaries who looked through Galileo's telescope was Cardinal Robert Bellarmine, a prominent Catholic theologian and a member of the Roman Inquisition, the same high tribunal of the Roman Church that had condemned Giordano Bruno to death eleven years earlier. Soon after meeting Galileo, Bellarmine asked for an opinion from the Jesuits of the Roman College on the "reality" of his discoveries. Even though Father Clavius and his colleagues warmly praised the scientist and his work, Bellarmine privately sent a letter to the inquisitor of Padua, demanding additional information about their visitor.

Back in Florence, Galileo attended a banquet given by Cosimo II, which was to have a long-term influence on his career. The Grand Duke frequently invited scholars to dine so he could listen to their ideas on philosophical subjects. Present on this day were two visiting cardinals, Maffeo Barberini and Ferdinand Gonzaga. The guests discussed a matter of physics—why some objects, like ice, float in water, while others sink. Cardinal Gonzaga sided with the followers of Aristotle who insisted that bodies float if their shape is wide and smooth. Galileo maintained that any object will float if its specific gravity is less than that of water. Cardinal Barberini, who took an active part in the argument, wholeheartedly supported Galileo. Not only had the scientist made a new and important ecclesiastical friend, but Cosimo II was so pleased with him he persuaded him to publish his views in a work called *Discourse on Floating Bodies*.

About this time, when everything was going so splendidly for him, Galileo quite unintentionally antagonized a Jesuit, a member of the powerful religious order that served as adviser to the Church on educational affairs. It happened in a controversy over sunspots.

In the course of his telescopic study of the heavens, Galileo had noted "dark spots in the solar disk." "Some are always being produced and others dissolved," he described them. ". . . In addition to changing shape, some of them divide into three or four, and often several unite into one . . . they have in common a general uniform motion across the face of the sun. . . . From special characteristics of this motion one may learn that the sun is absolutely spherical, that it rotates from west to east and around its own center, carries the spots along with it in parallel circles, and completes an entire revolution in about a lunar month."

Galileo firmly believed he was the first to observe sunspots. Actually they had been observed in ancient times and more recently a certain Johann Fabricius of Wittenburg had mentioned them. In any case, Galileo's first paper on them preceded a letter published under the pseudonym of "Apelles" but in fact written by a German Jesuit father, Christopher Scheiner, who claimed their discovery.

Galileo subsequently composed three *Letters on Sunspots*, which he sent to the publisher of "Apelles," criticizing the latter's interpretation of this phenomenon. The Jesuit, for instance, had stated that sunspots were small planets revolving around the sun; they could not be part of it since no blemishes could possibly exist on the face of the "celestial sun"! Galileo pointed out that the spots by their very nature must be on the sun's surface, or very close to it. Even more rashly, in his second letter he for the first time openly endorsed the Copernican system.

"You must be careful, Galileo!" How often he must have heard this warning. He was tired of being careful.

One of his former pupils, Father Benedetto Castelli, now a mathematics professor at the University of Pisa, sent him a worried letter. At a royal dinner party at the court of Tuscany, the Dowager Grand Duchess Christina, mother of Cosimo II, had expressed her convictions that the earth could not move because its motion would contradict the Holy Scriptures. This was bringing the camp of the "enemy" very close to home, and caused Galileo to do some serious thinking on the relation of science and faith in the modern world.

To Castelli he sent a letter in which he attempted to reconcile his scientific beliefs with the Holy Scriptures, making additional copies for other trusted friends. One copy fell into the hands of a Dominican priest, Niccoli Lorini. (The Dominican order was more rigid and orthodox than was the Jesuit.) Lorini, who was so ignorant about astronomy that he spelled Copernicus as "Ipernicus," forwarded Galileo's letter to the Holy Office in Rome, proposing that the "Galileists" be investigated.

Taking up the cudgel, another Dominican, Father Tommasco Caccini, preached a sermon in Florence against Galileo, in which he is said to have made a clever paraphrase of the Scriptures: "Ye men of Galileo, why stand ye gazing up into heaven?" The rest of his sermon was a denunciation of the Copernican system, mathematics in general, and all mathematicians and astronomers.

Back of Lorini and Caccini was an arrogant Aristotelian named Lodovico delle Colombe. Since "colombo" means pigeon in Italian, Galileo referred mockingly to these men as the "Pigeon League." Foolish and petty as their attacks seemed, he did not underestimate their potential danger. To strengthen his own position, he expanded the letter to Father Castelli into a lengthy and persuasive *Letter to the Grand Duchess Christina*, after which he begged permission of Cosimo II to go to Rome to justify himself. He arrived there on December 11, 1615, and lodged, in accordance with the Grand Duke's instructions, at the Florentine Embassy with "board for himself, a secretary, a valet, and a small mule."

The Romans had been rebuilding since his last visit, and the medieval city was transformed into a modern one, with monumental squares, statues, lovely gardens, and spectacular baroque fountains. Outwardly the welcome given Galileo was as warm as ever. He was invited everywhere, and wherever he went he argued the merits of Copernicus. "You have a way of bewitching people," a friend told him. For a while it seemed as though he had bewitched all Rome.

"We have here Sig. Galileo," wrote a certain Monsignor Querengo, "who often, in gatherings of men of curious mind, bemuses many concerning the opinion of Copernicus that he holds for true. . . . He discourses often amid fifteen or twenty guests who make hot assaults upon him, now in one house, now in another . . . what I liked most was that, before answering the opposing reasons, he amplified them and fortified them himself with new grounds with appeared invincible, so that, in demolishing them subsequently, he made his opponents look all the more ridiculous."

Cardinal Maffeo Barberini, whom he had met under such auspicious circumstances at the Grand Duke's dinner, acted as his sponsor in high Church and State circles. He had many visitors. Among them, surprisingly, was Father Caccini, the very man who had denounced Galileo in his sermon in Florence. Caccini stayed a long four hours, during which he alternated between making abject apologies and trying to draw Galileo into admitting he opposed the policy of the Church. Galileo was unimpressed. "I discovered a very great ignorance, no less than a mind full of venom and devoid of charity," he commented.

His triumph seemed complete. "From day to day I am discovering what a good inspiration it was for me to come here," he happily wrote the Tuscan secretary of state on January 8, "for such snares had been laid against me that I could not have hoped to save myself later."

Unknown to him, while he was in Rome, the Holy Office of the Roman Church carried through the investigation set in motion by Father Lorini. For the benefit of the qualifiers, "the experts on matters of heresy," the beliefs of Copernicus, and therefore of Galileo, were summed up in two exceedingly unscientific and foggy statements:

I. The Sun is the center of the world and hence immovable of local motion.
II. The Earth is not the center of the world, nor immov-

*able, but moves according to the whole of itself, also
with a diurnal [daily] motion.*

The qualifiers voted the first proposition "foolish and
absurd . . . heretical, inasmuch as it expressly contradicts the doctrine of the Holy Scripture." The second
proposition received the same censure.

On February 26, 1616, Cardinal Robert Bellarmine
summoned Galileo to appear at his palace, and in the
presence of several Dominican friars instructed him that
he must no longer *hold or defend* the views of Copernicus.

That was all. Bellarmine, a kindhearted and scholarly
man, showed no desire to pursue the matter further. Galileo was not at this time brought to trial and no formal accusations were made against him. The storm clouds that
the "Pigeon League" had stirred up were dissipated in
the lightest sprinkle. Grieved as Galileo was at the re-
striction placed upon him, he had the comfort that he
had not been forbidden to present the views of Copernicus as a hypothesis.

Angrily he learned that a rumor was spreading that
he had been called to account by the Inquisition and "had
to go around like a whipped dog." To put a stop to the
slander, he asked Bellarmine for a letter stating exactly
what had been said to him. In due time, the Cardinal
graciously obliged him. Since the Bellarmine letter was
to play a part in Galileo's later, less fortuitous brush
with the Inquisition, it is quoted in full:

"We, Roberto Cardinal Bellarmino, having heard that
it is calumniously reported that Signor Galileo Galilei
has in our hand abjured and has also been punished with

salutary penance, and being requested to state the truth as to this, declare that the said Signor Galileo has not abjured, either in our hand, or the hand of any other person here in Rome, or anywhere else, so far as we know, any opinion or doctrine held by him; neither has any salutary penance been imposed on him; but that only the declaration made by the Holy Father and published by the Sacred Congregation of the Index has been notified to him, wherein it is set forth that the doctrine attributed to Copernicus, that the Earth moves around the Sun and that the Sun is stationary in the center of the world and does not move from east to west, is contrary to the Holy Scriptures and therefore *cannot be defended or held.* [Italics ours] In witness whereof we have written and subscribed these presents with our hand this twenty-sixth day of May, 1616."

On his return to Tuscany Galileo made an effort to keep out of the limelight. He turned his attention to making a telescope for use at sea, and worked out other methods to make his astronomical discoveries useful to navigators. Sometimes his son Vincenzio, who was now living with Marina Gamba, came to see him. Sometimes he rode his mule up to the hill of Arcetri, overlooking Florence, to visit his two daughters, who were both nuns at the Convent of San Mateo.

His younger daughter, Livia, Sister Arcangela, was an unexceptional young woman, but the older, Virginia, now Sister Celeste, was intelligent, warmhearted, and compassionate. Of his three children, Sister Celeste was always Galileo's favorite. Eventually he bought a house at Arcetri so he could see her daily.

In 1620, his friend and patron, Cosimo II, died at the age of thirty. In deference to his father, the new Grand

Duke Ferdinand II retained Galileo at the court, though he did not have his father's passion for science and philosophy.

Against his better judgment Galileo eventually became involved in another skirmish in polemics, again with a Jesuit, an astronomer named Father Horatio Grassi. Father Grassi had cited the appearance of three comets in 1618 as proof that Copernicus was wrong. Galileo published an anonymous criticism, which Grassi answered. Galileo, a better scientist and a better writer than his adversary, expanded his first criticism in *The Assayer*, one of his most brilliant works, to which he recklessly signed his name. Once more he had made an enemy among the Jesuits who, in contrast to the Dominicans, had been for the most part friendly to him.

In 1624, to Galileo's delight, Cardinal Maffeo Barberini was appointed Pope Urban VIII. With this old friend as head of the Papal States, he had reason to hope that the ban against the Copernican theory would be lifted and that the conflict between the Church and science would be peacefully resolved. That spring Galileo journeyed to Rome to bring his personal congratulations. The new Pope granted him six private audiences, praised *The Assayer* unreservedly, promised Galileo a pension for the education of Vincenzio, and presented him a painting in a gold frame and some small sacred pictures. In addition, he lauded Galileo highly in a long letter to Grand Duke Ferdinand II.

It is understandable that these unprecedented marks of favor blinded Galileo to a sad truth—that Pope Urban VIII was no longer the same genial, tolerant person he had been as Cardinal Barberini. The vices of vanity and jealousy and arrogance had come with his high office.

He could afford to be gracious to his adherents when it suited him, but he had the power to be equally ruthless to any of them who crossed him, as Galileo was unwittingly doomed to do.

Unsuspecting, Galileo felt that now it would be safe to write the book of which he had long dreamed and that he had long postponed—a book that would show the truth of the Copernican theory on the basis of his own astronomical discoveries. To avoid disobeying the Church injunction not to hold or defend that theory, he hit on the ingenious plan of presenting his material in the form of conversations between three men of opposing views, whom he called Sagredo, Salviati, and Simplicio. He began work on *Dialogue on the Two Greatest Systems of the World; the Ptolemaic and the Copernican* (usually shortened to *Dialogue*) early in 1625. It was interrupted on several occasions, once by some intensive studies on magnetism, and again by a serious illness. By January, 1630, it was completed, an unwieldy manuscript of some five hundred pages.

Two of the three characters in the book were named after real people. Sagredo was the Venetian nobleman who had been Galileo's friend in his happy days at Padua. In *Dialogue*, he was also a Venetian nobleman, a man of the world with the best qualities of his class, interested in new developments of science, open to argument, though careful not to commit himself on theoretical issues.

Salviati was another friend, a Florentine nobleman whom Galileo had often visited. He was the scientist in *Dialogue*, a man of Galileo's own views who took avid pleasure in "deep speculation."

Sagredo had died in 1620 and Salviati in 1614. Galileo

had grieved for them both. Now he was to give them immortality.

Simplicio, the third character, was a composite of all the ignorant and opinionated persons who had plagued Galileo with their specious arguments. If he resembled any one of them, it was perhaps Lodovico delle Colombe, the head of the "Pigeon League." Simplicio took literally every word written by Aristotle, and held doggedly to Ptolemy's cumbersome plan of the heavens. Generously, Galileo portrayed him as a charming if simpleminded youth who cheerfully endured innumerable verbal defeats and came back for more of the same. For all his elaborate subterfuge, no intelligent reader could doubt that Galileo considered Simplicio a dunderhead, that the author and the scientist Salviati were the same, and that Sagredo represented the impartial observer.

From Rome came the encouraging news that the Pope in a private audience had declared that the "prohibition of Copernicus in 1616 was a nuisance." A Roman friend of Galileo, on learning that his book was finished, wrote, "You are awaited here more than any most beloved damsel." He arrived with his manuscript in May, 1630, then turned it over to Father Niccolo Riccardi, the Chief Licenser of the Church, for the official sanction he needed so it could be safely published.

Riccardi, a good-humored, enormously fat priest known by his intimates as "Father Monster," promised him quick action. The Pope received him warmly, listened to his account of the book, and assured him that the hypothetical treatment of his subject was entirely acceptable.

There followed painful delays. Riccardi, after a hasty

reading, concluded that the material was not as hypothetical as it should be and called in a mathematician, Father Raffaello Visconti, to edit it. Visconti changed a few words and then said in his opinion the manuscript was in proper shape. Riccardi, who was no astronomer, still hesitated, finally undertaking to revise it himself, page by page.

Like any writer, Galileo suffered acutely at the idea of having his work mutilated by an amateur, but there was nothing he could do about it. While he was waiting, news came of the death of Prince Cesi of the Lincean Academy, who had promised to publish the book. On the advice of other friends, Galileo asked Riccardi to let him have it printed in Florence. Months later, after the Florentine inquisitor had consented, Riccardi agreed to release the manuscript. Not until February, 1632, was Galileo able to present the first printed copy to Grand Duke Ferdinand II, to whom it was dedicated.

The *Dialogue* received ecstatic praise from the critics. The first edition was sold out almost immediately, so that it was June before the book was put on sale in Rome. Almost at once there was trouble.

"I have heard that they are having a commission of irate theologians to prohibit your *Dialogue*," wrote Galileo's staunch friend, Father Thomas Campanella, "and there is no one on it who understands mathematics." He added that "Father Monster" was making "fearful noises against" the commission, and that he was sure His Holiness was not informed about it.

In August came word that Rome had suspended the book's sale. Galileo was first stunned, then angry. He was certain this had been done without the knowledge of the Pope and persuaded his Grand Duke to prepare a message to him, requesting a mixed commission to investigate the matter.

Francesco Niccolini, the Florentine Ambassador in Rome, took the message personally to the Vatican. The Pope received him icily. "Your Galileo has ventured with things that he ought not and with the most grave and dangerous subjects that can be stirred up in these days," he said.

Could these be the words of the man who had showered Galileo with kindness?

The reasons for the Pope's change of heart were a mystery until long afterward. In spite of the ban of 1616, not all Church dignitaries were opposed to Copernicus, and there was some talk of adopting a less literal interpretation of the Holy Scriptures, should the findings of science warrant it. But then, as has been the case so often in the history of mankind, the voice of prejudice was louder than the voice of reason. Among those who cried most noisily against the *Dialogue* were the two Jesuits, Father Scheiner and Father Grassi, whom Galileo had mortally wounded in turn by his *Letters on Sunspots* and *The Assayers*. Either they or others of his opponents employed an extraordinarily clever maneuver to bring about his downfall. They let it be hinted to the Pope that Galileo had made fun of him, that his fool, Simplicio, was, indeed, a caricature of His Holiness.

One passage at least of the *Dialogue* gave substance to this allegation. In this passage, Salviati, the scientist, cited the ebb and flow of the tides as evidence that the earth moves (an error of Galileo, but that is beside the point). Simplicio replied that such talk was blasphemy "because it seems to cast a doubt on God's power to control the tides." Galileo had certainly forgotten where he had first heard this stupid argument. The Pope had not; he had used it himself in one of his many conversations with Galileo. Like all vain people, he was unduly vulnerable. It was easy to persuade him that Galileo had done this on purpose; he could not and would not ever forgive him.

Whatever Galileo suspected of these intrigues, the fact of the Pope's anger was plain. He had feared his book might be put on the Index—that is, banned in all Catholic countries. Now he realized he must face something much worse. Sooner or later he would be called before the Inquisition.

The Roman Inquisition was an outgrowth of the Medieval Inquisition. (A deputy inquisitor, it will be remembered, assisted at the medieval trial of Joan of Arc.) The extreme corruption and venality that blackened the name of the Inquisition in Spain did not exist in Rome. Torture to procure confessions was employed rarely by the Roman Inquisition and there was a Church ruling—not necessarily irrevocable—that it should not be applied to anyone over sixty. But even as with the Spanish Inquisition, to be called before the Roman Inquisition meant one had already been found guilty of heresy. The minimum penalty was public disgrace; the maximum—death.

Several anxious months passed during which Galileo's health steadily deteriorated. On October 1, 1632, the chief inquisitor of Florence came to his house with a summons from the Holy Office—the Congregation of the Inquisition—ordering him to appear in Rome within thirty days. He knew there was no escaping the summons but he begged for more time, pleading his poor health.

His request was denied. "He must come," the Pope sent word. "He can come by very easy stages, in a litter, with every comfort, but he must be tried here in person." On November 19, he received his second summons. He appealed again, offering a certificate signed by three doctors.

"We find that his pulse intermits every three or four beats," it read in part. "The patient has frequent attacks of giddiness, hypochondriacal melancholy, weakness of stomach, insomnia, and flying pains about the body. We have also observed a serious hernia with rupture of the peritoneum. All these symptoms, with the least aggravation, might become dangerous to life."

In response came a papal mandate. No more evasions would be tolerated. In case of further delay a commissioner would be assigned to bring Galileo back as a prisoner in irons.

Grand Duke Ferdinand II advised Galileo to leave immediately. Much as he respected his father's former tutor, even he dared not risk offending the Papal States. Long ago Sagredo had warned Galileo that Tuscany would never give him the protection he might have found in the independent Republic of Venice. Now his prophecy had come true. With his servants, Galileo set out in January on the painful journey that lasted twenty-three days, reaching the Florentine Embassy in Rome on February 13. A warm bed was ready for him there. The Ambassador's wife, Caterina Niccolini, whom he called "queen of all kindness," took care of him.

Several prelates of the Inquisition visited him at the Embassy in the next weeks. They seemed friendly and Galileo talked more openly than wisely, confiding that he still believed the Copernican theory, no matter what.

"Be more discreet, Master," Niccolini warned him. The visits, he pointed out, were not purely social. They were made only so that the case against him might be strengthened.

Throughout all this dreadful period, the Ambassador and his wife did everything possible for him, even risking their own prestige. In truth, they were genuinely fond of him. "We find a wonderful pleasure in the gentle conversation of the good old man," wrote Niccolini.

Their loyalty gave Galileo new strength and he planned his defense carefully, suddenly confident that he could make his case so strong no judgment could be granted against him. Gently, Niccolini endeavored to persuade him that any defense was useless. Galileo must submit "to whatever he may see they want in that business of the motion of the earth." Only by submission could he save his life.

He heard his friend's words, but neither his heart nor his mind yet accepted them.

His trial opened on April 12, 1633. It was held in the large council chamber of the Inquisition building, not far from the Vatican. Ten members of the Dominican order clad in black robes served as both judges and jury. The president of the court, Vincenzo Maculano da Firenzuola, and two of the other Dominicans sat on one side of a long table, on which was a crucifix, in the center of the chamber.

Galileo, who had officially surrendered to the Holy Office that morning, was brought in, escorted by a monk and a servant. The aged scientist was so feeble he could barely stand erect.

The clerk took his description: "Galileo Galilei, court mathematician, seventy years old, of Florence."

He repeated the oath: "I swear to speak the whole truth. . . . So help me, God, the Blessed Virgin, and all the saints of God."

He was asked if he knew why he had been summoned.

He answered that he supposed it was on account of his last book. The *Dialogue* was shown to him and he identified it as his.

They questioned him next about the events of 1616. Had not the Holy Office commanded him at that time to appear in Rome?

Surprised, he assured his judges that he had gone to Rome in that year *of his own accord*—so as to know what opinion it was proper to hold in the matter of the Copernican hypothesis and to be sure of not holding any but holy and Catholic views. The humble words seemed to come from afar, as though it was not he, the fiery Galileo, who had spoken them but some other more docile soul. Already he could see the drift of their questioning. They were trying to establish that the meeting at Cardinal Bellarmine's palace had been in effect a trial, that he had then been judged and condemned. It was not true. He had to make that point clear.

They asked him about certain conferences he had had with several prelates prior to Bellarmine's decree. He explained that the prelates had wanted to be instructed about Copernicus' book, which was difficult for non-scientists to understand. Firenzuola asked him what happened next.

He answered: "Respecting the controversy which had arisen on the aforesaid opinion that the sun is stationary and that the earth moves, it was decided by the Holy Congregation of the Index that such an opinion, considered as an established fact, contradicted Holy Scripture and was only admissible as a conjecture, as it was held by Copernicus."

Had he been informed of this decision, and if so, by whom?

Cardinal Bellarmine had told him of the decision of the Holy Congregation of the Index, he said.

He was told to state what Cardinal Bellarmine had told him about this decision and whether anything else was said on the subject.

He was ready with a clear answer on this point: "The Lord Cardinal Bellarmine signified to me that the aforesaid opinion of Copernicus might be held as a conjecture, as it had been held by Copernicus. . . ."

They asked him about Bellarmine's decree of February, 1616, and in what form that decree was made known to him.

He told them. "In the month of February, 1616, the Lord Cardinal Bellarmine told me that, as the opinion of Copernicus, if adopted absolutely, was contrary to Holy Scripture, it must neither be held nor defended but that it could be taken and used hypothetically. In accordance with this I possess a certificate of Cardinal Bellarmine, given on May 26, 1616, in which he says that the Copernican opinion may neither be held nor defended, as it is opposed to Holy Scripture, of which certificate I herewith submit a copy."

He had not been sure he was going to use Bellarmine's letter, but he saw no way out.

"When the above communication was made to you,

were any other persons present, and who?" he was asked next.

He remembered those shadowy robed figures in the meeting at Bellarmine's palace, and answered cautiously that some Dominican fathers were present but that he did not know them and had never seen them since.

They asked if any other command had been communicated to him on this subject in the presence of the Dominican fathers, by them or anyone else, and what was that other command?

He could only stare at them in bewilderment, repeat Bellarmine's order not "to hold or defend" the Copernican theory, and say that it escaped his memory whether the Dominican fathers were present before or came in afterward:

"I do not remember that anything else was said, nor do I know that I should remember what was said to me, even if it were read to me. I say freely what I do remember, because I do not think that I have in any way disobeyed the command, that is, have not by any means held or defended the said opinion that the earth moves and that the sun is stationary."

At this point the inquisitor informed Galileo that a command had been issued to him before witnesses. The command was that "he must not hold, defend, nor teach that opinion in any way whatsoever."

Galileo must have wanted desperately to cry out that this was not so. He had never been told not to "teach that opinion in any way whatsoever." The phrase was not in his letter from Bellarmine. But he could not accuse his questioners, who represented the Holy Church, of a misstatement. He stammered:

"I do not remember that the command was intimated to me by anybody but by the Cardinal verbally; and I remember that the command was 'not to hold or defend.' It may be that 'and not to teach' was also there. I do not remember it, neither the clause 'in any way whatsoever,' but it may be that it was; for I thought no more about it or took any pains to impress the words on my memory. . . ."

Coldly his examiners proceeded to the next point. After the aforesaid command was issued to him, had he received any permission to write the book that he had acknowledged was his?

Galileo admitted that he had not thought of asking for such permission. He had not considered that in writing it he was acting contrary to, far less disobeying, the command not to hold or defend the Copernican system.

The president of the council now asked whether, when he requested permission to print his book, he had informed the Master of the Palace about the 1616 command.

It was the most important question of his first hearing and Galileo answered it rather badly: "I did not happen to discuss that command with the Master of the Palace when I asked for the imprimatur, for I did not think it necessary to say anything, because I had no doubts about it; for I have neither maintained nor defended in that book the opinion that the earth moves and that the sun is stationary but have rather demonstrated the opposite of the Copernican opinion and shown that the arguments of Copernicus are weak and not conclusive."

To state that the *Dialogue* "demonstrated the opposite of the Copernican opinion" was certainly stretching the truth, but Galileo in his pain and distress hardly knew what he was saying. His signature on the protocol, the minutes of this first session, was so shaky as to be almost illegible.

It was a rule of the Inquisition that defendants be kept in strict seclusion during their trials. Because of his age and illness and high position in the Tuscan court, Galileo was not put in the dungeon but was given a suite of comfortable rooms. A servant of Niccolini looked after him. From the Embassy, Niccolini sent him cakes, cold meats, fruit, and his favorite wines.

He had little appetite for these delicacies, and no special privileges eased his inner agony. For many years he had known, with one part of his mind, that this reckoning might come. He had never really believed it. In every way he knew he had tried to win over ecclesiastical opinion to Copernicus and the new astronomy. Up until the last months, he had seemed very near success. Now at last he was forced to admit that he had lost.

Night after night he must have lain awake in anguish, trying to resolve the terrible conflict within him. As a man of science, he knew he had been right. As a devout Catholic—and he had always considered himself thus—he knew there was no course open to him but that of obedience to the Church.

The Inquisition moved slowly. On April 27, when deliberations had been going on for ten long weeks, Firenzuola, president of the council, came into his room and sat down at his bedside. The inquisitor described the meeting in a letter written the next day to Cardinal Francesco Barberini, a nephew of Pope Urban VIII.

"That no time might be lost, I entered into discourse with Galileo yesterday afternoon, and after many and many arguments and rejoinders had passed between us, by God's grace, I attained my objects, for I brought him to a full sense of his error, so that he clearly recognized that he had erred and had gone too far in his book. And to all this he gave expression in words of much feeling, like one who experienced great consolation in the recognition of his error, and he was also willing to confess it judicially. He requested, however, a little time in order to consider the form in which he might most fittingly make the confession, which, as far as its substance is concerned, will, I hope, follow in the manner indicated. . . ."

There is no record of what went on in Galileo's mind as he listened to Firenzuola's "many and many arguments." One can surmise that it was at this time he finally made up his mind to renounce his life's work.

Two days later, on April 30, he was called for another hearing, and asked whether he had anything to say. His statement—denying everything he believed most strongly—was ready:

"In the course of some days' continuous and attentive reflection on the interrogations put to me on the twelfth of the present month, and in particular as to whether, sixteen years ago, an injunction was intimated to me by order of the Holy Office, forbidding me to hold, defend, or teach 'in any manner' the opinion that had just been condemned—of the motion of the earth and the stability of the sun—it occurred to me to reperuse my printed *Dialogue*, which for three years I had not seen, in order carefully to note whether, contrary to my most sincere intention, there had, by inadvertence, fallen from my pen anything from which a reader or the authorities might infer not only some taint of disobedience on my part but also other particulars which might induce the belief that I had contravened the orders of the Holy Church.

"Being, by the kind permission of the authorities, at liberty to send about my servant, I succeeded in procuring a copy of my book, and, having procured it, I applied myself with the utmost diligence to its perusal and to a most minute consideration thereof. And as, owing to my not having seen it for so long, it presented itself to me, as it were, like a new writing and by another author, I freely confess that in several places it seemed to me set forth in such a form that a reader ignorant of my real purpose might have had reason to suppose that the arguments brought on the false side, and which it was my intention to confute, were so expressed as to be calculated rather to compel conviction by their cogency than to be easy of solution.

"Two arguments there are in particular—the one taken from the solar spots, the other from the ebb and flow of the tide—which in truth come to the ear of the reader with far greater show of force and power than ought to have been imparted to them by one who regarded them as inconclusive and who intended to refute them, as indeed I truly and sincerely held and do hold them to be inconclusive and admitting of refutation. And, as an excuse to myself for having fallen into an error so foreign to my intention, not contenting myself entirely with saying that when a man recites the arguments of the opposite side with the object of refuting them, he should, especially if writing in the form of dialogue, state these in their strictest form and should not cloak them to the disadvantage of his opponent—not contenting myself, I say, with this excuse, I resorted to that of the natural complacency which every man feels with regard to his own subtleties and in showing himself more skillful than the generality of men in devising, even in favor of false propositions, ingenious and plausible arguments. With all this, although with Cicero 'avidior sim gloriae quam sat est,' if I had now to set forth the same reasonings, without doubt I should so weaken them that they should not be able to make an apparent show of that force of which they are really and essentially devoid. My error, then, has been—and I confess it—one of vainglorious ambition and of pure ignorance and inadvertence.

"This is what it occurs to me to say with reference to this particular and which suggested itself to me during the reperusal of my book."

It would seem that no man could humble himself more than he had done. Yet, after he was dismissed, he returned to make an additional statement, in which he offered to revise the *Dialogue* so that it would become a refutation of what he knew to be true:

"And in confirmation of my assertion that I have not held and do not hold as true the opinion which has been condemned, of the motion of the earth and the stability of the sun—if there shall be granted to me, as I desire, means and time to make a clearer demonstration thereof, I am ready to do so; and there is a most favorable opportunity for this, seeing that in the work already published the interlocutors agree to meet again after a certain time to discuss several distinct problems of Nature not connected with the matter discoursed of at their meetings. As this affords me an opportunity of adding one or two other 'days,' I promise to resume the arguments already brought in favor of the said opinion, which is false and has been condemned, and to confute them in such most effectual manner as by the blessing of God may be supplied to me. I pray, therefore, this holy Tribunal to aid me in this good resolution and to enable me to put it in effect."

These two statements make up the recantation of Galileo, which ever since has been a subject of the widest speculation.

They were not exacted under torture, though he may have been shown the instruments of torture and threatened with them. Fear of death could have had little to do with them. He knew his life span was drawing to a close and in the midst of his disillusion and sorrow, death could not have seemed too fearsome. He made them because he felt it was his duty to do so, because there was no other way. If he had any consolation, it was that neither his words nor anything else in the world could change the truth; one day his science would triumph.

Temporarily Firenzuola released him in the custody of Niccolini, who was overwhelmed to see him. "It is a fearful thing to have to do with the Inquisition," the Ambassador wrote his Grand Duke. "The poor man has come back more dead than alive." He and Galileo's other friends were confident that the worst was over. His daughter, Sister Celeste, sent a loving letter. She was stunned with joy at the good news, she wrote, and chatted on about life in Arcetri:

"The potted oranges have been damaged by a storm . . . Your little mule become so haughty that she will be ridden by none . . . I have bought six bushels of wheat, so that as soon as it gets cooler, Piera [a servant] can go about making bread. She says that her desire for your

return is so much greater than yours, that if they were
put on a balance, yours would go highly up in the air."

The next interrogation of the Inquisition took place
on May 10. Firenzuola, on opening the session, informed
Galileo that according to the rules eight days were allowed for him to present a defense. Galileo saw no reason to postpone this empty formality and spoke at once.

He pleaded his "misunderstanding" about the decree
of 1616, that he had been unaware he was "not to teach
in any way whatsoever" the doctrine of Copernicus. He
concluded, ". . . It remains for me to beg you to take
into consideration my pitiable state of bodily indisposi-
tion, to which, at the age of seventy years, I have been
reduced by ten months of constant mental anxiety. . . ."

The final hearing was on June 20. Once more he was
bidden to speak the truth under threat of torture, and
again he stated that he had once held the Copernican
doctrine to be true but that he no longer did so. The
repetitions of his recantation—and many were demanded
—must have been harder to bear than his first statements.
When asked to confess the truth for the third time, he
could only say dully, "I am here to obey, and I have not
held this opinion since the decision was pronounced, as
I have stated."

There is a story that after all of this, Galileo murmured under his breath, "And the earth still moves." It
may be so; at least, no one can prove otherwise.

On Wednesday, June 22, 1633, Galileo was taken to
a large hall in the Dominican monastery. Clad in a white
shirt of penitence, he was made to kneel in the presence
of his judges while the sentence was read to him. As he
knelt, the long charge against him was reviewed, and

only after that did he hear his punishment. The *Dialogue* was to be prohibited. He was condemned to formal prison for a length of time to be determined by the Holy Office. For three years he was to come before them once a week to repeat the seven penitential psalms.

The sentence was not enforced. After a few final days with Ambassador Niccolini and his wife, he was sent to Siena in the charge of Archbishop Piccolomini, where he stayed for six months. In December, the Church grew kind and allowed him to return to Arcetri, on condition that he would not go to Florence or receive more than two visitors at a time.

His reunion with his beloved daughter, Sister Celeste, was tinged with melancholy. She had taken her father's agony as her own and it had sapped her fragile strength. The gentle nun lived on only until April, 1634.

Work had been the habit of Galileo's life. Even the Inquisition could not change that. He turned back to his former interest in motion, falling bodies, energy, heat, specific gravity. His book on these subjects, *Two New Sciences*, was the first great work on physics and laid the foundation for the laws of motion of Sir Isaac Newton, born the year of Galileo's death.

It was his last contribution to science. Soon afterward blindness overtook him. In the summer of 1638 he was permitted to live with his son in Florence, but his visitors were still limited. One of them came all the way from England, a young poet with flashing brown eyes named John Milton. Milton later referred briefly to this visit in *Areopagitica*, a speech addressed to Parliament against an order requiring the licensing of all books: ". . .There it was that I found and visited the famous Galileo, grown old, a prisoner to the Inquisition for thinking in

astronomy otherwise than the Franciscan and Dominican licensers thought."

Pope Urban VIII never restored Galileo to his freedom or released him from house arrest. His vengeance
outlived the astronomer. When Galileo died at Arcetri,
on January 8, 1642, at the age of seventy-eight, the Pope
forbade the Grand Duke to erect a monument in his
honor lest any word on it "offend the reputation of the
Holy Office."

"The state hath its own reasons that reason knoweth
not." The trial of Galileo, conducted by the Roman
Inquisition, had not been unfair by the standards of the
times. Its decisions remained on the records until 1885,
when they were quietly reversed. The stargazer of Tuscany was vindicated at last.

PETER ZENGER

On August 1, 1732, the citizens of the City of New York were in a turmoil of excitement. The new governor of New York and the Jerseys, appointed by the British Crown, had just arrived from England. People were justly curious about him. Though they had no say in his appointment, for an indeterminate number of years their welfare would be in his hands.

At the Black Horse Tavern, which in lieu of a popular newspaper served as a clearinghouse for news, men gathered in clusters, exchanging their few meager bits of information as they drank their ale. The name of their new governor was William Cosby, and he was formerly a brigadier general of the Royal Irish Army. He was a close friend of the English nobleman, the Duke of Newcastle. His wife was a sister of the Earl of Halifax. His last post had been governor of Minorca, but no one knew whether he had resigned or been

forced to quit. Before coming to New York, he had spent some time in London, securing repeal of a sugar bill detrimental to colonial interests. This, at least, was in his favor.

The colonists knew by experience that the Crown appointees, however impressive their titles, were not always honorable men. William Cosby, they reasoned, could hardly be worse than some of his predecessors, such as the notorious Edward Hyde, Lord Cornbury, whom Queen Anne had appointed governor back in 1703 and who had turned out to be a scamp, a spendthrift, and a drunkard. In the succession of New York governors, men like Cornbury were the rule rather than the exception.

Someone at the Black Horse Tavern may well have grumbled that whether the Crown's choice was good or bad was not the question: Free men should have the right to vote for a governor of their own choice. Anyone speaking so rashly would have been quickly silenced by his friends. Such sentiments were akin to treason, punishable by a stretch in the pillory or a public flogging.

Compared to Boston or Philadelphia, early eighteenth-century New York, with a population of less than ten thousand, was a small provincial town. There was an air of prosperity about it, with its neat rows of handsome red-brick buildings and cobblestone-paved streets, and its many well-dressed people, including a goodly sprinkling of imposing British officials and red-coated British officers. Manhattan Island, bought from the Indians in 1625 by the Netherlands East India Company for trinkets worth twenty-four dollars, had been conquered by the English in 1674, and New Amsterdam had been renamed New York. In the 1730's, most of the inhabitants were still of Dutch descent. About one in ten were Negro slaves; the English occupied many of the higher posts, and there were some Germans and other European nationals, but Dutch customs prevailed.

The townspeople saw their new governor, an imposing, haughty man in appearance, the second day of his arrival. At eleven in the morning he marched in a parade of important New York citizens from the governor's mansion, which was in the old Dutch fort near Bowling Green, to City Hall. A company of mounted halberdiers in full-dress uniform preceded him and British militia lined the streets. Later, when His Excellency returned to the fort, the soldiers drew up on the parade grounds and saluted him with three volleys.

Gradually reports about Governor Cosby seeped through to the Black Horse Tavern, and at first they were favorable. He was charming and well-bred and generous. At his parties at the governor's mansion, food was abundant and excellent and his wines were the very finest. Obviously he was a person of private means who did not have to steal from the colonies to enrich himself. Or so it seemed.

Another less pleasant story cropped up. The Governor, it was said, had been out driving in the country when his carriage was blocked by a farmer and his cart. Enraged because the farmer did not get off the road quickly enough to suit his pleasure, Cosby ordered his coachman to whip him. People went on hoping that this unsavory tale had been exaggerated in the telling.

At the next meeting of the New York Assembly, Governor Cosby was voted an annual salary of fifteen hundred pounds and an additional gratuity of 750 pounds for his services in repealing the unpopular sugar bill. Lewis Morris, the elderly and beloved chief justice of the New York Supreme Court, went to Cosby to inform him of this token of the citizens' appreciation. Far from being pleased, the Governor sneered because the sum was so small.

"Why didn't they add the shillings and pence?" he exploded.

Shocked and mortified, Justice Morris reported the Governor's reaction to the Assembly. There was some grim discussion, after which the members voted to increase the gratuity to a thousand pounds. Cosby gained 250 pounds by his outburst; he lost far more than money in public esteem.

Soon he showed his temper again.

Governor John Montgomerie, whom Cosby was replacing, had died the year before. In the little more than a year that New York had been without a governor, the president of the Council, a respected and well-to-do Dutchman named Rip Van Dam, served as acting governor. Now Cosby sent for Van Dam, waved in his face an order from the King, telling him that by this order he was entitled to half the salary of the office of governor from the time of his appointment until he reached New York a year later. On the basis of this order, he demanded that Van Dam refund him half of the monies the Assembly had paid him as acting governor, a sum of some nine hundred pounds.

The Dutchman was rightfully indignant. He had earned that money and it was his. He would not give Cosby a penny of it. In the next few days he had a chance to study the King's order carefully. Cosby's interpretation of it was somewhat erroneous. The order actually stated that *all* monies received for public services by either Cosby or the acting governor over the specified thirteen-month period should be divided equally, not only the sum paid Van Dam by the New York Assembly. A London friend of Van Dam's did some checking for him. Letters across the ocean traveled slowly; it was several months later that Van Dam learned that Cosby had been granted an allotment by the government before he left England. If their joint earnings were evenly split, in accordance with the King's order, Cosby would owe him, Van Dam, around thirty-five hundred pounds.

"We will settle our accounts fairly and squarely," he told Cosby blandly. "All that is needed is for you to pay me thirty-five hundred pounds."

Governor Cosby stormed. The insolence of the Dutchman! He would teach him a lesson he would not forget. He would sue. . . .

There was the question of how such a suit might be handled. He dared not sue in chancery, as was customary in litigation cases, since a jury would be called, and any jury of New York freeholders would be certain to favor Vam Dam, who was one of their own, a man they all knew and trusted. Nor was this suit a normal matter for the Supreme Court. On the advice of the attorney general, Richard Bradley, the Governor undertook a tricky legal procedure. By an ordinance dated December 4, 1732, Cosby proclaimed that the Supreme Court judges had authority to hear cases as Barons of the Exchequer in a "court of equity." Thereupon, Bradley brought action against Van Dam in the King's name—on the unstable theory that since Cosby represented the King, anything that benefited the governor would also benefit the King.

For his defense Van Dam hired the two best lawyers in New York, two young men named James Alexander and William Smith. When the case came up, they ignored the matter of who owed what and concentrated on one point. They claimed that it was illegal to set up a "court of equity" without the consent of the General Assembly, that in doing so Governor Cosby had exceeded his authority.

The Supreme Court of New York—which Cosby had temporarily transformed into his "court of equity" —was composed of three judges. Two of them, James De Lancey and Frederick Philipse, found it to their own best interests to side with the Governor. The chief justice, Lewis Morris, had the power of veto over the other two and possessed more courage than either. He ruled with the two lawyers that the "court of equity" was illegal and had no authority to act.

His verdict, dated April 9, 1733, concluded: "And as I take it, the giving of a new jurisdiction in equity by letters patent to an old court, that never had such jurisdiction before, or erecting a new court of equity by letters patent or ordinance of the Governor and Council, without assent of the Legislature, are equally unlawful, and not . . . sufficient warrant to justify this court to proceed in a cause of equity, and therefore by the Grace of God, I, as Chief Justice of this Province, shall not pay any obedience to them in that point."

Governor Cosby learned about Morris' verdict in New Jersey, and promptly sent him a vitriolic letter accusing him of lack of integrity and demanding a copy of his remarks in court. With the copy of his speech, the chief justice enclosed a letter that read in part:

"As to my integrity, I have given you no occasion to call it in question. I have been in this office almost twenty years, my hands were never fouled with a bribe; nor am I conscious to myself that Power or Poverty hath been able to induce me to be partial in the favour of either of them, and as I have no reason to expect any favour from you so am I neither afraid or ashamed to stand the test of the strictest inquiry you can make concerning my conduct. I have served the public faithfully and honestly, according to the best of my knowledge; and I have and do appeal to them for my justification."

There was only one way for any man in the Colonies, even such an important one as Chief Justice Morris, to appeal to the public for justification. He gave a second copy of his speech in court to a young German-born printer named John Peter Zenger, so it could be printed in quantity and distributed widely.

Up until now, this drama of local politics has been confined to a cast of eight characters: on one side, the arrogant Governor William Cosby, Attorney General Richard Bradley, the judges, De Lancey and Philipse; in opposition to their policies were Chief Justice Lewis Morris, the stubborn Dutchman, Rip Van Dam, the two young lawyers, James Alexander and William Smith.

All eight of these men were well-to-do and prominent. Ironically, they would mostly be forgotten were it not for this Peter Zenger, a poor printer with no social position at all, who spoke English haltingly and wrote it with difficulty, who worked as hard as any Negro slave to provide for his wife and children.

No one ever bothered to make a portrait of Peter Zenger, which is a shame. Only a few facts are known of his early life.

The Zenger family set sail for America in 1710, when Peter was thirteen. They were German refugees from the lower Palatinate on the Rhine, who, like thousands of others, had been driven from their homes by the French. The English Government advanced money to pay passage to the Colonies for these unfortunates, which they were obligated to pay back from future earnings.

The long and stormy crossing took six to seven weeks. Passengers were crowded below decks in the dark and unpleasant hold. To add to their misery, a typhus epidemic broke out. (Robert Hunter, then New York governor, reported that some four hundred and fifty of the refugees en route for America died in a single month.) It is believed that Peter Zenger's father was among the casualties. His widow, Hannah Zenger, Peter, and a younger brother and sister landed safely at the port of New York.

Most of the Palatinates were employed in the pine forests up the Hudson, in a project to produce tar and turpentine for British ships. The Zenger family might have gone to one of these river communities had Peter's father lived, but the work there was not for women or children. It is probable that Hannah Zenger found a position as a household servant in New York and kept her two youngest with her.

It is known that on October 26, 1710, she signed a paper apprenticing her oldest son Peter to the New York printer, William Bradford. By this legal agreement, Peter had to work as Bradford's servant and shop assistant for eight years. He received board and food but no wages and he learned the printing trade. So far as is known, he was treated as a member of the Bradford family and was neither overworked nor underfed. Such apprenticeships were common for youths of poor families who wanted to learn a trade. While Zenger was working for Bradford, another colonial boy named Benjamin Franklin was serving as an apprentice to his brother James in a Boston printing shop.

William Bradford was then the only printer in New York. Previously he had been Pennsylvania's first printer, having settled in Philadelphia after coming from England in 1685. The first thing off his press was an accurate copy of William Penn's Pennsylvania Charter. Certain prominent Philadelphians who had distorted the charter for their personal benefit raised such a stir that Bradford was summoned before the Governor and the City Council and put under a five-hundred-dollar bond. Three years after this episode he published a pamphlet that offended the Society of Friends. His press was seized and he was taken to court, but because the jury disagreed he was released. By this time he had had enough of Philadelphia politics and moved to New York. For the rest of his life, his motto was prudence.

In New York Bradford printed almanacs and religious works in English, Dutch, and French, as well as official reports and paper money for the government, and in 1715 he issued a prayer book in the Mohawk Indian language. Possibly young Peter helped him set type on it. None of this output could have provided much entertainment—there were no novels or poetry or humor—but then, he was not there to be amused but to learn.

He was twenty-one when his long apprenticeship

ended, and he left New York at once, possibly to satisfy a long-suppressed desire to see more of his adopted country. In Chestertown, Maryland, he set up his own printing shop and got married. His young wife died after giving birth to a boy named John, but he stayed on and within two years had become official printer for the entire Province of Maryland. On October 27, 1720, Zenger applied for his naturalization papers; he was granted citizenship nearly three years later, on July 6, 1723.

In the meantime he had returned with his small son to New York to work as a journeyman for his former patron, William Bradford. He may have been in the shop the day that seventeen-year-old Benjamin Franklin, having quit his brother's printing shop in Boston, wandered in and asked for a job. Bradford turned him down, advising him to go to Philadelphia, where Franklin became that city's most famous citizen.

Soon after his return to New York, Peter Zenger married a second time. His bride, Anna Catherine Maulin, was an attractive, intelligent young woman of a good family. She helped him in the shop and kept house as well. Everything indicates that the two loved each other deeply and that their marriage was a happy one.

Anna Zenger is known today as the "mother of Sunday schools." In her time, children went to church with their elders, squirming and fidgeting on hard benches as the preacher delivered a sermon that might last several hours. Anna suffered with them and for them. Convinced that this grueling ordeal did nothing for their souls or their minds, she persuaded the parents to let her hold Sunday classes where she taught boys and girls

Bible stories in simple language. This was the beginning of the institution of Sunday schools.

In 1725, William Bradford made Peter Zenger his partner and in the same year started New York's first newspaper, the *Gazette*. It was a dull paper devoted almost entirely to legal notices and government advertising, devoid of current events or human interest. Naturally it mirrored the view of the British Crown and the English officials, causing someone to say it was a paper for "those who had," not for "those who had not."

It is indicative of Zenger's disinterest in this sheet that he stayed with Bradford only a year longer. Their partnership was disbanded after they produced one book together. In 1726, no doubt with Anna's encouragement, Zenger set up his own printing shop on Smith Street (now William Street), which was then in the heart of New York City.

Sixteen years had passed since he had disembarked at the port of New York, a frightened, shabby lad who knew not a word of English. Now, at twenty-nine, he was the head of his own business, a married man with two children, his first-born, John, and another boy born in 1725 named Pieter. (Four more were added to his family in the next years: Nicolas, in 1727; Elizabeth, the following year; Evert, in 1732, and the sixth, Frederick, in 1734.) With no proof to the contrary, one can imagine him as a big blond young man, good-humored, slow to anger and hardworking, hands stained with printer's ink, who except on Sundays rarely appeared without the leather apron of his trade.

While Bradford held a monopoly on government printing, there was plenty of other work, less profitable, to be sure, for a good printer in this thriving community. He did Dutch religious tracts, in 1730 printed New York's first arithmetic book, called *Vanema's Arithmetica*, and a variety of miscellaneous jobs. Even so, it was not easy to feed and buy shoes for his growing family.

Through a friend he learned to play the organ. When he had become sufficiently good at it, the Old Dutch Church offered to pay him twelve pounds a year to play at Sunday services. It seemed a stroke of luck at the time, but months passed without a mention of money. Had the church elders forgotten him? How can one submit a bill to a church without seeming to lack piety? One day Zenger drew up a solemn petition, requesting that the church authorities permit him to take up a collection from the congregation for his back salary. The petition may have been presented humorously but it shamed the elders into paying him. Peter Zenger was an honest man, and he expected others, no matter how highly placed, to be honest with him.

In the absence of a people's press, whenever anyone had something important to say, he had to get it printed himself. Sometimes Zenger was asked to print political tracts that the prudent Bradford declined to handle because of their controversial nature. From these tracts and from talking to the men who wrote them, Zenger became aware of the existence of injustice even in this country that had been so kind to him.

There was the sad situation of his fellow German Palatine refugees, for example, the families who had come to America at the same time as he and been sent to work along the Hudson in the English-sponsored tar-making project. The project had collapsed because the pines of that region proved unsuitable for the production of tar in large quantities, and misery had struck the river communities. Rather than providing them a more profitable way to earn a living, the English had commandeered their men for an expedition against Canada, leaving women and children to face starvation or servitude. Some families became so desperate they turned to the Indians for help. The Indians gave them permission to settle at Schoharie, where many went, in defiance of a British order forbidding them to do so.

It was wrong, very wrong, to bring helpless people to the Colonies and then treat them like cattle. Zenger might not have much education, but he knew what was right. It was not by accident that Chief Justice Lewis Morris asked him to print his speech about the illegal "court of equity." Zenger already had a reputation as a man who was not afraid to take the side of truth.

That, by publicizing this speech, Morris would further incur Governor Cosby's displeasure was a foregone conclusion. To the Duke of Newcastle, on May 3, 1733, Cosby sent a bitter letter:

"Things are now gone that length that I must either discipline Morris or suffer myself to be affronted, or, what is still worse, see the King's authority trampled on and disrespect and irreverence to it taught from the Bench. . . ."

In August, four months later, he summarily dismissed Morris as chief justice, a post he had held so long and faithfully, and commissioned James De Lancey in his place. Frederick Philipse automatically became second justice. Thus, instead of three justices, the Supreme Court of New York now had but two, both supporters of Governor Cosby.

It was hardly a year since Governor Cosby had as-

sumed his post in New York, and the Black Horse
Tavern was buzzing with a list of his misdeeds, over and
above his dismissal of Lewis Morris and his wretched
attempt to dupe Rip Van Dam of his salary. On a trip to
Albany, Cosby had destroyed a deed made with the
Mohawk Indians to protect them against the rapid set-
tling of their country, solely so he might receive a fee
when a new grant was executed. There were several
other instances when he had granted lands to settlers
only on the condition that a third of the grant be reserved for his personal use. The man the friendly New
Yorkers had first called generous had turned out to be
greedier than any of his predecessors. There were rum-
blings in the tavern that no caution would still.

A new political organization sprang into being. It was
called the Popular Party and was made up of men whose
indignation was aroused by Cosby's highhanded methods. The Popularists persuaded Lewis Morris to bring
his case to the people by standing for election as Westchester representative of the General Assembly. The
election was scheduled to be held at Eastchester Green
in October, 1733. As was the custom, Nicolas Cooper,
the High Sheriff of Westchester County, placed posters
on the church and at other public places, announcing the
day and place. The posters omitted to give the time of
the election, however, an oversight that aroused suspicion among the Popular Party membership.

Some fifty of them showed up on Eastchester Green
at midnight the night before the election and kept watch
all night long. Others met in New York and headed on
horseback toward New Rochelle, stopping at various
houses along the way to enjoy bountiful repasts prepared for them in advance and to collect new recruits.

By the time they reached the house of one William LeCount of New Rochelle, their number had so snowballed there was not room for them inside. They built a large fire in the street and sat around it till dawn.

The next morning a parade of some three hundred horsemen verged on Eastchester Green. At the head of it were two trumpeters and three violin players, followed by four voters, each carrying a banner embroidered in gold with "King George" on one side and "Liberty and Law" on the other. The candidate, Lewis Morris, rode next, and behind him, the rest of the horsemen. Never had so many showed up to vote for one assemblyman since the country was settled.

At Eastchester Green, the fifty men who had been on guard all night scrambled to their feet, jumped on their horses, and joined the others. With horns blasting, they rode three times around the green, then dispersed to nearby taverns for a hearty breakfast.

The opposition did not appear until about eleven that morning—Governor Cosby's choice as candidate, a schoolteacher named William Forster who had paid Cosby some four hundred dollars for the nomination, escorted by the two judges, De Lancey and Philipse, and a mere hundred and seventy horsemen. At high noon Sheriff Cooper galloped up on a handsome horse with a splendid saddle trimmed with scarlet and silver.

The election could now begin and the sheriff read His Majesty's Writ, showing he had the right to conduct it. He needed only a glance to see that Morris' three hundred and fifty supporters, to which were now added thirty-seven somberly clad Quakers, could outvote Forster's party. But though an oral vote was considered sufficient unless there was some doubt about the outcome, the sheriff insisted on a written poll. There was a two-hour delay to get the ballot boxes ready. The voting was not secret and each man announced his choice as he approached the table where the sheriff sat.

When it came the turn of the Quakers, the first stated he was voting for Lewis Morris.

"Do you have property?" the sheriff asked him. In colonial New York, a man had to have property to have the right to vote.

"I do," the Quaker said.

The sheriff ordered him to swear on the Bible that this was true. The Quaker explained that taking an oath on the Bible was forbidden by his religion but that he would gladly take a solemn affirmation as to the truth of his statement, a practice legally accepted in both England and America for those of his faith. Sheriff Cooper, who was a law unto himself, disqualified him, as well as all the other thirty-seven Quakers.

In the end it made no difference. Lewis Morris won by a large majority. The cheers that broke out could be heard all over Eastchester.

It is believed that Peter Zenger was present at the election, and though he could not vote, since he was not a property owner, that he took notes on everything that went on. A full account of the election, including the illegal ban on Quaker votes, appeared in the first issue of a new newspaper called the *Weekly Journal* on November 5, 1733.

The *Journal*, like Bradford's *Gazette*, was a small paper, folded to make four pages printed in double columns, each page about eight by twelve inches. It offered "subscriptions at three shillings per quarter and advertisements at three shillings the first week and one shilling every week thereafter." Only one name appeared on the masthead: "Peter Zenger, Printer." It was the first newspaper in the American colonies to expose corruption of English rule.

It must be admitted that the *Journal* was not planned by Zenger alone. Back of it were Lewis Morris; his son, Lewis Morris, Jr.; the lawyers James Alexander and William Smith; Cadwalader Colden, a prominent New York scholar and politician; and perhaps Rip Van Dam. These men, who for political reasons did not want their names used, wrote most of the *Journal's* articles and editorials. James Alexander apparently served as editor-in-chief. But it was Zenger who did the printing—and took full responsibility for it.

The appearance of the *Journal* was a major event in New York. Whereas few bothered to read Bradford's pedantic *Gazette*, everybody bought the *Journal* and everybody talked about it. It was a medley of witticisms, satire, lampoons, squibs, ballads—the latter thought to be written by Zenger—and some extremely well-written political articles. In its second issue it defended the liberty of the press: "The Liberty of the Press is a Subject of the greatest Importance and in which every Individual is as much concern'd as he is in any other Part of Liberty."

Most of all, it campaigned against Governor Cosby and his policies, in pieces signed noncommittally "Cato" or "Philo Patriae" or "Thomas Standby."

In successive issues the Governor was accused of voting as a member of the Council during its legislative sessions, of demanding that Assembly bills be presented to him before the Council saw them, of adjourning the Assembly in his own name instead of the King's—all in

violation of the rules by which a governor was bound—
and of other crimes against the people. "A Governor
turned rogue, does a thousand things for which a small
rogue would have deserved a halter. . . ." read one
editorial. "A Governor does all he can to chain you, and
it being difficult to prevent him, it is prudent in you
(in order to keep out of prison) to help him put the
chains on and to rivet them fast."

As the *Journal* continued to appear, week after week,
Cosby's cries of pain crossed the ocean. "A press supported by him [Alexander] and his party," he wrote,
"has begun to swarm with the most virulent libels.
. . . They [Van Dam and Alexander] are so implaca-
ble in their malice that I am to look for all the insolent,
false and scandalous aspersions that such bold and profligate wretches can invent." But though he knew who
stood behind the *Journal*, he had no way of proving it.

Bradford's *Gazette* was assigned a new editor—a special friend of Governor Cosby named Francis Harison.
Harison was a cocky little man who had been whee-
dling easy jobs for himself for about twenty years. In
turn he had been governor's council, recorder of the
City of New York, and judge of the admiralty. Once
when he was assigned to settle a boundary dispute between New York and Connecticut, Harison learned that
some fifty thousand acres were to be turned over to New
York and wrote friends in London, advising them to
snap them up before the colonists could get them. The
trouble was he gave his friends the wrong acreage, as
they learned to their sorrow when they tried to get
land grants. This incident brought Harison a reputation
for both underhand dealings and stupidity.

With Harison on the editorial staff, the *Gazette*

launched into flowery prose. It spoke of the "harmoney and good understanding between the several branches of the legislature—whereby nothing came to be demanded on one side but what was for the public general good and welfare of His Majesty's people," and of "all those blessings which we enjoy under a government greatly envied." Sometimes it blossomed into verse:

> "*Cosby, the mild, the happy, good and great*
> *The strongest guard of our little state . . .*"

For a while the *Gazette* ignored the *Journal*, as if stony silence could force its rival out of existence. In contrast, the *Journal* had a good deal of fun at the expense of Bradford's sheet. One mock advertisement was obviously directed to Francis Harison:

"A large spaniel of about five foot five inches high has lately strayed from his kennel with his mouth full of fulsome panegyrics, and in his ramble dropped them in the *New York Gazette*. When a puppy he was marked thus (FH), and a cross in the middle of his forehead; but the mark being worn out, he has taken upon him in a heathenish manner to abuse mankind by imposing a great many gross falsehoods on them. Whoever will strip the said panegyrics of their fulsomeness and send the beast back to his kennel, shall have the thanks of all honest men, and all reasonable charges."

The "spaniel" endured the barbs of ridicule just so long and then lashed back in the *Gazette:*

"Supposing another should turn the tables upon the authors of these infamous and fictitious advertisements, how easily might it be done? The real or imagined defects of the AMSTERDAM CRANE, the CONNECTICUT MAS-

TIFF, PHILLIP BABOON, SENIOR, PHILLIP BABOON, JUNIOR, the SCYTHIAN UNICORN and WILD PETER FROM THE BANKS OF THE RHINE might be enlarged upon, and placed in a most ludicrous light."

This example of Harison's poor wit is worth quoting only because it identifies the backers of the *Journal*. Rip Van Dam was the "Amsterdam Crane. The "Connecticut Mastiff" was lawyer William Smith; "Phillip Baboon Senior and Junior" were Lewis Morris, father and son. The "Scythian Unicorn" was apparently James Alexander, though no one knows why, while "Wild Peter from the Banks of the Rhine" was, of course, the *Journal's* printer.

In the war between the two papers, the *Journal* had an even greater advantage than its humor and effective writing. Peter Zenger and his supporters were all known to be honorable men, with no black marks on their record. Governor Cosby and Francis Harison could not compete in this respect, and everyone knew it. Copies of the *Journal* reached England, with the result that Parliament warned Cosby to watch his step. In New York, the proud Governor sensed that his colonial subjects, who should have given him loyalty and respect, were laughing at him behind his back. It was an unbearable situation, and he vowed to have revenge.

To silence the troublemakers, the Governor ordered Chief Justice De Lancey to get a grand jury indictment against the *Journal* on the ground of libel. De Lancey made the attempt twice but failed both times. The jurors claimed that since the editors did not sign their names, there was no one to indict.

Finally, in October, 1734, De Lancey, under orders of

the Governor, brought an indictment to the grand jury against Peter Zenger, specifying that "certain low ballads" in the *Journal* were libelous. "Sometimes heavy, half-witted men get a knack of rhyming," said De Lancey loftily, "but it is time to break them of it when they grow abusive and insolent and mischievous with it."

In the name of "His Majesty's Council" Cosby released an order that four of the most offensive issues of the *Journal* be "burnt by the hands of the common hangman, or whipper, near the pillory." The mayor and other city magistrates were instructed to witness the burning. Again he met with frustration. The court refused to accept the order, the aldermen protested it as arbitrary and illegal, and the magistrates forbade anyone within their authority, including the hangman, to have anything to do with it. Nearly all copies of the condemned issues disappeared. At the hour of the scheduled burning citizens stayed indoors and the streets of New York were empty. Only Francis Harison was there to supervise, and in place of the hangman, Harison's Negro slave set the tiny blaze. At the Black Horse Tavern and elsewhere in the city, people laughed at Cosby's folly.

The popularity of the *Journal* could not alter the fact that Cosby was still governor, lashed firmly to his position by the Crown appointment. Sometime in 1734, Lewis Morris sailed to London to try and get him recalled. He failed because there were too many important people in England who wanted Cosby to stay safely on the other side of the ocean. To James Alexander, Morris wrote:

"Everybody here agrees in a contemptible opinion of Cosby . . . and it may be you will be surprised to hear that the most nefarious crime a Governor can commit is not by some counted so bad as the crime of complaining of it. . . ."

Possibly it was in England that Morris learned what happened in Minorca while Cosby was governor there. By his greed and his arrogance, he had also exasperated the Minorcans, and they, too, had repeatedly and vainly tried to get him recalled. Eventually he overstepped himself. At a time when England and Spain were at peace, Cosby seized the cargo of a Spanish merchant ship, had it sold at auction, and took the proceeds for himself. In spite of the fact that his act might have caused the outbreak of a new war, all that happened to him was that he was ordered to reimburse the Spaniards and called home. His high-placed friends in England forestalled any formal reprimand. By granting him the governorship of New York, Parliament apparently felt they were rid of him at last.

While Lewis Morris continued his fruitless campaign in England, Cosby in New York decided on the drastic step of arresting Peter Zenger.

"It is ordered," read the warrant, "that the sheriff for the City of New York do forthwith take and apprehend John Peter Zenger for printing and publishing several seditious libels dispersed throughout his journals or newspapers, entitled *The New York Weekly Journal;* as having in them many things tending to raise factions and tumults among the people of this Province, inflaming their minds with contempt of His Majesty's government, and greatly disturbing the peace thereof. And upon his taking the said John Peter Zenger, to commit him to the prison or common jail of the said city and county."

Peter Zenger was taken into custody on November 17, 1734, and held in the jail on the third floor of New York's City Hall (now Federal Hall, at the corner of Wall and Nassau Streets, where the John Peter Zenger Museum is open to the public). He was forbidden to see his wife, children, friends, or lawyers, and refused pen, ink, and paper. The *Journal* was scheduled for the next day. It missed its publication date for the only time in its existence.

The following Wednesday, when the prisoner was brought before Chief Justice De Lancey, he complained vociferously about the harsh treatment he had received. After that he was permitted to speak to his wife Anna and other visitors through a small opening in his cell door and allowed to have writing materials. On November 19 the *Journal* appeared on schedule; it told the story of his arrest and imprisonment. His remarkable wife had calmly taken over the printing end of the paper, setting the type and running the press, with the aid of a journeyman and her sons. Throughout her husband's imprisonment she continued to see that their paper appeared on time each week—the first American woman to run a newspaper. It is believed that during this period she even wrote some of the articles and editorials.

Anna undoubtedly would have claimed that any other woman in her position would have done the same. Though the women of New York had very likely never heard the word "emancipation," on many occasions they had shown they could do a man's work. It was not uncommon for widows to carry on their husbands' businesses efficiently. One woman ran a thriving blacksmith shop after her husband's death. Another acted as her hus-

band's attorney while he was in Europe getting cus-
tomers for his foreign trade. Margaret Filipse, an
eighteenth-century "career woman," owned a number
of ships that she sent out regularly to foreign ports.
Women frequently went into the wilderness to make
trade agreements with the Indians; they had a special
talent for Indian languages and the Indians often preferred dealing with "white squaws" rather than their
men. James Alexander's wife, on her own, ran a store
and amassed a considerable fortune.

In prison, Peter Zenger was being questioned night
and day. Who was the editor of the *Journal?* Who wrote
the copy? Who financed it? The printer stubbornly refused to give his captors any satisfaction. The *Journal*
was all his, he said. He was responsible for everything
in it.

With feigned pity, the *Gazette* commented on "the
pretended patriots of our days . . . who are so tenacious
of their own [safety] as to neglect that of their poor
printer." For once Bradford's paper was on the side of
truth. No one of the *Journal*'s true editors and writers
stepped forward to go to prison in Zenger's place, although James Alexander and William Smith did volun-
teer their services as his counsel.

On a writ of habeas corpus, Zenger was brought before Chief Justice De Lancey. Alexander and Smith demanded that a reasonable bail be set for him. In response to De Lancey's questioning, Zenger swore he was
worth no more than forty pounds, excepting the tools
of his trade and his clothes. The court promptly set bail
at four hundred pounds. Over the protests of his lawyers that no man should be asked for a bail ten times
his fortune, he was taken back to prison. There is no

explanation as to why some of his backers, several of whom were quite wealthy, did not pay his bail for him.

His case was brought to the grand jury. They found no valid charge against him, but he was still not released. On January 28, 1735, after he had spent two months in prison, Attorney General Richard Bradley filed a charge against him of "false, scandalous, malicious and seditious libels." Since the court term had just been terminated, nothing more could be done until the new court term three months later.

When the term opened on April 15, Alexander and Smith promptly petitioned to contest the proceedings. Their petition was denied. Chief Justice De Lancey further accused them of contempt and disbarred them from legal practice in New York! Disconsolately, the two men consulted with their client. They could no longer act for him, at least openly. He must petition the court to appoint a new lawyer as his counsel.

The court's choice was a fashionable society lawyer named John Chambers, competent but not brilliant. It was too much to hope that he would risk offending Cosby and the chief justice by putting up a strong defense. Actually, he tried harder than anyone expected him to.

By law, Peter Zenger's case had to be tried by a "struck jury." This meant that the clerk of the court should, in the presence of witnesses, "strike off" the names of the jurymen from the Freeholders Book. (A freeholder was a property-owning citizen with the right to vote.) The list the clerk produced obviously had not come from the Freeholders Book. There were non-property owners on it who had no legal right to serve on a jury. Several of the names suggested were men dependent on Governor Cosby's bounty—his baker, tailor, shoemaker, and candlemaker.

To the surprise of Zenger's friends, John Chambers found the courage to protest this flagrant infraction of legal practice. Judge De Lancey, with every evidence of sincerity, claimed he had no idea how the "error" had occurred and ordered a proper jury "struck off."

The twelve men selected on that jury deserve to be mentioned by name: Thomas Hunt (the jury foreman), Harmanus Rutgers, Stanley Holmes, Edward Man, John Bell, Samuel Weaver, Andries Marschalk, Egbert van Borsom, Benjamin Hildreth, Abraham Keteltas, John Goelet, and Hercules Wendover.

For nearly nine months the defendant had been held in jail. The *Journal*, which over this period was filled with editorials on justice and on freedom of the press and attacks on Governor Cosby's unscrupulous methods, omitted all mention of the sufferings of its printer. One can guess, from contemporary descriptions, that his cell was sweltering in the summer and wretchedly cold as winter approached, that prison fare was miserable, and that Zenger survived it only by grace of the food Anna smuggled to him. His confinement must certainly have left him emaciated and haggard, but that he still refused to name his editors is proof that his morale remained unshaken.

On August 4, 1735, the German printer who held no sacrifice too great for the cause in which he believed, was brought to trial. Chief Justice James De Lancey and his associate justice, Frederick Philipse, presided. Attorney General Richard Bradley was prosecutor for the "court of the King." The jury was sworn in.

The court-appointed lawyer, John Chambers, presented Zenger's case, basing his plea on the assumption that the *Journal* printer should not be held responsible for the paper's editorial policy. He did the best he could under the circumstances, but that the prisoner would be found guilty seemed foreordained.

He was finishing his speech when an elderly white-haired gentleman, seated in the rear of the courtroom, rose and walked slowly and with some difficulty down the aisle toward the bench.

"May it please Your Honor," he said in a strong and resounding voice, "I am concerned in this cause on the part of Mr. Zenger, the defendant."

This courtly stranger, who was elegantly dressed and wore a magnificent wig, had the air of one accustomed to command respect. He was Andrew Hamilton, the outstanding lawyer in all the Colonies and one of Philadelphia's most distinguished citizens, a member of the Pennsylvania Council and the Philadelphia Assembly, an architect as well and designer of the Pennsylvania State House, which in the not-too-distant future would become known as "Independence Hall."

Though eighty years old and in feeble health, he had come to New York at the request of James Alexander to defend Peter Zenger and the freedom of the press. Of all the achievements of his illustrious career, none would bring him more lasting fame than his defense of this poor and obscure printer.

His first statement took the court by surprise: "I do (for my client) confess that he both printed and published the two newspapers set forth in the information —and I hope that in so doing he has committed no crime."

The court had subpoenaed Zenger's journeyman and

two of his sons to testify that Zenger had printed two issues of the *Journal* labeled "libelous." In view of Hamilton's admission, the prosecuting attorney, Bradley, moved for the dismissal of these witnesses, as their testimony was now unnecessary. Hamilton affably agreed:

"If you brought them here only to prove the printing and publishing of these newspapers, we have acknowledged that, and shall abide by it."

With this acknowledgment, Bradley—too quickly—assumed that the case was closed and that there was nothing more to be said: "Indeed, sir," he addressed Justice De Lancey, "as Mr. Hamilton has confessed the printing and publishing of these libels, I think the jury must find a verdict for the King. . . ."

"Not so, Mr. Attorney," Hamilton interrupted him. "There are two words to that bargain. I hope it is not our bare printing and publishing a paper that will make it a libel. You will have something more to do before you make my client a libeler. For the words themselves must be libelous—that is false, scandalous, and seditious —or else we are not guilty."

A libel could not be so called unless it was false. That was the basis of Hamilton's defense. Anything that was true could not be called a libel—by the attorney's own words, "scandalous, seditious, and false." To substantiate his claim, Hamilton quoted from English law to show precedent where men accused of libel had been allowed to defend themselves on the grounds that what they had written was true.

Prosecuting Attorney Bradley continued to argue that whether the person defamed was a private individual or a public figure, living or dead, whether the libel was true or false, it was nevertheless a libel. There was absolutely nothing to be said in defense of a man who had so "notoriously scandalized" the Governor and the principal magistrates and officers of the government. If these two newspapers were not libelous, he did not know what a libel was. . . .

While he blustered on, Hamilton waited patiently. Then, in measured tones, he addressed the bench: "May it please Your Honor, I agree with Mr. Attorney that government is a sacred thing, but I differ widely from him when he would insinuate that the just complaints of a number of men who suffer under a bad administration is libeling that administration. Had I believed that to be law, I should not have given the Court the trouble of hearing anything that I could say in this cause. . . .

"No, the falsehood makes the scandal, and both make the libel. And to show the Court that I am in good earnest, and to save the Court's time and Mr. Attorney's trouble, I will agree that if he can prove the facts charged upon us to be false, I shall own them to be *scandalous, seditious, and a libel.* So the work seems now to be pretty much shortened, and Mr. Attorney has now only to prove the words *false* in order to make us guilty."

"We have nothing to prove," the prosecuting attorney burst out angrily. "You have confessed the printing and publishing." By his shouting, he no doubt hoped to distract the jury from the simple fact that there was no one who could disprove the *Journal's* accusations against the Governor and his associates. Indeed, he knew very well it was impossible to do so.

"If a libel is understood in the large and unlimited sense urged by Mr. Attorney," continued Hamilton, undisturbed, "there is scarce a writing I know that may not be called a libel, or scarce a person safe from being called to an account as a libeler. For Moses, meek as he was, libeled Cain; and who is it that has not libeled the Devil? . . ."

He turned to the jury: "Gentlemen: The danger is great in proportion to the mischief that may happen through our too great credulity. A proper confidence in a court is commendable, but as the verdict (whatever it is) will be yours, you ought to refer no part of your duty to the discretion of other persons. If you should be of the opinion that there is no falsehood in Mr. Zenger's papers, you will, nay (pardon me for the expression) you ought, to say so—because you do not know whether others (I mean the Court) may be of that opinion. It is your right to do so, and there is much depending upon your resolution as well as upon your integrity.

"The loss of liberty, to a generous mind, is worse than death. And yet we know that there have been those in all ages who, for the sake of preferment, or some imaginary honor, have freely lent a helping hand to oppress, nay to destroy, their country.

"This brings to my mind that saying of the immortal Brutus when he looked upon the creatures of Caesar, who were very great men but by no means good men. 'You Romans,' said Brutus, 'if yet I may call you so, consider what you are doing. Remember that you are assisting Caesar to forge those very chains that one day he will make you yourselves wear.'

"Power may justly be compared to a great river," he continued. "While kept within its due bounds it is both beautiful and useful. But when it overflows its banks, it is then too impetuous to be stemmed; it bears down all before it, and brings destruction and desolation wherever it comes. If, then, this is the nature of power, let us at least do our duty, and like wise men (who value freedom) use our utmost care to support liberty, the only bulwark against lawless power, which in all ages has sacrificed to its wild lust and boundless ambition the blood of the best men that ever lived.

"I hope to be pardoned, Sir, for my zeal upon this occasion. It is an old and wise caution that when our neighbor's house is on fire we ought to take care of our own. For though (blessed be God) I live in a government where liberty is well understood and freely enjoyed, yet experience has shown us all (I am sure it has to me) that a bad precedent in one government is soon set up for an authority in another. And therefore I cannot but think it my, and every honest man's, duty that (while we pay all due obedience to men in authority) we ought at the same time to be upon our guard against power wherever we apprehend that it may affect ourselves or our fellow subjects.

"I am truly very unequal to such an undertaking on many accounts. You see that I labor under the weight of many years, and am bowed down with great infirmities of body. Yet, old and weak as I am, I should think it my duty, if required, to go to the utmost part of the land where my services could be of any use in assisting to quench the flame of prosecutions upon informations, set on foot by the government to deprive a people of the right of remonstrating (and complaining too) of the arbitrary attempts of men in power.

"Men who injure and oppress the people under their administration provoke them to cry out and complain, and then make that very complaint the foundation for new oppressions and prosecutions. I wish I could say that there were no instances of this kind."

From a mere case of libel, Andrew Hamilton, with his eloquence, had transformed the trial of Peter Zenger to a defense of the rights of free men everywhere. Now he was ready to conclude.

"The question before the Court and you, Gentlemen of the Jury, is not of small or private concern. It is not the cause of one poor printer, nor of New York alone, which you are now trying. No! It may in its consequence affect every free man that lives under a British government on the main of America. It is the best cause. It is the cause of liberty. And I make no doubt but your upright conduct this day will not only entitle you to the love and esteem of your fellow citizens, but every man who prefers freedom to a life of slavery will bless and honor you as men who have baffled the attempt of tyranny, and by an impartial and uncorrupt verdict have laid a noble foundation for securing to ourselves, our posterity, and our neighbors, that to which nature and the laws of our country have given us a right—the liberty of both exposing and opposing arbitrary power (in these parts of the world at least) by speaking and writing truth."

Attorney Bradley, in his closing comments, "observed that Mr. Hamilton had gone very much out of the way, and had made himself and the people very merry," but insisted once more that since the printing and publishing of the paper had been admitted, the jury had no choice but to vote the defendant guilty. Justice De Lancey warned the jurors that regardless of Hamilton's suggestions to the contrary, their task was simply to determine if the words in the information were libelous; the law was to be left to the court.

The jury felt otherwise. They were out of the court-room a bare ten minutes. When they returned, Thomas Hunt, as their foreman, announced their verdict:

"Not guilty."

"Huzzahs and cheers," as Peter Zenger wrote later, broke out in the crowded courtroom.

That evening the victory was celebrated by a dinner in honor of Andrew Hamilton at the Black Horse Tavern. Conspicuously absent from this happy affair was Hamilton's client, Peter Zenger. Although he was technically free, he had been taken back to his cell until the next day—when friends arrived with the funds to pay for his keep during the eight and a half months he had been in custody!

He bore no grudge at being omitted from the celebration and later wrote Hamilton a warm note of gratitude.

Hamilton left New York the next day to return to Philadelphia. As he departed he was saluted by the guns of several ships in the harbor—as a public testimony of the glorious defense he had made in the cause of liberty in the province. Some five weeks later the Common Council of the City of New York voted to present Hamilton with the freedom of the corporation in honor of his "learned and generous defense of the Rights of Mankind and the Liberty of the Press." As an additional memento, Hamilton was given a gold box made by the silversmith La Roux, inscribed with the coat of arms of the government and the colony, and filled with gold coins donated by New York's leading citizens.

A few months afterward, James Alexander and William Smith were reinstated to the bar. About the same time, Francis Harison, the notorious "little spaniel," was found guilty of a piece of chicanery and had to flee the country. He died in England, penniless. Governor Cosby survived the humiliation of his defeat only for a year, dying in 1736. Lewis Morris, the former chief justice, returned to America to become Governor of New Jersey. His son, Lewis Morris, Jr., became speaker of the New York Assembly, and his two grandsons, Lewis Morris III and Gouverneur Morris, were both signers of the Declaration of Independence.

As for Peter Zenger, he quietly returned to his shop to resume printing the *Journal*. As long as Cosby lived, he continued his attacks on the Governor's corrupt administration, ignoring the advice of friends who feared for his life and wanted him to leave New York.

After Cosby's death, the Crown appointed a more liberal-minded governor, George Clark, and a comparative calm settled on the New York scene. In 1737, Zenger was made public printer of New York, in belated acknowledgment of his dogged courage. A year later he became public printer for New Jersey as well. After his death in 1746, Anna Zenger published the *Journal* for two years by herself. It was then taken over by Zenger's son John until 1751, when publication ceased.

Andrew Hamilton's defense of Peter Zenger was widely distributed throughout the Colonies and helped to form the philosophy of the new generation who were to drive English tyranny from America forever. The verdict of Zenger's twelve-man jury, which anticipated modern libel laws by three-quarters of a century, has remained a landmark in American history. Thereafter no governor of any colony dared try to suppress the public press.

History awarded a proper place to Peter Zenger only after his lifetime. The loyal and faithful printer has come to be known as the founder of freedom of the press in America, the first of the Four Freedoms on which American democracy is based.

WS.

ROBERT EMMET

The trial of Robert Emmet, Irish patriot, opened at ten o'clock the morning of Monday, September 19, 1803, at the Green Street Courthouse, in Dublin. The charge was high treason—conspiracy and rebellion against the British Crown that then governed Ireland.

The defendant's two lawyers, Leonard McNally and Peter Burrowes, were both secretly in the pay of his accusers, and there was no witness to speak in his defense. The Crown had four attorneys (John Townsend, William Conyingham Plunket, William Ridgway, and a Mr. Mayne), as well as a long stream of witnesses to give evidence of the prisoner's guilt.

A little before nine o'clock mounted soldiers escorted Robert Emmet from his prison to the courthouse, through a laneway from Halston Street. Until time for him to appear he was kept waiting below the courtroom in a brick-walled cell with an arched ceiling so low he could barely stand erect.

When the court opened, the guards led him, in chains and with fetters on his ankles, to the prisoner's dock, facing judges and jury. He was a slight, pale young man of twenty-five with brown hair and eyes and regular features. Since the day before he had eaten nothing. For more than twelve hours he would stand in the prisoner's dock. His expression was serene and occasionally contemptuous.

For love of Ireland he had done the things for which he was to be judged. Love of a woman had helped lead him to his doom. He was certain he would be condemned and he was resigned to it, knowing that if it were all to do over he would not and could not have acted otherwise. He was sustained with the knowledge that it was Ireland, not he alone, who was on trial—for the crime of wishing to be free.

For more than six hundred years, Ireland had suffered from the oppressive measures of British rule. The Irish Parliament was made up largely of British appointees and in no way represented the Irish people. Dublin Castle was the seat of this Irish Parliament, and to the common people "the Castle" was synonymous with the British rulers and the Irish who collaborated with them.

The majority of the Irish were Catholics, still living with the searing memory of the harsh Penal Laws, the cruelest measures ever legally enacted by one country on another. By the Penal Laws, no Catholic could be a member of Parliament, a magistrate, lawyer, soldier, sailor, juryman, voter, sheriff, policeman, schoolmaster, or even a private tutor. Catholic schools were forbidden, nor could a Catholic child be sent abroad for the education

refused at home. A Catholic could not buy land, inherit land, or receive land as a gift from a Protestant. He could not own a horse worth more than five pounds. Catholics could not marry Protestants, and a Catholic who converted a Protestant could be condemned to death.

Though most of the Penal Laws had been revoked, at least on paper, the poverty, misery, and bitterness they had induced remained unabated.

The harsh treatment of Irish Catholics had not directly affected the distinguished and wealthy Emmet family, who were Protestant. Robert Emmet was born in a large and stately mansion across from Dublin's fashionable St. Stephen's Green on March 4, 1778, at the time America was fighting what seemed a losing battle for her independence. His father, Dr. Robert Emmet, was State Physician of Ireland and held other important official posts. Unlike most of Ireland's upper classes, Dr. Emmet never hesitated to speak out on the need for Parliamentary reform and gave regularly to Dublin's many poor and destitute. Mrs. Emmet, a woman of warm and tender nature with high principles about honor and moral conduct, assisted her husband in his charities.

Robert was the youngest of seventeen brothers and sisters, of whom only four survived childhood. The oldest, Christopher Temple Emmet, was a promising young lawyer, handsome and talented. As a child, Robert may have heard him rehearse this passage from one of his speeches:

"America! America! the land of arts and arms, where that Goddess, Liberty, was wooed and won, and twelve young eagles springing from her nest bore freedom upward on her soaring wings."

That there were thirteen, not twelve, states in the new United States did not make the lines less stirring.

Christopher died when he was twenty-eight and Robert was eleven. Robert's second brother, Thomas Addis Emmet, had just received his medical degree at the University of Edinburgh. Dr. Emmet summoned him home, insisting he must switch to law as a career so he could replace Christopher at the bar.

Thomas Addis lacked the oratorical power of Christopher, but he had a quiet intelligence combined with determination and integrity. Within three years he had completed his law studies. One of his first clients was James Napper Tandy, an Irish patriot accused of subversive activities against the Crown. His defense was so brilliant that the government, in an effort to buy him for their side, offered him a court post, but Thomas Addis, whose revolutionary ideals had been nourished in Edinburgh, turned them down.

Robert's one sister, Mary Anne, had the same principles as the rest of the Emmets. As a young girl she wrote several political pamphlets, one on the false patriotism of the Irish who worked at the Castle. She later married a lawyer named Robert Holmes, as dedicated to the cause of Irish freedom as she was.

Of all this talented family, young Robert was the least impressive—an undersized, quiet child who kept his thoughts to himself. At school he showed a special aptitude for mathematics and chemistry. At home one day he did an experiment involving corrosive sublimate (mercuric chloride) and that evening, while studying his algebra, he became violently ill. While concentrating, he had been biting his nails, thus swallowing traces of the poison. Rather than disturb his sleeping family, he looked up an antidote for corrosive sublimate in his father's medical encyclopedia. It recommended chalk. He found some in the coach house, but chewing on it brought him no relief. All night he tried to forget his excruciating pain by working out algebra problems in his mind, and the next morning at the breakfast table his face was "as small and yellow as an orange."

To ask help for trouble he had brought on himself was contrary to his nature, even at this early age.

In secret he composed poetry. His first surviving effort, written at the age of twelve, was titled "Erin's Call" and began:

> *Brothers arise: Our country calls—*
> *Let us gain her rights or die;*
> *In her cause who nobly falls,*
> *Decked with brightest wreaths shall lie;*
> *And Freedom's genius o'er his bier*
> *Shall place the wreath and drop a tear. . . .*

With time his verses improved in style but all had the same theme—the freedom of Ireland.

When he was fourteen he got hold of a copy of John Locke's *The Origin, Extent and End of Civil Government.* Robert found this heavy work fascinating reading, and his copy, which still exists, shows underlining and marginal notes in his handwriting on almost every page. One paragraph marked for emphasis stated that a people owe no obligation to a government if force, not choice, compels them to submission.

At fifteen he entered Dublin's Trinity College, as Christopher and Thomas Addis had done before him. Already he knew much of Ireland's unhappy history.

The year before, Thomas Addis had joined a secret patriotic organization, the Society of United Irishmen, a fraternal union of all Irishmen, Catholic and Protestant alike. Its aim was to fight the legal restrictions that burdened Ireland and to end English oppression forever. The plan—at first—was to accomplish its work by parliamentary reform, not by force.

Through his older brother, Robert met a number of the society's leaders, among them its founder, Theobald Wolfe Tone, son of a Belfast coachman, a fiery reckless young man filled with patriotic zeal, and the cofounder, tall handsome Thomas Russell, a former army officer who had renounced his military career to join Wolfe Tone.

At Trinity, meanwhile, Robert worked hard at his studies. Latin and French came naturally to him since they, rather than English, were commonly spoken in the Emmet home. He still excelled in mathematics and chemistry and in fact did well in all his subjects. The Reverend Archibald Douglas, who knew him during his college days, wrote of him later, "So gifted a creature does not appear in a thousand years."

One of his classmates was a plump, rosy-cheeked youth named Thomas Moore, the future author of "Believe Me, If All Those Endearing Young Charms," "The Last Rose of Summer," and of another poem that would immortalize Robert Emmet, "He Lived for His Love, for His Country He Died." In his *Memoirs*, Thomas Moore would speak of him as "wholly free from the follies and frailties of youth."

Robert gave the impression of being reserved and mild, but when he spoke before the college Historical Society he became transformed, at once "excitingly powerful and inspired" and able to hold his listeners by both his eloquence and the boldness of his opinions. In a debate on whether an aristocracy or democracy was most favorable to the advance of science and literature, Robert Emmet defended democracy so ardently that Thomas Moore claimed his words resounded in his ears for years. The conservative college authorities were less happy about what seemed to them dangerous ideas emanating from the Historical Society and arbitrarily locked their meeting room. The members, Robert Emmet among them, promptly and gleefully rented a room in Dublin, where they could continue their discussions undisturbed.

In December, 1796, at the age of eighteen, Robert Emmet took an oath of allegiance to the Society of United Irishmen, as Thomas Addis had done. Soon he was recruiting new members from among his fellow collegians. Under the guise of a debating society, the college students formed their own branch of the UI. Thomas Moore never joined them, although for the society's publication, *The Press*, he wrote an inflammatory piece urging students to be a "scourge to tyrants" so they could serve their "sunken and degraded country." Robert Emmet gently rebuked him. It might be dangerous to all of them, he pointed out, to call public attention to the political activities of the college. Unknown to either of them, the cruel and brutal head of the Dublin secret police, Major Charles Henry Sirr, who had set spies among the unsuspecting collegiates, already had a full account of their activities.

A split occurred within the ranks of the United Irishmen in December, 1797, between those who felt revolution was inevitable and the moderates, such as Thomas

Addis, who wanted Irish independence but felt it could be achieved by nonviolent means. The moderates triumphed and Thomas Addis was made one of the directors. Robert, who had considerable artistic talent, designed his insignia of office, a woman representing Ireland, or Eire, playing on a harp. This emblem became the seal of the society's branch in the south of Ireland.

Thomas Addis had held his post only about three months when, on March 13, 1798, he was taken into custody by the police at his father's home on St. Stephen's Green and escorted to Kilmainham jail. There was no specific charge against him, although he was rightly regarded as a strong opponent of English rule. Arrested the same night were most of the UI executive committee, all victims of the Castle's net of informers. To Dr. Emmet and his wife, Thomas Addis' arrest was a shattering blow from which they never recovered. For Robert, it was a catalyst that hardened to steel the romantic patriotism that had flooded his spirit since childhood. A few weeks later he was faced with his own first crucial test.

In April, the Lord Chancellor of Ireland, Lord Clare, a hatchet-faced man with a penetrating stare, visited Trinity for the purpose of ferreting out the liberals or patriots among the students. He had them brought before him one by one, made each take an oath of loyalty to the Crown, then questioned them in detail about their political beliefs. His manner was insulting. "This young gentleman's reason seems to be affected," he said repeatedly. Some of the students were intimidated and told all they knew, including the fact that Robert Emmet was secretary of one of the college's UI branches. (There were now four of them.) The Lord Chancellor no doubt planned an especially severe grilling for the young brother of Thomas Addis Emmet. But Robert did not give him that pleasure.

Even to remain in college, he was not going to give information that might endanger others; he stayed away from his classes during Lord Clare's inquisition. At the close of the questioning, Robert and eighteen others were scheduled to be expelled for seditious activities. Robert did not wait for the expulsion. With his father's permission, he sent a letter of resignation to the college board of fellows, at the same time denouncing their violation of the right of free speech. This magnificent gesture ended his university education and with it any hope of a professional career.

After the arrest of Thomas Addis and his comrades, the leadership of the United Irishmen fell to Lord Edward Fitzgerald, a gallant young man from one of Ireland's most distinguished and aristocratic families, who had long favored revolution. Acts of provocation intensified, as though the English were deliberately trying to force the patience of the Irish beyond endurance. Already, the oppressed peasants and workers were arming for a struggle that seemed inevitable. The United Irishmen numbered over two hundred thousand, and Fitzgerald estimated a minimum fighting force of ten thousand. It is believed that Robert served briefly as an emissary between Fitzgerald and his imprisoned brother, Thomas Addis. The date of the uprising was set for May 22, 1798, but on May 19, Fitzgerald was captured, like his comrades betrayed by a Castle informer. In his attempt to escape he was severely wounded and died in Newgate prison a few days later, apparently as the result of blood poisoning.

The uprising took place without him. All over Ireland, men armed with pikes and old muskets, a green cockade on their hats and a handful of wheat in their pockets, left their cabins and slipped into the darkness to join their comrades. The "entire male inhabitants of Wexford" were rebel soldiers, according to one government informant. The uprising involved most of the men in Wicklow, Kildare, Carlow, and Kilkenny. At Ballitore, an ex-Austrian army officer, Malachy Delaney, was in command. He had won the people's confidence by distributing copies of Thomas Paine's *Rights of Man*, the "Koran" of the United Irishmen, according to Wolfe Tone. (Paine's *Common Sense* had shown Americans the road to independence. *Rights of Man* had caused him to be outlawed from England.)

The Castle, seeing the rebellion get out of hand, retaliated with brutality, calling up soldiers and yeomen to scour the countryside for rebels. When prisons overflowed, prison ships took the surplus.

In Dublin, the riding school on Marlborough Street was turned into a flogging arena where prisoners were whipped with cat-o'-nine-tails until their bones showed through their flesh. A vicious torture called "pitchcapping" was invented. Many United Irishmen wore their hair cut short, earning for themselves the name of "croppies." Soldiers rounded up all those with short hair, United Irishmen and others, and forced them to wear a cap of coarse linen or strong brown paper covered with boiling pitch, hence the name, "pitchcapping."

Arrests extended to anyone suspected of liberal connections. Women were not exempt, and were arrested, merely on suspicion of favoring the rebels. Dublin lamplighters were publicly flogged, accused of putting water into street lamps so that rebels could assemble in darkness. Martial law was proclaimed for the city.

Such stringent measures suppressed rebellion in Dublin, but in the open country the fighting went on for weeks. Gradually it died out except for a few bands of guerrilla fighters who refused to admit defeat. One of these bands, led by Michael Dwyer of County Wicklow, hid in the mountains for the next five years, resisting the combined efforts of the Irish yeomanry and the British army to capture them.

The United Irishmen had hoped that the French, who were now at war with England, would come to their rescue. On October 10, 1798, a fleet of eight French ships headed for the coast of Ireland. Among their officers were several Irish exiles, including the founder of the United Irishmen, Wolfe Tone. The English learned of the plans and sent a fleet after the French ships. Some of them escaped, but the *Hoche*, with Wolfe Tone aboard, was captured. Tone was sentenced to the gallows but committed suicide before the sentence could be carried out. The defeat of the French ships marked the official end of the Irish Rebellion of 1798.

While unquestionably Robert Emmet was working with the rebels, there is no record as to his duties at this period. Even the informers, whose detailed reports to the Castle would prove invaluable to future historians, were silent about him. There is no doubt that he suffered bitterly at the defeat and that he resolved even then to continue the fight.

In the meantime, harrowing experiences had been the lot of his brother Tom. At Newgate he was confined in total darkness in a narrow cell. He had no bed clothing and slept on a stone shelf raised several inches from the floor. His diet was water and stale bread, with never enough of either to satisfy thirst or hunger. The prison attendant threw his bread to him as to a dog and placed the water on the floor so roughly that a portion of it spilled over. The prisoner had no way to keep himself clean, or even to wash his hands and face. The only ventilation, from a loophole above his cell door, gave barely enough air to sustain life. Within six weeks he had become so emaciated that he lacked the strength even to hunt for his bread.

He was near death when a kindly official took pity on him and had him transferred to larger quarters, where friends were allowed to visit him. His wife, Jane, obtained permission to share his lot, and she stayed with him in his cell for the next year.

In March of 1799, Thomas Addis Emmet and three other prisoners, Arthur O'Connor, Sam Neilson, and one Samuel Turner, who was actually an informer, were transferred by prison ship to Fort George in Scotland. The physical conditions were better than those in Dublin, but the men, all closely confined in one cell, began to have bitter arguments. Sam Turner, the spy, cleverly encouraged each of them to think the others were traitors.

Into this charged atmosphere twenty-two-year-old Robert Emmet arrived on a visit to his brother early in 1800. His idealism and boundless admiration for the courage and sacrifices of the prisoners in the name of freedom put an end to their petty bickering and renewed their dormant hopes. Robert stayed at Fort George near his brother for some two months.

The Castle was duly informed that Robert was very active among the remaining members of the United Irishmen, and it was hinted that he had carried secret instructions to his brother. A warrant was issued for his arrest, but he was not to be found. After Tom's arrest, his parents had moved to their country estate, the Casino, of Milltown, some seven miles south of Dublin, to get away from their town house with its memories of happier days. Robert stayed with them part of the time, but when he learned the police were after him, he knew he had to get out of the country for a while. Moreover, he had conceived an ambitious plan, to go to France and see if he could enlist the First Consul, Napoleon Bonaparte, to support the bleeding Society of United Irishmen in a new uprising.

He set sail for the Continent—the exact date is not known—in the company of Malachy Delaney, the ex-Austrian officer who had been active in Kildare and Wexford in 1798. He landed in Hamburg and then went on to Paris.

In Paris he was welcomed by Irish exiles and many others. Polish patriots treated him as a comrade because of his devotion to democracy. He made friends among the American colony and found a home in the large and hospitable mansion of Joel Barlow, a future American ambassador. At the Barlows, he met Robert Fulton and no doubt heard his dream of making a ship that would be powered by steam. His interest in chemistry won him the friendship of a number of French scientists.

His birth and breeding made him eligible to the most elite salons of French intelligentsia, among them that of Madame de Staël, one of the celebrated women of her age. Madame de Staël's granddaughter, the Comtesse d'Haussonville, on whom he made a deep impression, left a vivid description of him:

"His countenance pleasing and distinguished, his hair brown and his complexion quite pale, the eyebrows arched and the eyes black and large with dark eyelashes, which gave his looks a remarkable expression of pride, penetration and mildness. His nose aquiline, and his mouth slightly disdainful. Energy, delicacy and tenderness are expressed in his melancholy features. Such was, however, the total absence of affectation, and his simplicity, that nothing seems to have at first attracted attention to Robert Emmet. The modesty of his character, joined to a sort of habitual reserve, hid the working of his mind to the ordinary circumstances of life, but were any subject started which was deeply interesting to him, he appeared quite another man."

In furtherance of his plans for Ireland, Robert paid a call on Talleyrand, the cynical and shrewd French Minister of Foreign Affairs under Napoleon Bonaparte.

England signed its peace with France on May 25, 1800. The English, freed of fear of a French invasion from Irish shores, gradually released some of their United Irishmen prisoners. Thomas Addis was set free, on the condition of permanent exile. Robert met him and his wife and children in Amsterdam, in August of 1802. The two brothers were still close to each other. In spite of his ordeal, Tom had lost none of his patriotic fervor, but he dared not return to Ireland or aid Robert other than with advice.

Early in the autumn, Robert went back to Paris, saw Talleyrand again, and after that met Napoleon Bonaparte. Both Bonaparte and Talleyrand were convinced that the peace with England would not last. In theory they were interested in a new Irish uprising, but Napoleon said he had been informed that the Society of

United Irishmen was practically extinct and that before he sent any more French forces on vain missions—such as the one in which Wolfe Tone had participated—the Irish must reorganize. Robert agreed with him on this point, although he had taken a strong dislike to the French dictator.

On this second visit to Paris, he began a self-appointed task of rounding up Irish expatriates and exiles. The seasoned veterans of 1798 looked askance at first on the idealistic young conspirator, but one of them quickly recognized that Robert Emmet had the qualities of a leader. This was Thomas Russell, the big handsome man who had organized the United Irishmen with Wolfe Tone. Gradually Robert won over others.

An agent was sent to them—no one is sure of his name—with the news that preparations were under way in Ireland for a new uprising and with an urgent plea that Robert come home. It is now known that the agent had been sent by William Pitt, the English Prime Minister, and that indeed, from beginning to end, Robert Emmet and all his activities were under the constant scrutiny of the Castle and the British Crown. His weakness —as well as part of his greatness—was that he could not suspect anyone to whom he had once given his confidence. He hastily made arrangements to return to Ireland.

Before he left the Continent he returned to Brussels to say good-by to Tom and his family. Thomas Addis was planning eventually to go to America and he wanted Robert to go with him. His wife, Jane, it is said, went down on her knees to implore Robert to abandon what she felt to be a futile endeavor. But there was, for Robert, no turning back from the course he had chosen. He never again saw his brother, who later became one of America's most distinguished lawyers.

All his adult life, Robert Emmet had let himself be guided by Tom. As he set sail for Ireland after his sad farewell, he knew that henceforth he was on his own. From now on he must make decisions for himself and others. It was a terrifying responsibility but one that seemed to him inevitable.

He reached Dublin in December, 1802. Soon afterward, his father died, leaving him about three thousand pounds. There was no doubt in Robert's mind as to what he would do with the money. It was at once set aside for the work to which he would dedicate the rest of his life.

One at a time he chose his close assistants, most of them from the working class rather than from the middle class and intelligensia that had furnished the United Irishmen an undue quota of spies and cowards.

Jemmy Hope, a weaver and a staunch UI veteran, was his first choice. Of all those who worked with him, no one was more trustworthy or loved. Among others in his close confidence were Michael Quigley, a bricklayer and carpenter; John Hevey, a tobacconist; Thomas Freyne, a gentleman farmer from Kildare; and Denis Lambert Redmond, a coal merchant, who called their young chief "the most brilliant and most inspiring creature who ever walked on earth." There were also, among others, W. P. McCabe, an innkeeper; Felix Rourke, a brewery clerk; Nicholas Stafford, a baker; Henry Howley, a carpenter; and Miles Byrne, a leader of the men of County Kildare in 1798 who had since been working as a bookkeeper in Dublin. Bernard Duggan, a cottonworker, was another admitted to Emmet's inner circle, but this was a mistake. Not until long after Duggan's death was it revealed that the Dublin chief of police, Major Sirr, had paid him five hundred pounds a year as an informer.

With better judgment, Emmet chose as his assistant a County Wicklow man, Big Arthur Devlin, another veteran of the Rebellion of 1798 who had joined the British army to escape arrest. When he learned of Emmet's forthcoming uprising, Big Arthur deserted the army and came to Dublin to join him, bringing some fifty other Wicklow men from his regiment. Emmet had been lodging at Harold Cross, outside Dublin, with a Mrs. Palmer, but was looking for a house to use as his central headquarters. It was Big Arthur who found a suitable place, a two-story house with an aura of middle-class respectability about it, on Butterfield Lane in Rathfarnham, a few miles south of Dublin. In April, 1803, Emmet leased it under the name of "Mr. Ellis."

Nearby lived Big Arthur's uncle, Bryan Devlin, a farmer, with his wife and seven children. They were all patriots. Mrs. Devlin was the aunt of the famous Wicklow outlaw, Michael Dwyer, while Bryan Devlin had suffered more than two years in the Wicklow jail on the charge of aiding the rebels. His second daughter, Anne, a dark-haired spirited young woman of twenty-three, volunteered to serve as Robert Emmet's housekeeper at Butterfield Lane, and soon was an active participant in his activities.

They had almost no furniture. Their beds were mattresses spread on the floor and they ate from packing boxes. Sometimes as many as thirty men showed up for dinner. The neighbors were duly curious, deciding the new tenants were either in debt or counterfeiters. What was Mr. Ellis' profession? they asked Anne. Was he an attorney?

"Aye, is he?" she said. That was all the satisfaction she would give.

Thomas Russell returned from Paris and came to live at Butterfield Lane, giving the same loyalty to young Emmet as he had to the martyred Wolfe Tone. He brought word that Napoleon's interest in their undertaking was waning, and that there was no use counting on French aid. Emmet was almost relieved. His distrust of the great Bonaparte had increased. Far better to fight their own battles than to risk an ally of dubious motives. From all over the country, his scouts brought word that the veterans of '98 were ready and waiting. Even without the French, their hopes for success were high.

At Emmet's suggestion, Big Arthur Devlin and the weaver, Jemmy Hope, went to the Wicklow mountains to try and enlist the support of Michael Dwyer. They found him and his men living in an underground cave in the wilderness of the Glen of Imaal. Dwyer was plainly skeptical about Emmet and his insurrection and said he did not think his followers would risk another defeat. Hope and Big Arthur dejectedly returned to Emmet.

A few days later, however, Michael Dwyer arrived at Butterfield Lane with three companions, all big, burly, roughly-dressed men. They stayed three days, during which Dwyer neither ate nor slept. On the third day he caught sight of a neighbor woman standing outside the house and ordered his men to get ready to leave that night, saying he would not stay in a house that was being watched. Just before he left he told Emmet he could depend on his help. The slender young patriot had won his trust.

Jemmy Hope next took a tour through Ulster, the county organized by Wolfe Tone and Thomas Russell, to sound out the former United Irishmen there. Cold at first, they soon warmed to Jemmy's enthusiasm, particularly when they learned that Thomas Russell was part of the movement. Thus, slowly and steadily, the secret army grew. Several thousand Kildare men promised support. Michael Dwyer could command a force from Counties Carlow, Wicklow, and Wexford of more thousands. There were several hundred Wexford United Irishmen refugees in Dublin, ready to serve under Miles Byrne. Jemmy Hope enlisted some five thousand working-class Dubliners, all personally devoted to him.

Emmet rented two buildings in Dublin as depots for arms and ammunition, one on Patrick Street, the other on Thomas Street. With the aid of Quigley, the carpenter, he built secret cupboards and hidden passageways in the Patrick Street depot, to be used in an emergency. Later he rented other ammunition depots. In the last weeks he rarely visited any one of them for more than an hour or so, appearing without warning and leaving abruptly.

Emmet never made a decision without consulting his comrades, and when he made up his mind about something he spoke mildly. Yet they all give him implicit obedience, in part because they came to trust his judgment, in part because of his charm, his dedication, and a certain purity about him that inspired confidence.

Only once did he overrule them. Miles Byrne and his experienced fighters felt that their limited funds should go for standard weapons such as pikes, pistols, and blunderbusses. Emmet insisted they try out an invention of his. Putting his knowledge of chemistry to a practical use, he had at the Patrick Street depot perfected a rocket, a conical iron tube filled with a mixture of gunpowder, niter, and sulphur, and attached to a fuse.

Emmet, Thomas Russell, and Miles Byrne took the rocket out to the country to test it. After placing it against a trestle, they lit the fuse. With a noise between a scream and a hiss, it tore along almost parallel with the ground, pouring out flames and fire until it struck the earth, where it tore out a great pit before it was extinguished. After this convincing demonstration, Miles Byrne and the others yielded. The "Congreve Rocket" the weapon was called later, though Robert Emmet's model preceded that of William Congreve.

Blunderbusses and pistols were being stored on Patrick or Thomas Street, and the men constructed their own pikes. Emmet supervised everything. Pike handles were made of red deal, a form of pine wood, rather than the customary ash, because red deal was easier to obtain. The men invented a "folding pike," which could be concealed beneath their coats, and they hollowed out blocks of wood, filled them with gunpowder, nails, stones, and broken iron, and attached fuses. These "square bombs," as they called them, were designed to stop approaching cavalry.

By the end of June, Robert Emmet felt certain of a force of several thousand to start his insurrection in motion. How did he think he could overthrow the British yoke with so few? His plan was fantastically simple, and even later, when all was lost, it was generally agreed to have been extremely practical.

The gates of Dublin Castle lay open until far into the night, flaunting the arrogant self-confidence of the English usurpers. Inside, the Viceroy and other officials walked about freely and unprotected. The Castle had only a small guard.

Emmet planned to have a first detachment of patriots enter the Castle gates in a stream of coaches—as though they were visitors. Once inside, they were to fire off rockets to call up the others. If only five thousand responded, the outcome was certain. Dublin Castle would be in Irish hands. The government, deprived of its leaders and central quarters, would be temporarily disorganized. By the time the British could send forces to recapture the Castle, the gates would be closed. Emmet counted on the dramatic news that the green flag was flying from the Castle to inspire the whole country to rise.

Other minor assaults were planned for the same day at Pigeon House Fort on Dublin Bay, the Royal Artillery Barracks at Island Bridge, and another at the ammunition magazine in Phoenix Park. The date set for this combined operation was July 23, 1803, though only a trusted few were told of it.

Until that year, women had played no part in Emmet's life, but sometime in the spring or early summer he fell in love, desperately and completely. The object of his affection was the daughter of an old family friend, John Philpot Curran, the most famous liberal lawyer in Ireland. Emmet had first met Sarah Curran as a child. She was twenty-two when he saw her again at the home of a mutual friend, a slender, fragile girl with dark eyes, soft auburn hair, and very white skin lightly flecked with freckles. "She is kind, she is lovely," he wrote of her ecstatically, "and heaven only knows how good."

The Curran family lived in a big stone house known as the Priory, about half a mile from Butterfield Lane.

Sarah's father was a widower. She had a brother named Richard and a spinster sister, Amelia. When Emmet came calling, he had difficulty seeing Sarah alone, nor in the beginning did she pay much heed to her intense young suitor. But her more observant father noticed how Emmet's eyes followed his younger daughter and instructed Amelia to warn him to make his visits less frequent. Patriotism was fine in its place, so Barrister Curran must have reasoned, but he had no desire for a son-in-law who had never finished college and had no profession but the dubious one of revolutionist.

It is the nature of love to flourish when there are obstacles to surmount. Only after her father's ultimatum did the willful and enchanting Sarah give her heart to Robert Emmet. They met secretly whenever they could, and when it was not possible to see each other they wrote long and affectionate letters, which pretty Anne Devlin delivered.

Since Sarah was the daughter of a patriot, Emmet was certain she would understand his dreams and aspirations. Rashly, he confided everything to her, where his depots were, what they contained. The two sweethearts made up a code for writing of these secret things, and as a further precaution promised to destroy each other's letters, a promise neither fulfilled.

Plans for the insurrection approached completion. Knowing one mistake might be fatal, Emmet swore that nothing must go wrong. Then, on July 16, a week before the fateful day, something went very wrong indeed. At the Patrick Street depot, where some of Emmet's men were making rockets, a spark ignited the powder. There was a dull roar. The police arrived on the scene to find windows shattered, a room wrecked, and three men lying wounded. They were taken to the hospital, where one of them, John Keenan, died a few hours later. The police searched the house but did not find the secret cupboards in which most of the ammunition was stored.

Emmet was sure the police would set a guard on the depot but, incredible as it seemed, that night there was no one near it. Miles Byrne and Big Arthur, in several trips, emptied the secret cupboards, storing arms and ammunition at the Thomas Street depot, at Butterfield Lane, and at the homes of trusted comrades.

Even with this salvage, the explosion was a staggering blow. How much did the men at the Castle suspect? How could they not suspect something? Yet, judging from the account in the official *Dublin Evening Post*, the authorities were not at all concerned. While "alarmists had not been idle," the newspaper item read, inquiries indicated that "nothing of a political nature" was involved. Somewhat reassured, Emmet and his comrades decided to go ahead as planned.

The truth—not revealed until many years later—was that William Wickham, chief secretary of the Castle, and Alexander Marsden, the undersecretary, knew exactly what was going on, but were under instructions from William Pitt in England to let Emmet proceed. Not even their superior, the Lord Lieutenant (the Viceroy) of Ireland, was informed of these devious political maneuvers.

For the next week Robert Emmet slept on a pallet on the floor of the Thomas Street depot, eating food sent in from a cookshop or in a tavern. There were a dozen men with him there, including Quigley, the carpenter, Nicholas Stafford, the baker, and a tailor named Terence Colgan, who was employed to make some truly handsome uniforms for the leaders with white cashmere pantaloons and green jackets trimmed with gold epaulettes.

In this confused and crowded atmosphere, it was almost impossible to complete the innumerable tasks still to be done. In the midst of the pounding and hammering, Emmet did find time to do one thing he felt of supreme importance: the writing of a proclamation to the people of Ireland, to be printed and distributed, explaining the reasons for the uprising and making a stirring plea for Irish freedom.

Saturday, July 23, arrived—a fine, hot morning. In Dublin was the usual Saturday-morning scene of rattling carts, bleating beasts being led to market, noisy drovers, bustling housewives. There was no undue movement of troops and the gates of Dublin Castle were open, with coaches going in and out. Since the day before, men in country clothes had been streaming into Dublin, rugged in physique and determined in bearing. They came from Kildare and elsewhere to join "General Emmet's" army.

Emmet rode out very early to Butterfield Lane to collect his mail. He destroyed most of it but thrust into his breast pocket a letter Anne Devlin had brought him from Sarah. Big Arthur was there and he gave him some final instructions, including the sending of a messenger to Michael Dwyer in the Wicklow mountains to urge him to come at once with as many men as he could rally. (The messenger never was able to find Dwyer, for which Emmet was later thankful.) Then he returned to Thomas Street.

In the depot thousands of pikes had been brought out from behind false partitions and stacked against the wall in readiness for that night's attack, along with bushels of

musket balls and numerous square bombs. Some of the
men were making hand grenades, and there was con-
sternation when Quigley confessed he had forgotten
where he had hidden the fuses. Ladders to be used by re-
inforcements to scale the Castle gates still lacked cramp
irons; the smith sent them over so late that only one ladder was completed—not ten, as Emmet had planned.
The depot became increasingly noisy as more men piled
into it. Major Sirr's spies, who were watching, must
surely have reported the unprecedented activity.

Sometime that morning Emmet conferred with the
Kildare leaders. They were disappointed that there were
so few guns; they had not expected to fight with pikes.
To appease them, Emmet borrowed some money and
sent out a scout to try and buy more blunderbusses.
Nevertheless, in the early afternoon many of the out-of-
towners left Dublin to return to their homes. Their departure was not for lack of courage but because of a
persistent rumor, perhaps started by informers, that the
rebellion was to be postponed.

It was a day of disaster, unforeseeable and unavoid-
able, that in the aggregate would prove fatal.

At about seven in the evening, Emmet called a halt to
the activity and read aloud from the freshly printed
Proclamation:

"The Provisional Government to the People of Ireland:

"You are now called upon to show the world that you
are competent to take your place among nations; that
you have a right to claim their recognizance of you as an
independent country, by the only satisfactory proof you
can furnish of your capability of maintaining your independence—your wresting it from England with your

own hands. . . . Our object is to establish a free and independent republic in Ireland. . . . We war not against property, we war against no religious sect, we war not against past opinions or prejudices, we war against English dominion."

It had seemed urgent to Emmet that his men should hear these words before the battle began, so that the reason they were fighting would once more be impressed on them. "Good," several of them murmured. "Very good."

And then Ned Condon, who had gone out to get the hackney coaches in which they planned to ride to the Castle, came running in, a look of dismay on his face. An officer had stopped him to ask where he was going with so many carriages. He had lost his head and fired. The hackney drivers had taken fright and driven off.

If Emmet was shaken at seeing the collapse of this cherished part of his plan, he let no one know it. Very well, they would go on foot. They still had enough men to take the Castle. Michael Dwyer with his contingent would soon arrive, or so he believed. Thomas Russell was raising an army up in Ulster. Kerry and Limerick Counties were sure to rise when Dublin was taken. . . .

Thus did he continue to reassure his men, though in his heart he was afraid—not for himself but for their undertaking. Before his eyes the fruits of his months of labored planning were withering away, as if some terrible curse had been set on them. But he could not give up. Too many had put their trust in him.

Shortly after eight o'clock, too late to call off their attack and too soon to proceed with much hope of success, Michael Quigley came rushing in, red-faced and out of breath.

"They are on us! The soldiers are coming!" he cried.

No soldiers were near. Quigley had made a mistake, but there was no way of investigating his story. All that Emmet knew was that it was better to die in action than penned up in a coop.

"Come on, boys!"

He and several others slipped on their green and white uniforms. Men hurriedly threw pikes from the upper windows of the depot to others gathered below. Less than three hundred set out on foot. In short order all but forty or fifty had disappeared into the shadows. By the time they turned into Patrick Street, about halfway to the Castle, there were, according to one witness, no more than fifteen men with their young leader. It was about then, probably in the shadow of St. Patrick's Cathedral, that Robert Emmet finally relinquished the dream that had sustained him since childhood and gave the order to disperse.

About eleven o'clock that night he, Quigley, and five others, still in their fine uniforms, walked into the house on Butterfield Lane, their faces dejected and gray with fatigue. Anne Devlin, the young housekeeper, was there impatiently awaiting news.

"Bad welcome to you," she cried out at the sight of them. "Is the world lost by you, cowards that you are, to lead the people to destruction and then to leave them?"

"Don't blame me, Anne, the fault is not mine," Emmet told her wearily.

As she heard the story of their tragic day, her heart softened with pity. Before dawn she sent them across the fields to her father's farm, where they would be safe until horses and dark cloaks to cover their bright uniforms could be found for them. She stayed on to warn away any latecomers from this house that was sure to be searched sooner or later. In the course of the day she directed a dozen or so other comrades of Emmet to her farm.

From them Emmet learned of the sporadic fighting in different parts of Dublin the night before and of the arrests already made. That they were all in grave danger he had no doubt, just as he was still certain that one day Ireland would be free. He tried to cheer his men by suggesting they might still get French aid and start again, but he could not fool himself. He knew his own part in that struggle was over.

They were all sitting around the crowded Devlin kitchen on Monday afternoon. Hevey, the baker, an apron around his waist, was churning butter for Mrs. Devlin. Most of them were in uniform. A neighbor woman walked in, looked around in amazement, and then, making some feeble excuse, backed out hastily. From there she dashed over to the house of George Grierson, the King's printer, who lived nearby, to report that "fifty French officers" were staying with the Devlins. Emmet knew of this because the Grierson's butler, who had overheard her, soon rushed in to warn them. It was fortunate that Grierson had just sat down to his dinner, he said. Otherwise he would have taken off at once for the Castle.

The refugees left at once. That night they slept at the home of an old farmer, John Doyle, known as "Silky Jock." One of their group knew the Doyle family and thought they would be secure there, but Silky Jock turned out to be a scared old man and they left early. The following night they stayed in a comfortable farmhouse owned by a Mrs. Rose Bagnell, and the night after that they slept in the fields.

That afternoon they decided to separate. Their chances were far better if each man was on his own. Miles Byrne wanted Emmet to take refuge with Michael Dwyer, but he refused, saying he could not bear to face Dwyer after their failure. Nor would he consider the alternative of fleeing to France. He could not run away and abandon his comrades.

He did not mention the other reason he wished to stay in Ireland—Sarah Curran. After dividing the little money he had among his men, he took leave of them and went to stay with Mrs. Palmer at Harold Cross, the lodging in which he had resided before moving to Butterfield Lane. Mrs. Palmer liked him and he could count on her discretion. He did not worry, if he knew, that a nearby tavern was run by Simon Doyle, the son of "Silky Jock," the farmer who had given them such a grudging welcome, and he found consolation in the fact that Harold Cross was not far from the Priory, where Sarah lived.

Meanwhile a storm had broken loose in Dublin Castle. The night of the insurrection, Chief Justice Lord Kilwarden had been driving with his nephew and daughter. Some drunken rowdies, aware only that this was the night the common people were to have their revenge, dragged them out of the carriage and in the skirmish both Kilwarden and his nephew were killed. His daughter managed to make her way to the Castle to tell her story. The worst part was that Lord Kilwarden was one of the few Irishman in power who treated the patriots with justice. Though Emmet was in no way responsible for the tragedy, he shared the burden of it.

Dublin was put under martial law. Hundreds were arrested, and no one was more assiduous than Secretary Marsden in trying to get the prisoners to name their comrades and leaders. In some cases he was successful. To the Viceroy he wrote cynically, "This has been a most unfortunate business, but however severe in its present circumstance it will excite a feeling which may materially serve us hereafter."

Two days after the insurrection, a contingent of yeomen came to Butterfield Lane, ransacked the house, and tried to get Anne Devlin to tell them where "Mr. Ellis" was. She put on a stupid look and said she was only a servant and cared for nothing but that her salary be paid. They pricked her with bayonets and even jabbed her small sister who was staying with her, but could not make Anne talk. Then they took her out in the courtyard, saying they were going to hang her. When she again defied them, they strung her up on an upturned wagon long enough for her to lose consciousness. Not then nor ever did she tell them anything.

After Emmet moved to Harold Cross, he sent for Anne and asked her if she would continue to deliver his letters to Sarah. Anne, whose loyalty to him was boundless, agreed willingly. She also brought Sarah's letters to him, including two that were long, chatty, and indiscreet, and that he kept in his jacket next to his heart, disobeying Sarah's instructions to burn them. Though Sarah passed Mrs. Palmer's house, where her sweetheart was staying, on at least two occasions, there is no evidence she ever saw him again.

Emmet seldom left the house, but occasionally he had visitors. Simon Doyle, the tavernkeeper, delivered eggs and butter to the Palmers and it is believed it was indirectly through him or his father, Silky Jock, that Major Sirr, the Dublin chief of police, learned a suspicious stranger was staying there. The Doyles were never paid for this valuable information, though there is record of a thousand pounds paid by the English to a gentleman farmer named Richard Jones, a friend of the Doyles. Major Sirr also received three hundred pounds for Emmet's arrest.

On August 25, Emmet spent the morning in the back parlor working on a letter to the Viceroy, half plea and half threat, to the effect that only if the government would cease the merciless punishment of the prisoners in custody would there be any chance for peace in the country. He broke off his writing to go have dinner with Mrs. Palmer. They were beginning their meal when Major Sirr broke in.

"You are under arrest," the major said.

Sirr left a soldier to guard Emmet while he searched the rest of the house. There was a scuffle in his absence. Emmet attempted to escape, but the soldier knocked him down with the butt of his pistol. When Sirr returned, Emmet was leaning against the wall with blood pouring down his cheek. The soldier was holding two letters he had taken from his prisoner's jacket, the letters from Sarah that Emmet had been unable to force himself to destroy.

He was taken to Kilmainham jail, the great gray building constructed some years before to incarcerate those imbued with the "dangerous" ideas of independence engendered by the American and French Revolution. Since he was a "gentleman" of good family, he was not put in a cell but in a pleasant, well-furnished room with a desk and a good bed, and with only the barred windows as proof of his captivity. After five days he was taken to Dublin Castle and examined by Lord Chancellor Redesdale, Secretary William Wickham, and Attorney General Standish O'Grady. O'Grady presided.

"What is your name?" they demanded first.

"Robert Emmet," he said. "Having now answered my name I must decline answering any other questions."

His examiners told him, kindly enough, that it would be in his own interest to answer them. He replied, equally politely, that he must persist in declining.

"Where did you first hear of the insurrection?" they asked.

"I decline answering any question."

They continued to pound him with questions. Was he in Dublin the night of July 23? Had he been in France for two years? Had he seen the Proclamation of the Provisional Government? He would tell them nothing. The attorney general grew red with anger.

Abruptly he demanded, "By whom were the letters written that were found on your person?"

His examiners believed they were from his sister, Mary Anne Holmes, but Emmet had no way of knowing this. He was frightened for Sarah, and because of her, he broke his silence.

"As to the letters taken out of my possession by Major Sirr, how can I avoid their being brought forward?" His voice was anxious. "Has anything been done in consequence of those letters being taken? May I learn what has been done upon them?"

"You cannot be answered as to this," O'Grady told him gloatingly.

Emmet pleaded with them: "You must, gentlemen, be

sensible how disagreeable it would be to one of yourselves to have a delicate and virtuous female brought into notice. What means would be necessary to bring the evidence in those letters forward, without bringing the name forward? Might the passages in those letters be read to me?"

His interrogators were sure now that the letters were not written by Emmet's sister. Thinking they had a good weapon in them, they hinted that the author of the letters might well be protected if he gave information about his organization and his colleagues. His composure returned.

"May I know when my arraignment will take place?" he asked haughtily.

O'Grady let the interview come to an end, and Emmet was taken back to Kilmainham.

One redeeming feature of his imprisonment was the solicitude shown him by his jailer, a pleasant-faced man named George Dunn. Dunn did everything possible to make him comfortable. When they were alone, he confided that he had always been sympathetic to the cause of Ireland. Emmet believed him. Pure in heart himself, it was always difficult for him to detect hypocrisy in others. When Dunn volunteered to deliver messages to his friends, Emmet gave him a note to his cousin, St. John Mason, who was also a prisoner. Dunn shortly brought back an answer, which Emmet took as proof of his good faith. After the exchange of several more letters, Mason, a well-to-do businessman, offered Dunn a bribe to help arrange their escape and that of four other prisoners. Dunn seemed amenable but then suddenly announced that the authorities had become suspicious and he could do nothing. Neither Mason nor Emmet guessed that Dunn was an informer and that Dr. Edward Trevor, the prison supervisor, had seen all their correspondence.

Still trusting Dunn, Emmet committed the gravest indiscretion of his life. He gave the jailer a note addressed to Sarah Curran, in which he advised her to destroy all his letters and warned her of the two letters his captors had found.

The letter was never delivered. Early the next morning, Major Sirr with some of his men arrived at the Priory. Barrister Curran was not at home. Amelia, Sarah's sister, and her brother Richard, were having breakfast. Sarah was still in bed. The major stormed up the stairs to her bedroom and burst in, demanding Robert Emmet's letters. The shock was too much for Sarah, who screamed hysterically. In the resultant confusion, Amelia calmly took the letters from their hiding place and fed them into the fire before Sirr realized what she was doing.

Major Sirr later claimed that he had taken a stack of correspondence "a yard square" between Emmet and Sarah, all devoted to the subject of "public massacre and wrong." Other evidence indicates that the two letters Robert Emmet carried next to his heart were the only ones the court ever saw.

Sarah was not arrested, nor did Major Sirr ever further bother any of the Curran family. The Castle authorities felt they did not wish to antagonize Sarah's father, Barrister Curran, who had recently showed a willingness to work with them. In truth, when this former lawyer of the rebels learned of his daughter's relationship with Robert Emmet, he disowned her and turned her out of his house.

For several years she stayed with friends in Cork, and gradually she seemed to recover from her deep shock. Sometimes she sang melancholy songs in her sweet, pleasing voice. A British officer fell in love with her and proposed marriage. She accepted him, perhaps because she was tired of living on charity. She died in the first year of their marriage—long after her true love had met his destiny.

On the same day that Major Sirr visited Sarah, Thomas Russell was arrested and Robert Emmet's mother died. Happily for his peace of mind, he did not know of this triple tragedy. He had named Sarah's father as his lawyer, but Curran would have nothing to do with the case—not, as Emmet thought, because of Sarah, but because he was through defending Irish patriots. Leonard McNally, whom Emmet mistakenly believed to be his friend, took his place. McNally served as counsel for a large number of the rebels, winning their confidence and promptly reporting to the Castle what his clients told him. With him worked the attorney Peter Burrowes, who had also sold himself to the Castle. But that Robert Emmet's lawyers were not on his side mattered very little.

The day of the trial, Monday, September 19, 1803, Dublin seethed with excitement. Dr. Robert Emmet had been a public figure. His son and namesake was a romantic one. Everyone had heard of how he had resigned from Trinity College rather than betray his fellow students, and of how he had been to France and talked with Napoleon. They knew, too, that he had filled Dublin storehouses with pikes and blunderbusses and ammunition, and that, dressed in a gold-trimmed uniform of emerald hue, he had led an army toward the Castle. It was no wonder that he stirred the imagination of the oppressed and wretched working class of Dublin. They crowded outside the courthouse, on the streets, gathered in taverns to discuss the gallant young man who had sacrificed everything because he wanted them to have a better life. Inside, the trial went on, hour after hour.

Attorney General Standish O'Grady, who had previously examined Emmet, opened the proceedings. His duty, he said, was to state as concisely as he could the nature of the charge. He went far beyond conciseness as he held up to ridicule Emmet's "provisional government," pointing out tauntingly that it was made up of such members of the lower orders as "an eminent bricklayer" [Quigley] and "a bankrupt clerk [Miles Byrne] sitting on the second floor of a malt house, meditating without means and marshaling armies that never enlisted."

The witnesses for the prosecution were called, one by one, to the stand. All were under oath, all forced to testify under penalty of a thousand-pound fine.

The first was Joseph Rawlings, who had done legal work for Dr. Emmet before his death. He was supposed to say that Robert had uttered treasonable sentiments on his return from Europe. Instead, all he could remember was that Robert had heartily disliked Napoleon Bonaparte. He was quickly dismissed.

George Tyrrell, who had leased Emmet the house on Butterfield Lane, testified that Emmet had used the name of "Robert Ellis." Michael Frayne, a neighbor, related that he had called on "Mr. Ellis" and been invited to dinner, but had not stayed: "There being no chairs, we felt a little awkward."

John Fleming, a somewhat simple-minded hostler at

the White Bull Inn adjoining the Thomas Street depot, was next. Fleming had been in Robert's confidence but Major Sirr had easily persuaded him to turn state's evidence. He knew the depot, he said, had seen men there making pikes and ball cartridges, had seen a supply of blunderbusses and pistols.

"Look at the prisoner at the bar," he was instructed.

"I know him. Mr. Emmet there," Fleming said uncomfortably.

Had he seen him before? "I have. The Tuesday morning after the blowing up in Patrick Street."

He was followed by Terence Colgan, the tailor who had made the men's uniforms. Now he claimed that he had been kidnaped while he was drunk, taken to the depot, and forced to make the uniforms. But he admitted that he would never have testified of his own accord, and did so only so he would be freed to earn bread for his family.

After him came Patrick Farrell, a middle-aged grocer, surly and sharp-spoken. He had been caught eavesdropping at the Thomas Street depot one day, and the men had dragged him inside. Some of them had wanted to drop him then and there, but Robert Emmet had prevented them. Farrell repaid this favor by describing what he had seen.

Leonard McNally intervened at his client's request. "Did you hear any printed paper read?" he asked, referring to the Proclamation Emmet had written. Farrell said he had heard part of it. "Was anything said about the French?"

"Not the smallest, as I heard," Farrell admitted: "they said they had no idea as to French relief but to make it good themselves."

McNally then asked him what the men said about the Proclamation.

"The observation I heard, listening like another," Farrell said, "was that it was very good."

This was the one and only time Emmet asked his lawyer to cross-examine a witness. He was anxious to defend not his life, but his intentions and his principles. Several times when Burrowes rose to cross-examine, he stopped him, saying, "No, no. The man's speaking truth."

Every so often McNally cross-examined on his own. The evidence he extracted was always unfavorable to his client.

The next witnesses were official: the soldiers and the magistrate who had found the military supplies and batches of the Proclamation. The long Proclamation, "The Provisional Government to the People of Ireland," was read in its entirety.

As hours passed without a break, it was obvious to all that only will power kept the prisoner, laden with chains, from collapsing. A spectator slipped him a bit of lavender, but he had held it to his nostrils only a moment when the court ordered him to put it aside. "The smile that crossed his face as it was taken from him was slightly disdainful," someone commented.

More soldiers were called, and after them, John "Silky Jock" Doyle, the old farmer at whose house Robert and his friends had stayed on leaving Butterfield Lane. He injected the only humor in the proceedings, when he described how he had awakened from a drunken slumber to find himself in bed with several "French generals" in green and gold uniforms.

Joseph Palmer, the son of Robert's landlady at Harold

Cross, was summoned next. Reluctantly he testified that their lodger had gone by the name of "Mr. Hewitt." He said, under questioning, that Major Sirr had come there and arrested their lodger, and that the major had come into his (Joseph's) room where he was lying sick in bed. When he was asked if the prisoner was the person who had been arrested, the young man hesitated. Only after Robert smiled and nodded his head to him did Joseph Palmer identify him.

Major Sirr was on the stand after that, describing in glowing terms his own part in the prisoner's arrest. When Mrs. Palmer's lodger tried to escape, Sirr said, he "instantly ran to the back part of the house, as the most likely part for him to get out at. I saw him going off, and ordered a sentinel to fire, and then pursued myself, regardless of the order. . . . I overtook the prisoner, and he said, 'I surrender' . . ."

Of the entire trial, there was no part more agonizing for Robert Emmet than when copies of Sarah's letters were put on the table and excerpts read to the jury. The presiding judge, Lord Norbury, offered with obvious malice to have other parts of the letters read if the prisoner wished. The matter was not pursued, certainly to avoid affront to Sarah's father.

When the prosecution had called all its witnesses, the court gave the floor to Leonard McNally for his defense. There was none, McNally said. His client had instructed him to make no observations on the evidence. He presumed that the case was therefore closed.

The second prosecuting attorney, William Conyingham Plunket, was visibly upset. A former friend of the Emmet family, he had once called the English "invaders" and sworn he would protect Ireland "with the

last drop of his blood." Like Barrister Curran, he had renounced his former sympathies and, to prove his loyalty
to the Crown, had prepared a long speech of rebuttal to
Emmet's defense. Though Emmet had made no defense,
he insisted on delivering his speech anyway.

Much of it consisted of lofty praise of English rule.
"God and Nature have made the two countries essential
to each other," he said at one point, referring to Ireland
and Great Britain, "let them cling to each other to the
end of time." In a dramatic finale, he pointed his finger at
Emmet and shouted, "His followers are a bloodthirsty
crew, incapable of listening to the voice of reason, and
equally incapable of obtaining rational freedom, if it were
wanting in this country, as they are of enjoying it."
Throughout, Emmet listened with a disdainful expression.

"A masterly performance," Secretary Wickham
termed Plunket's address. Two months afterward he was
granted the coveted appointment of solicitor general,
and, much later, in 1830, he became Lord Chancellor of
Ireland.

It was nine o'clock; the court had convened for
twelve hours. Lord Norbury, the presiding judge, did
the summation. The jury did not even leave the box.
After a few minutes of whispered consultation, the foreman addressed the court.

"My lords, I have consulted with my brother jurors,
and we are all of the opinion that the prisoner is guilty."

According to custom, the clerk asked whether the
prisoner had anything to say regarding why a judgment
of death should not be pronounced against him.

No, Emmet said, he had nothing to say on that point.
"But as to why my character should not be relieved

from the imputations and calumnies thrown out against it I have much to say."

He had been standing for more than twelve hours in chains without rest or refreshment, but his voice, when he began speaking, was, according to witnesses, clear and distinct, "perfect in its modulation and exquisite in its cadences." What he said has become a classic, reprinted everywhere. It was read by Abraham Lincoln by firelight in his Kentucky cabin, and it has served as an example of oratory for innumerable young lawyers.*

"My Lords," he began, "I have no hopes that I can anchor my character in the breast of this court. I only wish your lordships will suffer it to float down your memories until it has found some hospitable harbor to shelter it from the storms with which it is at present buffeted. Were I to suffer only death after being adjudged guilty I should bow in silence to the fate which awaits me; but the sentence of the law which delivers my body over to the executioner consigns my character to obloquy.

"A man in my situation has not only to encounter the difficulties of fortune and the force of power over minds which it has corrupted or subjected, but the difficulties of established prejudice. The man dies, but his memory lives, and that mine may not forfeit all claim to the respect of my countrymen I seize upon this opportunity to

---

* There exist many versions of Emmet's speech. The government distorted it for their own purposes and even Emmet's friends were guilty of inserting their own thoughts in their own words. The version here is given with the permission of Helen Landreth, author of *The Pursuit of Robert Emmet,* who thoroughly examined and analyzed contemporary documents to produce as accurately as anyone can determine Emmet's language and opinions.

vindicate myself from some of the charges alleged against me.

"I am charged with being an emissary of France. It is alleged that I wished to sell the independence of my country. No, I am no emissary, and my ambition was to hold a place among the deliverers of my country, not in profit, nor in power, but in the glory of the achievement. Never did I entertain the remotest idea of establishing French power in Ireland.

"Connection with France was indeed intended, but only as far as mutual interest would sanction and require. Were they to assume any authority inconsistent with the purest independence it would be the signal for their destruction. We sought aid, and we sought it—as we had assurances we should obtain it—as auxiliaries in war and allies in peace.

"Were the French to come as invaders or enemies, uninvited by the wishes of the people, I should oppose them to the utmost of my strength. Yes, my countrymen, I should advise you to meet them upon the beach, with a sword in one hand and a torch in the other. I would meet them with all the destructive fury of war. I would animate my countrymen to immolate them in their boats before they had contaminated the soil of my country. If they succeeded in landing, and if forced to retire before superior discipline, I would dispute every inch of ground, burn every blade of grass, and the last entrenchment of liberty should be my grave. What I could not do myself, if I should fall, I should leave as a last charge to my countrymen to accomplish because I should feel conscious that life, even more than death, would be unprofitable when a foreign nation held my country in subjection." (This latter statement applied, of course, as much to the English as to the French.)

"But it was not as an enemy that the succors of France were to land. I looked, indeed, for the assistance of France, but I wished to prove to France and to the world that Irishmen deserved to be assisted, that they were indignant to slavery, and ready to assist the independence and liberty of their country!

"I wished to procure for my country the guarantee which Washington procured for America! To procure an aid which, by its example, would be as important as its valor—disciplined, gallant, pregnant with science and with experience, which would perceive the good, and polish the rough points of our character. They would come to us as strangers, and leave us as friends, after sharing our perils, and elevating our destiny. These were my objects, not to receive new taskmasters, but to expel old tyrants!

"My object, and that of the Provisional Government, was to effect a total separation between Great Britain and Ireland—to make Ireland totally independent of Great Britain, but not to let her become a dependent of France."

Here the presiding judge, Lord Norbury, interrupted, saying that the court was not there to listen to treason. Emmet resumed mildly:

"When my spirit shall have joined those bands of martyred heroes who have shed their blood on the scaffold and in the field in defense of their country an virtue, this is my hope, that my memory may animate those who survive me.

"While the destruction of that government holds its dominion by impiety agains which displays its power over man a the fields, which sets man upon his brother, and lifts his hand, in religion's name, against the throat of his brother who believes a little more or less than the government standard, which reigns amidst the cries of orphans and the widows it has made . . ."

Lord Norbury broke in at this point to comment sarcastically on "the massacres and murders committed in one night" by the men under Emmet's command. His objection gave Emmet an opportunity to elaborate on the plight of his people.

"I swear by the throne of Heaven before which I must shortly appear, by the blood of those murdered patriots who have gone before me, that my conduct has been governed only by the convictions I have uttered, and by no other view than that of their cure, and the emancipation of my country from the inhuman oppression under which it has so long and too patiently travailed, and that I confidently and assuredly hope that (wild and chimerical as it may appear) there is still strength and union enough in Ireland to accomplish this noble enterprise. Of this I speak with confidence, of intimate knowledge, and with the consolation that appertains to that confidence. Think not, my lords, that I say this for the petty gratification of giving you a transitory uneasiness. A man who has never yet raised his voice to assert a lie will not hazard his character with posterity by asserting a falsehood on a subject so important to his country, and on an occasion like this. Yes, my lords, a man who does not wish to have his epitaph written until his country is liberated will not leave it in the power of envy to impeach the probity which he means to preserve even in the grave, to which tyranny here consigns him.

"Again I say, that what I have spoken was not intended for your lordships, whose situation I commiserate rather than envy; my expressions were for my countrymen. If there be a true Irishman present, let my last words cheer him in the hour of affliction. . . ."

Angrily, Lord Norbury said that the court could not listen to a discourse of this kind. Emmet insisted quietly on the right to say what he deemed to be important:

"I have always understood it to be the duty of a judge, when a prisoner has been convicted, to pronounce the sentence of the law. I have also understood that judges sometimes think it their duty to hear with patience and to speak with humanity—to exhort the victim of the law, and to offer with tender benignity his opinions of the motives by which he was actuated in the crime of which he was adjudged guilty. That a judge has thought it his duty so to have done I have no doubt; but where is the boasted freedom of your institutions, where is the vaunted impartiality, clemency and mildness of your courts of justice, if an unfortunate prisoner whom your policy, and *not justice*, is about to deliver to the hands of the executioner is not suffered to explain his motives sincerely and truly, and to vindicate the principles by which he was actuated?"

As he spoke on he moved about the prisoner's dock as well as his chains would permit him. His body swayed slightly and his gestures were eloquent.

"My lords, it may be a part of the system of angry justice to bow a man's mind by humiliation to the purposed ignominy of the scaffold; but worse to me than the purposed shame or the scaffold's terrors would be the tame endurance of such foul and unfounded imputations as have been laid against me in this court.

"You, my lord, are a judge. I am the supposed culprit. I am a man. You are a man also. By a revolution of power we might change places, though we never could change character. If I stand at the bar of this court and dare not vindicate my character, *what a farce is your justice!* If I stand at this bar and dare not vindicate my character, *how dare* you calumniate it! Does the sentence of death which your unhallowed policy inflicts upon my body condemn my tongue to silence, and my reputation to reproach? Your executioner may abridge the period of my existence, but while I exist I shall not forbear to vindicate my character and my motives from aspersions; and as a man to whom fame is dearer than life, I will make the last use of that life in doing justice to that reputation which is to live after me, and which is the only legacy I can leave to those I honor and love, and for whom I am proud to perish. As men, my lords, we must appear on the great day at one common tribunal, and it will then remain for the Searcher of all hearts to show a collective universe, who was engaged in the most virtuous actions, or actuated by the purest motives, my country's oppressors or—"

Again Lord Norbury tried to silence him. He had had a patient trial, the judge told him, but it was an insult to the court to expect them to sit and listen to expressions of treason. Robert Emmet, however, was not ready to stop yet.

"My lords, will a dying man be denied the legal privilege of exculpating himself in the eyes of the community from a reproach thrown upon him during his trial, by charging him with ambition, and attempting to cast away for a paltry consideration the liberties of his country? Why then insult me, or rather why insult justice by demanding of me why sentence of death should not be pronounced against me. I know, my lords, that the form prescribes that you should put the question; the form also confers the answering. This, no doubt, may be dispensed with and so might the whole ceremony of the trial, since sentence was already pronounced at the Castle before your jury was impaneled. Your lordships are but the priests of the oracle, and I submit, but I insist on the whole of the forms."

He paused, overcome with weariness. The court urged him to proceed.

"I have been charged with that importance in the efforts to emancipate my country as to be considered as the keystone of the combination of Irishmen, or as it has been expressed, 'the lifeblood and soul of this conspiracy.' You do me honor overmuch; you have given to the subaltern all the credit of the superior. There are men concerned in this conspiracy who are not only superior to me, but even to your own conception of yourself, my lord; men, before the splendor of whose genius and virtues I should bow with respectful deference, and who would not deign to call you friend—who would not disgrace themselves by shaking your bloodstained hand. . . ."

This personal attack was more than Lord Norbury could endure and he glared at Emmet, saying that it was he who was responsible for the bloodshed.

"What, my lord," said Emmet in an incredulous tone, "shall you tell me on my passage to the scaffold, which that tyranny of which you are only the intermediate minister has erected for my death—that I am accountable for all the blood that has and will be shed in this struggle of the oppressed and the oppressor? Shall you tell me this, and must I be so very a slave as not to repel it?

"I do not fear to approach the Omnipotent Judge, to answer for the conduct of my short life; and am I to stand appalled here before a mere remnant of mortality? Let no man dare, when I am dead, to charge me with dishonor; let no man taint my memory by believing that I could be engaged in any cause but my country's liberty and independence. The Proclamation of the Provisional Government speaks my views. No inference can be tortured from it to countenance barbarity or debasement. I would not have submitted to a foreign oppression for the same reason that I would have resisted tyranny at home."

Lord Norbury interrupted again in a long discourse intended to show how foolish Emmet had been to desert his own high and safe social station.

"You, sir, had the honor to be a gentleman by birth," Norbury said in part, "and your father filled a respectable situation under the government. You had an eldest brother whom death snatched away, and who when living was one of the greatest ornaments of the bar. But you have conspired with the profligate and abandoned, and associated yourself with hostlers, bakers, butchers, and such persons, whom you invited to council when you erected your provisional government. Your sentiments and your language are a disgrace to your friends, your education, but more particularly to your father, who if alive would not countenance such opinions."

Emmet indignantly came to the defense of his father's memory.

"If the spirits of the illustrious dead participate in the concerns of those who were dear to them in this transitory scene, dear shade of my venerated father, look down on your suffering son, and see has he for one moment deviated from those moral and patriotic principles which you so early instilled into his youthful mind, and for which he has now to offer up his life."

And now he had nearly finished.

"My lord, you are impatient for the sacrifice. The blood you seek is not congealed by the artificial terrors which surround your victim; it circulates warmly and unruffled through its channels, and in a little time it will cry to heaven. Be yet patient! I have but a few more words to say. My ministry is ended. I am going to my cold and silent grave; my lamp of life is nearly extinguished. I have parted from everything that was dear to me in this life for my country's cause, and abandoned another idol I adored in my heart, the object of my affections. My race is run. The grave opens to receive me, and I sink into its bosom. I am ready to die. I have not been allowed to vindicate my character. I have but one request to make at my departure from this world. It is *the charity of its silence.*

"Let no man write my epitaph; for as no man who knows my motives now dares vindicate them, let not prejudice or ignorance asperse them. Let them rest in obscurity and peace. Let my memory be left in oblivion, and my tomb remain uninscribed, until other times and other men can do justice to my character. When my country takes her place among the nations of the earth, then, and not till then, let my epitaph be written.

"I have done."

It was over. Lord Norbury pronounced the expected death sentence. The prisoner was taken to Newgate prison and given a meal, but immediately afterward was transferred to Kilmainham under heavy guard. Exhausted as he was, he spent part of the night writing letters, one to Sarah, which was never delivered, and another to Secretary Wickham, thanking him in veiled terms for not having Sarah's name mentioned at the trial. Then he slept.

The next morning Leonard McNally was allowed to visit him.

"How is my mother?" he asked his lawyer.

When McNally evaded his question, Robert Emmet repeated it, adding, "What would I not give to see her!"

The lawyer who had so constantly betrayed him pointed heavenward. "You will see her this day."

Emmet was staggered for a moment but then gained control of himself. "It is better so," he said.

A few hours later the sheriff came to get him. Emmet told him he had one last request, that he might die in his green and white uniform. It was impossible, the sheriff said. Shrugging, Emmet admitted he had not expected the request to be granted but that he still wanted it remembered that he had wished it.

To his jailer, George Dunn, and the prison governor, Edward Trevor, he said good-by politely, entrusting to them two more letters, one to his brother, Thomas Addis, and the other to young Richard Curran, Sarah's brother. Both were filled with his great love for her. Then he walked out with the sheriff and his guard to the waiting carriage.

It moved slowly between rows of silent spectators and stopped at St. Catherine's Church on Thomas Street.

In front of the church a crude gallows had been erected. From a high transverse beam a noose dangled about five feet above a single narrow plank. Emmet, his hands tied behind his back, was helped up a ladder to the plank. He looked down at the thousands who stood beneath him and he spoke his last words:

"My friends, I die in peace, and with sentiments of universal love and kindness toward all men."

They pulled a black cap over his head and placed the noose around his neck. Then the executioner kicked the plank off its ledge. When the body finally hung limp and lifeless, he cut it down, laid it on the platform, and with a blow of a butcher's knife severed the head. "This is the head of Robert Emmet, a traitor," he shouted over and over in a monotonous tone as he held it high.

The assembled crowd slowly dispersed. Some stray dogs slipped up to lick the pools of blood. A sergeant beat them away with his gun butt. He pretended not to notice when some women timidly crept forth to dip their handkerchiefs in the blood.

Robert Emmet, the young man who hoped to make Ireland free, was dead. The memory of Robert Emmet and his love, Sarah Curran, lives on, forever dear, in the hearts of his Irish countrymen.

THE DREYFUS AFFAIR

On the morning of October 15, 1894, Captain Alfred
Dreyfus, probation staff officer of the French General
Staff, left his home on the Avenue du Trocadero and
walked along the wharves of the Seine the short distance
to the Ministry of War headquarters on Rue Saint-
Dominique. He was a slender man of thirty-five, with
light brown hair already thinning across his high forehead and blue, nearsighted eyes that peered straight
ahead through rimless glasses. Though he was not a
brawny, athletic type of man, even in civilian clothes his
bearing and carriage were proof enough of his military
training.

The sun had not yet dissipated the soft gray haze
hanging over the river. There was an autumn crispness
in the air. The chestnut trees along the boulevards were
discarding their many-pronged leaves. It was a morning

to make a man count his blessings, and Captain Dreyfus had many to count.

He was happily married to a loving and loyal wife. He had two charming children, three-year-old Pierre and the baby, Jeanne. Unlike many of his fellow officers, he had no financial worries. A sizable private income supplemented his modest army pay. He was well launched on the military career he had desired since childhood.

Now he was headed for an inspection at the Ministry where he had been summoned to appear in mufti (civilian dress) at nine o'clock. The summons was unusual but he did not think of questioning it. The first lesson in the army is to obey without asking why. He was on time at the Ministry office.

A fellow officer, the handsome and intelligent young Major Georges Picquart, was waiting for him. Picquart had passed his probation period and was a regular Staff member. He had never been very friendly with Dreyfus, but then, neither had any of the other officers. Dreyfus kept to himself and did not invite intimacy. That he was Jewish, at a time when the poison of anti-Semitism was being widely disseminated, also set him apart.

After a brief and formal greeting, Picquart escorted Dreyfus into the office of General le Mouton de Boisdeffre, chief of the General Staff.

To Dreyfus' disappointment, the general was not there. He liked De Boisdeffre and felt indebted to him. Several years before, the general had paid a visit to the Ecole de Guerre, where Dreyfus was then studying to be an officer, and had listened to the students discuss artillery positions. The views expressed by young Dreyfus had so impressed De Boisdeffre that, to the astonishment of the other students and instructors, he had taken him out for a walk and urged him to elaborate his ideas. Dreyfus firmly believed that his later appointment to the select General Staff was due only to the general's recommendation.

There were three civilians in his office and one officer, the Marquis, Major du Paty de Clam, a tall, baldish fussy man who wore a monocle and sported a tiny mustache. The major was a member of the Third Bureau of the General Staff. (It should be explained that the General Staff, which was France's central military organization, had four bureaus in all. The first dealt with army maneuvers; the second, with espionage; the third, that of Major du Paty, with military operations and training; the fourth, with military transportation. The probation officers, who were still learning the routine of the General Staff, usually served on each bureau in turn.)

"The General will be here shortly," Du Paty informed Dreyfus curtly. "I have a bad thumb and will appreciate your writing a letter for me while we are waiting."

The general never did appear.

Dreyfus took a chair at a small desk and wrote down the major's dictation, a series of disconnected phrases. The major came to the words, "A note on the hydraulic brake of the 120mm. gun," then stopped and glared at the captain.

"You are trembling."

"Am I?" Dreyfus looked up and shrugged. "Perhaps my fingers are cold."

"Watch yourself, this is a serious matter." Du Paty scowled at him and continued: "Some modifications will be introduced by the new plan. . . . A note concerning Madagascar . . . The provisional Firing Manual for Field Artillery . . . I am off to maneuvers . . ."

What was it all about? Dreyfus understood nothing.

Suddenly the major rose, assumed a theatrical pose, and shouted, "Captain Dreyfus, I arrest you in the name of the law. You are accused of high treason!"

Had he gone mad? The captain sprang to his feet, so shocked he could only stammer incoherently. The three civilians, who were really policemen, gathered around him. All were making incredible accusations, insisting that he must confess.

Confess to what? "Show me the proof of the infamy you pretend I have committed," Dreyfus said, when he finally gained control of his voice.

"The proofs are overwhelming." The major drew out his revolver and placed it on the table before Dreyfus. The gesture meant that for the honor of the army that he was being accused of betraying, he should shoot himself.

Dreyfus refused to touch it. "But I am innocent. . . ."

Another officer came in—Major Hubert Joseph Henry of the Second, or Intelligence, Bureau. He was a huge man with a broad red face, a low forehead, and small, sly, closely-set eyes. The snobbish officers avoided Henry because of his peasant background. Inordinately ambitious, Henry was willing to grovel for the crumbs of social recognition.

The questioning was over. Du Paty dismissed Dreyfus with a vindictive glance and ordered Henry to accompany the "prisoner" to Cherche-Midi prison. In the cab, Dreyfus, still bewildered, asked Major Henry what it was all about.

"I haven't the slightest idea," Henry lied.

A cell had been prepared for him at the prison. A guard left him alone there with the nightmare that had become a reality. In the space of a few hours the world he had known and loved had vanished, leaving him only walls of stone and bars of iron. He had never been an emotional person, but the shock was too much for him. He screamed his rage at the top of his lungs and smashed himself against the walls.

His cries evoked the sympathy of the prison governor, Major Forzinetti, who could not believe that such a man was a desperate spy. But he had been ordered to keep the imprisonment a secret and there was nothing he could do.

For three days the captain was left in solitude, unable to communicate with his wife or anyone at all from the outside world. It was the beginning of a fearful ordeal that was to last twelve years.

Alfred Dreyfus, the youngest of seven children, three girls and four boys, was born in the textile town of Mulhouse, in Alsace, on October 9, 1859. His father was the head of a prosperous cotton spinning mill. When he was eleven, the Franco-Prussian War of 1870 broke out. From his window the boy watched the thrilling sight of the French cavalry riding to battle on their fine steeds. Later he suffered the torment of the Prussian occupation. It was then that he resolved he would become a soldier and help restore France to her glory.

At the end of the war Alsace was ceded to Germany. Dreyfus senior, a patriot, preferred exile to German rule and moved to Switzerland, leaving his oldest son, Jacques, to manage the Mulhouse factory. Eventually

Jacques was joined by the other two older brothers, Mathieu and Léon. Alfred, with no taste for business, persuaded his father to sponsor his training as a French army officer.

His choice meant many years away from home, first at the Collège Sainte Barbe in Paris, and then on to the military school, Ecole Polytechnique. He proved a brilliant scholar and won a reputation as a daring horseman and a skilled fencer.

His studies absorbed him completely. The gay life of Paris had no appeal for him. A mask of cold reserve concealed his timidity and lack of social graces. His more frivolous fellow students thought him a bore. That his father died and left him an income amounting to about five thousand dollars a year increased their resentment, particularly because of his Jewish birth. Many of the cadets belonged to the impoverished aristocracy who found it convenient to blame the Jews for their financial difficulties. Happily for Dreyfus, he was too immersed in his work to be aware of the antagonism he inspired.

Following his graduation in 1880, he spent two years in the Fontainebleau artillery school as a second lieutenant, and a year in a regiment at Mans as first lieutenant, following which he was transferred back to Paris. By 1889, when he was thirty, he was a captain serving in the Central School of Explosives at Bourges.

His brother Mathieu visited him there. He was distressed to find that Alfred was still a bachelor, so single-minded he took no time to enjoy himself. In an effort to expand his younger brother's horizons, he introduced him to some friends, among them the Hademards, a

Jewish family of Bourges with a distinguished and scholarly background. They had an attractive daughter named Lucie, a small, quiet girl with great dark eyes. She proved an excellent listener for a young man who had never before found anyone in whom to confide. Soon Alfred was calling on her regularly. Sympathy and friendship ripened into love and they were married on April 21, 1890.

On that same day he was notified of his admission to the Ecole de Guerre, a top military school restricted to candidates for the French General Staff. The honor was a good omen for a marriage that was just starting.

The school was in Paris and after their honeymoon he and Lucie went there to live. They were sublimely happy together, finding no need for companionship other than their own. Dreyfus was now competing with the most brilliant young officers of France, working as he never had before. Lucie, gentle and unobtrusive, never objected to his long hours.

During his second year at the Ecole de Guerre, a newspaper was launched, *La Libre Parole* (The Free Word), edited by Edouard Drumont, a fanatical anti-Semite who used the paper as a means of expounding his theories of race hatred. Drumont had mastered a technique that would later be adapted by Adolf Hitler: If you tell a big enough lie often enough, you will pass it as the truth.

La Libre Parole spewed out its poison on all "non-Christians" but was especially vicious in its attacks on Jewish army officers, whom it claimed were all potential traitors. Overnight it had an enormous circulation. Dreyfus often saw his fellow officers reading, and apparently enjoying, this wretched sheet. He lived too much in his own private world to consider the possibility that its contents might ever affect him personally.

It was in his third year at the Ecole de Guerre that General de Boisdeffre, head of the General Staff, singled him out. In 1893, just after the birth of his second child, Jeanne, Captain Dreyfus was appointed to the General Staff as a probationer. It was a magnificent triumph—a triumph of which all French officers dream and which few achieve. As soon as his probation period was over, Dreyfus would be a regular General Staff member! Nothing could alter that, or so he trustingly believed until that hideous day he was arrested and charged with betraying his own country.

How had it come about? Why had such a terrible charge been made against a man who loved France more than life itself?

The corrosive evil of *La Libre Parole* had seeped into the General Staff headquarters; some of the officers were furious at the admission of a Jew to their inner circle. Colonel Jean Sandherr, head of the Second Bureau, was so infected with the disease of anti-Semitism that he labeled Dreyfus a "security risk," with the result that he was not assigned to Sandherr's department but to the First Bureau, dealing with maneuvers. In spite of this discriminatory attitude, no one had anything definite against this eager and ambitious young officer.

Ever since the Franco-Prussian War, espionage had been a touchy matter with the top military echelon. Relations with Germany were still uneasy, nor was Italy trusted. Certain information had leaked out that indicated an informer in a confidential post. There was espionage going on, and there was also counterespionage and counter-counterespionage. The situation had become so complicated that even the Second Bureau sometimes had difficulty figuring out who was in the pay of whom.

A German Embassy charwoman regularly turned over to the Second Bureau the contents of the Embassy wastebaskets, which were duly studied by Colonel Sandherr and his assistant, Major Henry. Once they intercepted a message between the German Military Attaché, Colonel von Schwarzkoppen, and the Italian Military Attaché, Lieutenant Colonel Pannizzardi, that read:

"Enclosed are twelve detail maps of Nice that the Scoundred D——left with me for you."

It was suspicious, but that was all. "Scoundrel D——" might not be a spy at all. If he was, it was a fair certainty that his name did not begin with "D"— secret agents were not usually so stupid as to use their own initials. Nonetheless, the message was filed for future consideration.

Then one day came a thunderbolt. An officer named Bruecker produced a sheet of lightweight graph paper, handwritten on both sides, that he had rifled from the incoming mail of German attaché, Von Schwarzkoppen. Written in French, it read:

"I have no news to indicate that you wish to see me; however, I am sending you some interesting information.

"1. A note on the hydraulic brake of the 120mm. gun and on the way it was found to work.

"2. A note on the supporting troops. Some modifications will be introduced by the new plan.

"3. A note on the modification of artillery formations.

"4. A note concerning Madagascar.

"5. The provisional Firing Manual for Field Artillery (March 14, 1894).

"This last document is extraordinarily difficult to procure, and I have it at my disposal only for a very few days. The Minister of War has issued a limited number to the corps, and the corps are responsible for them. Each officer who has a copy has to send it back after the maneuvers. If, therefore, you will take notes of whatever is of interest to you, and hold it at my disposal, I shall take it back. That is, unless you want me to have it copied in full and send you the copy. I am just off to the maneuvers."

This document, called a *bordereau*, or schedule, was to become world famous.

Here was proof that there was a spy within French army circles, and it was written obviously in the spy's own handwriting. Major Henry was away at the time. Colonel Sandherr discussed the matter with a few of his fellow officers. In the general excitement, they overlooked the obvious fact that the information contained in the *bordereau* was worthless to the Germans or anyone else. For the honor of the army the spy had to be identified.

Colonel D'Aboville of the Fourth Bureau suggested that the informer might be a probationer—someone who moved from bureau to bureau. The others accepted his suggestion readily. Why not? The search was narrowed.

A file of probation officers was brought forth. They went down the names until they reached the "D's," and stopped short and looked at each other. *Alfred Dreyfus.* The Jew. But of course. . . . "The Scoundrel D———."

The matter of handwriting had to be considered next.

They took samples of Dreyfus' handwriting from his personal file and compared them hopefully with the writing of the *bordereau*. It was not difficult for them to convince themselves there were similarities.

General de Boisdeffre, the Chief of the General Staff, General Gonse, his deputy chief, and General Auguste Mercier, the French Minister of War, were duly informed of the existence of the *bordereau* and the clue as to its possible author. Major du Paty de Clam, who seems to have relished melodramatic spy stories, made himself part of the investigation. A handwriting expert, a precise and careful banker named Monsieur Alfred Gobert, was summoned and presented with the *bordereau* along with samples of the handwriting of Captain Alfred Dreyfus.

His verdict was: "The *bordereau* could have been written by a person other than the writer of the samples submitted."

An evasive opinion that meant nothing, the Staff officers decided in annoyance. They dismissed Gobert and sent for the celebrated Monsieur Alphonse Bertillon. Bertillon is known for his system of identifying criminals according to the bone structure of their skulls,—a system then being used by police departments all over the world. Because of this weird "anthropometric" method of criminal detection, fingerprinting was denied official acceptance for some twenty years. Bertillon also considered himself an authority on handwriting, on the basis of a system of numbers and symbols so complex that no one could grasp what it was all about.

When they instructed Bertillon to compare the two handwritings, the General Staff officers took the precaution of assuring him they had overwhelming proof that the same person was the author of both. Bertillon did not take it on himself to contradict military opinion. He worded his conclusion:

"If the hypothesis is discarded that the author of the *bordereau* forged another's handwriting while preparing it, it appears to be manifest that the identical person wrote both the samples and the incriminating document."

General Mercier, the Minister of War, and the General Staff officers decided that Bertillon's ambiguous statement implicated Dreyfus sufficiently to warrant his arrest. For reasons of their own, they ignored evidence that indicated he could not have been involved. Dreyfus had not been "off to maneuvers," as the *bordereau* stated. Also, the *bordereau* had certain Germanic twists of phrasing, whereas Dreyfus wrote flawless French. When Major Henry returned from his leave, he was brought up to date about what had happened. It is possible he knew at once the true author of the *bordereau*. No one was ever sure on this point. But from then on, no one on the Staff was more vehement against Dreyfus than he.

Dreyfus was summoned to the Ministry, accused, arrested, taken to prison. On the same day Major du Paty de Clam paid a call on Lucie Dreyfus.

"Madame, I have a very sad mission to fulfill," he told her.

Her dark eyes widened in fear. "My husband is dead?"

"No, worse than that . . . he is in prison. . . . You must tell no one."

She assured him calmly it must be a mistake, her husband could not have done anything wrong. She pleaded to see him, but the major flatly refused. He ordered her apartment searched, hoping to find graph paper like that on which the *bordereau* had been written, or other incriminating material. There was nothing.

After Dreyfus had been in prison three days, Major du Paty began visiting him in his cell, behaving in the most peculiar manner. He ordered Dreyfus to write letters, standing, sitting down, lying down, and with his gloves on. Once he arrived at night, flashing his lantern in the prisoner's face, as though to surprise an expression of guilt. Another time he brought a photostat of the *bordereau*, tore it in pieces, mixed the pieces with photostats of the captain's own handwriting, and demanded that he separate the two. Dreyfus did as he was told without a mistake. Human company, even that as unpleasant as the snobbish marquis, had brought him back to his senses. Now he saw his arrest as merely a case of mistaken identity. Soon his name would be cleared. . . .

On October 29, when he had been in prison two weeks, an item appeared in *La Libre Parole*: "Is it a fact that on orders from the military a very important arrest has been made? The prisoner is accused of high treason. If this news is true, why the silence?"

It was Major Henry who had sent the query to the editor, Edouard Drumont, through a mutual friend, one Major Esterhazy, about whom there will be more later. Soon all the rabid elements in Paris were proclaiming that a Jewish officer was guilty of treason, that he had confessed, that absolute proofs were held against him. Drumont, with his usual neglect of truth, blasted General Mercier, the Minister of War, as "irresponsible" for trying to hush up the matter.

Under this pressure, Mercier, who had previously been lukewarm about Dreyfus, promised an immediate trial.

Lucie, released of her promise of silence to Du Paty, wired her husband's brothers in Alsace. Mathieu, who was closer to Alfred than the others, took the next train to Paris. Like Lucie, he knew that his younger brother could not be guilty of the slightest indiscretion. They went together to see an elderly Catholic lawyer of great integrity named Edgar Demange. Demange first refused to take the case because the army was involved, but changed his mind when he learned the flimsy evidence on which the charge was based and the role of racial hatred in prejudging the accused.

The trial began on December 19, 1895, in a gloomy courtroom at the Hôtel du Cherche-Midi, not far from the prison. Seven officers served as both judges and jury. Colonel Maurel, who had the highest rank, was the presiding judge. Major du Paty was there, as were Major Henry and General Gonse. The handsome Major Georges Picquart represented General Mercier. Picquart took it for granted, like the others, that Dreyfus was guilty. Demange represented Dreyfus, and the prosecuting attorney was a Captain Brisset. There were three handwriting experts, including Bertillon. The press was there and a scattering of the general public.

Dreyfus, in his full-dress uniform, held himself at attention as a soldier should. When he was asked to give his name, rank, and address, his naturally high-pitched voice cracked, creating an unfavorable impression. This weakening of his voice happened sometimes when he was upset.

Demange took the floor, intending to point out to the press that the *bordereau* was the only official evidence against the prisoner. Before he could complete his statement, the trial was declared secret and the press and public dismissed. Demange guessed then what the decision would be, but Dreyfus himself was only puzzled. The newspapers had unjustly condemned him in advance of his trial. Why should journalists be forbidden to hear the testimony that would clear his reputation?

His nervousness left him when the questioning began. He explained why he could not have known about the 120mm. gun and the other items on the *bordereau*, and that the statement, "I am off to maneuvers" could not have applied to him since General Staff probationers did not go to maneuvers. He said he had renounced wealth and comfort for a military career and that he was happy in his family life; it would have been folly to risk all he had to betray his country.

Major du Paty de Clam was called to the witness stand. He stressed that Dreyfus had trembled when the *bordereau* was dictated to him. At what phrase had the witness trembled? Demange asked. The major, fearing a trap, glared and refused to answer. Later on he popped up again to say he had figured out a motive for Dreyfus' treachery. The Dreyfus factory in Mulhouse had burned down. A German company had insured it. Could it be that the payment given Dreyfus as compensation was in excess of the damage? Even the prejudiced judges looked skeptical at this far-fetched theory.

The questioning of Dreyfus resumed. He made his answers as complete as possible, and he spoke without hesitating. The court's first session ended with his testimony. All in all, things looked hopeful for him, too hopeful to suit the already deeply committed Ministry of War.

That night General Mercier and Colonel Sandherr prepared a brief from material furnished by Major du Paty de Clam, aimed to raise doubts about Dreyfus' character. It included the "Scoundrel D——" letter and even scraps retrieved by the charwoman from the German Embassy wastebasket that might, by a long stretch of the imagination, indicate a spy was at work. The brief was sealed in an envelope, along with a note to the court that it be given to the judges *after* the testimony was concluded. In so doing, the military had placed itself above the law, since it is contrary to legal procedure to introduce evidence without the knowledge of the defendant and his lawyer.

The next day several fellow officers of Captain Dreyfus were brought to the stand. Few had anything good to say about him. Some claimed they had been suspicious of him because he wanted to know too much. Others suggested he had used his money to win the favors of young women. Their testimony showed that he was unpopular with them, but not that he had betrayed his country.

The testimony of the three handwriting experts was divided. Bertillon confused everyone with an involved dissertation on how certain differences between the handwriting of Dreyfus and that of the *bordereau* might indicate that Dreyfus had disguised his handwriting.

Major Henry was summoned as a witness. The huge peasant had planned a dramatic stratagem. The previous March, he declared loudly, an *unimpeachable* personage had informed him there was a traitor in the War Ministry. In June, the same person had repeated his warning. He paused, stood up, turned, pointed to Dreyfus, and shouted, "There is the traitor!"

Dreyfus jumped to his feet in protest. His lawyer, Demange, demanded to know the name of the "unimpeachable personage," pointing out that under Article 101 of French law, the accused had the right to be faced with his accuser. Henry refused. "There are secrets in an officer's head that even his kepi [his officer's cap] must not know," he said mysteriously.

The presiding judge, Colonel Maurel, intervened. They would not insist on the name of his informant, he stated blandly, if Major Henry would swear on his honor that this person had told him the traitor was Captain Dreyfus.

Henry raised his hand toward the crucifix and said, "I swear it."

Only Dreyfus himself knew positively that he was lying.

Henry's statement, plus the nebulous material in the sealed envelope that Maurel had read to his fellow judges, produced the desired effect. On December 22, the third day of the trial, Dreyfus was pronounced guilty. He was condemned to dishonorable discharge from the army and deportation for the rest of his life.

"At last I am approaching the end of my sufferings," Dreyfus had written Lucie the day before the trial. The day after the decision, his letter was concerned only with her: "I pity you more than myself. . . . Your heart must bleed."

The dreadful ceremony for the dishonorable discharge took place on January 5, in the courtyard of the Ecole Militaire. A mob gathered in front of the school. They were so disorderly that a double line of guards had to be stationed in the quadrangle. Soldiers from every regiment of the Paris garrison were assembled in military precision around the courtyard. A trumpet sounded and a sergeant of the guard marched in, leading four soldiers with drawn swords. Dreyfus walked between them. His face was drawn and he marched rigidly, like a marionette. The group came to a halt before General Paul Darras, who was waiting on horseback.

The general pronounced the fearful words: "Alfred Dreyfus, you are unworthy of carrying arms."

Choking, Dreyfus called out with all his strength, "An innocent is dishonored. Long live France!"

An adjutant sergeant tore the epaulets from his shoulders and wrenched from his trousers the red stripes that marked him as a General Staff officer. Then he took Dreyfus' sword and broke it in two. Shorn of his cherished insignia, Dreyfus was marched between two lines of officers, his face distorted by his mighty effort to conceal his suffering. As he passed, a fanatic young officer stepped forward and struck him on the cheek with the hilt of his sword, leaving a bloody gash.

"I am innocent," Dreyfus shouted at regular intervals. "Long live France!"

The spectacle moved even the hostile spectators and they fell silent.

A few days later he was taken to the port of La Rochelle with a trainload of convicts. A rumor spread at the station that the "traitor" was aboard, and a crowd gathered, muttering threats of violence. The guards kept him in his cramped cell until nightfall when they risked bringing him from the train. The moment he appeared, the mob was cursing and striking him.

He stood quite still, making no attempt to defend himself. Had he been in their place, he told himself, he would have felt as they did. Against his wishes, his guards sprang to his assistance. They had their orders and could not allow him this easy escape from his misery.

On February 21, 1895, he was put on board a prison ship bound for Devil's Island off the Coast of Guiana. He was chained to the floor in a felon's cell in the forecastle. Tortured by hunger and cold he was tormented even more by mental agony. For hours at a time he wept.

Devil's Island is a rock some two miles long and four hundred yards wide. Its climate is so foul that even an attempt to raise goats there failed. At one time a leper colony had occupied the island, but now the lepers were gone and their cabins burned. Here Dreyfus arrived on April 13, condemned to be the island's sole prisoner for as long as he lived.

His lodging was a stone hut some thirteen feet square, specially built for him. It had a small room at one end where a guard was constantly on duty. The guards had orders never to speak to him and never to let him out of their sight. In his first months he was permitted to walk beneath the blistering tropical sun in the bleak, treeless area beyond his hut. He prepared his own meager meals, using tin cans as dishes, washed and mended his clothes, cleaned his quarters.

Whatever he did, he was never beyond the shadow of his armed and silent guards. He was cut off from his fellow men, and yet he was never alone. Of all his hardships, the lack of privacy was the worst. Eyes were always watching him.

His one solace came from Lucie's letters, which arrived regularly on the fortnightly ship. "Let us hope that we have finally surmounted the most arduous stage of our calvary, and that the future holds only happiness." "I am convinced that with a will of iron . . . untiring perseverance, we can overcome every difficulty." "I have ever before my eyes your beloved face." Only her words gave him the courage to live.

After an eternity of eighteen months, he was abruptly confined solely to his hut and at night placed in double irons attached to his bed in such a way that it was impossible for him to move. Night after night he lay sleepless in the sweltering heat, harassed by vermin, his ankles chafed and bleeding from the fetters. Bitterly he told himself that he had reached the limit of human suffering.

The double irons were the inspiration of the Colonial minister, André LeBron, who had taken literally an administrative order to employ every "measure of safety" to prevent his important prisoner from escaping. In later years Dreyfus forgave nearly everyone connected with his misfortunes but he could never forgive LeBron. This cruel torture lasted forty-four consecutive nights.

Other "measures of safety" were instituted. A double wall was built around his cabin. The nearest one was eight feet high and five feet from his windows, cutting out both light and air. The other, of thick planks of wapa trees, enclosed a space about 130 feet long and 55 feet wide. At infrequent intervals he was allowed to exercise on this narrow walk that did not even give him the comfort of a glimpse of the sea.

The packages of books and periodicals from his brother Matthieu ceased coming. Lucie's letters came less frequently; sometimes he received only cut and mangled copies. Often he was ill with dysentery or with attacks of cerebral congestion. He suffered from bites of enormous mosquitoes, from the enervating heat, from insomnia. A prison physician who visted him in April, 1897, reported his poor health and also that the long unbroken silence had made it difficult for him to speak. "Sentences no longer come readily . . . he is obliged to repeat himself to convey a thought."

To keep his sanity he studied English by translating passages from Shakespeare, or reconstructed from memory problems in integral and differential calculus.

From France had come rumors of a plot to rescue the prisoner Dreyfus. Unfounded and fantastic as these rumors were, his captors increased the number of his guards from five to thirteen. Guards were placed on his roof and along the palisade, and as a further precaution were encouraged to inform on one another. An observation tower was built, topped with a Hotchkiss gun, kept loaded and pointed toward the sea. No ship was allowed nearer than three miles from shore. The men on night duty marched back and forth constantly, and the measured tread of their wooden shoes was an added torment to the sleepless prisoner. Triangular panels were placed over the iron grating of his windows. Half-suffocated in his darkened cell, Dreyfus choked and coughed, unable to breathe the fetid and noisome air.

While the French Government was spending enormous sums to guard one heartsick, weakened man, it seemed to Alfred Dreyfus that the whole world had forgotten him. The very opposite was true. His first trial was only the prologue to a mighty drama, involving other trials, duels, upsets in government, suicides, and even murder.

About a year after Dreyfus had been sent to his earthly hell, Colonel Sandherr, chief of the Second Bureau, suffered a paralytic stroke. Major Henry was sure that in reward for his loyalty he would be promoted to Sandherr's place. The appointment went instead to Georges Picquart, now a lieutenant colonel. This efficient and intelligent man gradually began to make order out of the disorder of the colossal files on spies and counterspies.

Before Sandherr left his post, he had shown Picquart the safe in which the secret file on Dreyfus was kept—the material shown to the seven judges but to no one else—advising him not to touch it, that it was best "to let sleeping dogs lie." Later, General de Boisdeffre advised Picquart to study the Dreyfus file. De Boisdeffre had not forgotten his first favorable impression of Dreyfus. If Picquart could figure out why such a man had committed treason, he said, it would help him in his other Intelligence work. Picquart, looking over the secret file, was shocked at the meagerness of the evidence against the condemned man.

Fifteen months after the Dreyfus case had been marked officially closed, a member of the Second Bureau brought Picquart the latest result of its espionage—a special delivery letter of the type known in Paris as a *petit bleu* (literally, a "little blue thing") because of its color. It was written by a woman friend of the German Military Attaché, Von Schwarzkoppen, but not mailed, and was addressed to a French artillery officer—Major Count Ferdinand Walsin-Esterhazy.

Who was this Major Esterhazy? Picquart was curious and did a little investigating. What he learned set him wondering further. Then, by an odd coincidence, he received an application for service on the General Staff from this same Major Esterhazy.

As he read it over it occurred to him that he had seen this spidery handwriting before. He looked up the *bordereau*. Unable to accept the evidence of his own eyes, he summoned Bertillon and asked his opinion. For once this handwriting "expert" made no long speeches. "This is the man who wrote the *bordereau*," he said simply.

Picquart went immediately to General de Boisdeffre to report that Esterhazy, not Dreyfus, had written the *bordereau*. "Well, we were wrong, weren't we?" the general conceded. He advised Picquart to take the matter up with General Gonse.

It was then that Lieutenant Colonel Picquart had the greatest shock of his hitherto uncomplicated life. "You should have kept the two cases separated," General Gonse snapped. "The Dreyfus case is closed."

The Dreyfus family did not think it was closed, Picquart reminded him. They were still trying to have it reopened.

"What do you care for this Jew anyhow?" Gonse demanded.

Picquart stared at him in amazement. "But he is innocent!"

"If you keep silent, no one need find out anything," Gonse said.

"General," cried Picquart, "what you say is abominable. I do not yet know what I am going to do. But I will not carry this secret to my grave." He must have guessed that he was signing a death warrant to his own military career.

Major Esterhazy was not arrested. He was not even questioned.

A few months later, the government released a statement to the Paris newspaper, *L'Eclair*, saying that now that the need for secrecy was past, the real proof of the guilt of Alfred Dreyfus could be revealed: a letter from the German Military Attaché to his Italian counterpart that included the words, "Decidedly, this beast of a Dreyfus has been demanding." So confidential was this letter, the statement continued, that it had been handed secretly to the judges of the Dreyfus trial. Not even Dreyfus' defense attorney had known about it.

Edgar Demange, Dreyfus' lawyer, read the newspaper story with excitement. He had no idea that the letter referred to mentioned only "Scoundrel D——," not "this beast of a Dreyfus." No one knew that except a few Staff officers. But as a lawyer he recognized at once what Georges Picquart did not realize—that the trial had been illegal since evidence had been introduced without informing the accused or his lawyer. At last he had a basis on which to ask for a new trial.

Lucie and Mathieu Dreyfus were overjoyed at this hopeful news. Lucie appealed to the Pope and to the French Chamber of Deputies for support. There was no response from either. Then Mathieu persuaded a young literary critic named Bernard Lazare to write a pamphlet about his brother's case, so far as the facts were known. Called *A Judicial Error*, it was published in Belgium to avoid persecution. Copies were sent to the press and to important people. There was no evidence it did any good. It was suspect in any case, since it was sponsored by the family of the accused.

The one man who knew the truth—and wanted to tell it—was removed beyond temptation, or so his superiors believed. Lieutenant Colonel Georges Picquart had been sent on an inspection tour of the eastern frontier by General Gonse. From there he was ordered to the Italian frontier, and then on to Algiers and Tunisia.

In Picquart's absence, Major Henry was acting head of the Second Bureau. Henry took it on himself to start a "Picquart file," which he filled with a mass of material intended to compromise his missing chief. Since Picquart's record was impeccable, this required considerable invention on Henry's part, including steaming open Picquart's mail and pasting and clipping excerpts in an attempt to distort the truth. The monocled Major du Paty helped him in this game. On his own, Henry also began making additions to the Dreyfus file, for which he enlisted the aid of a skilled forger, Lemercier-Picard.

In his exile, Picquart became annoyed at the irregularity with which he received his mail and wrote to find out what had happened. In reply he received an incoherent blast from Major Henry, accusing him of incompetency, of willful wrongdoing, of opening letters to Major Esterhazy without authorization, and of making public the secret Dreyfus file. The hysterical letter made clear to the exile the depths of the plot in which he had become involved. He could no longer doubt the real reason why he had been sent away, or that his enemies would stop at nothing.

Shortly after this Picquart fell from his horse. He was not hurt, but the fall struck him as a warning. He had told General Gonse he would not carry the secret to his grave. The long fight between his conscience and his duty as an officer was almost over.

That night he wrote out a statement in which he said that Major Esterhazy was a German agent, that acts charged to Dreyfus had been committed by Esterhazy, and that Dreyfus had been tried with a preconceived judgment of his guilt. Two months later, when he finally obtained leave and could return briefly to Paris, he gave the statement to his lawyer and friend, Louis Leblois, with instructions that in case of his death it should go to the President of the French Republic.

Leblois, an upright and honorable man, could not rest knowing the horrible secret that an innocent man had been condemned as guilty. Before Picquart left, he won his consent to reveal as much of the story as possible without mentioning Picquart's name. As his confidant, Leblois chose the esteemed and venerable senator from Alsace, Vice President of the Senate, Auguste Scheurer-Kestner.

Scheurer knew the fine reputation of the Dreyfus family in Alsace and had already suspected that the charge against Dreyfus might be based on anti-Semitism. Without the name of the officer who had supplied the information about Esterhazy he could do nothing officially, but he did hint to the President of the Senate that there was new evidence of Dreyfus' innocence. His indiscretion boomeranged. The press heard about it, called Scheurer a "dummy of a syndicate of Jews," suggested he ought to take a seat in the Prussian Parliament, and attacked his private life.

In the meantime, the Paris newspaper, *Le Matin*, had a scoop. From one of the handwriting experts, they got hold of a photostat of the *bordereau*, which they reproduced under the headline "The Proof." Mathieu Dreyfus and Bernard Lazare promptly prepared a second edition of *A Judicial Error*, including this famous document as it had appeared in *Le Matin*, along with testimony from their own handwriting expert as to why it could not have been written by Alfred Dreyfus.

Shortly after its publication, a stockbroker named Castro called on Mathieu Dreyfus, saying that he recognized the handwriting of the *bordereau*. In fact, he had had some rather unfortunate business dealings with the man who had written it. He produced some letters signed by Major Count Ferdinand Walsin-Esterhazy.

It was a glorious moment for Mathieu and Lucie Dreyfus. Now, at last, the name of the true criminal could be brought forth and the name of their loved one cleared. Or so they thought, little guessing that the War Department already knew about Esterhazy. By the French criminal code, a private citizen with knowledge of a crime can bring a charge and the charge must be investigated. Accordingly, on November 15, 1897, Mathieu Dreyfus charged Esterhazy with being the author of the *bordereau*.

Major Count Ferdinand Walsin-Esterhazy—who was he? His full story was not pieced together until later. Born in France of an aristocratic Hungarian family, he had been orphaned at an early age and had spent his childhood and youth at Austrian military schools. He had served in the Austrian army and the Papal army before becoming a French officer. There he acquired a reputation for extravagance, gambling, drinking, and women. He married into the French aristocracy and soon squandered his wife's dowry. From then on he was always in debt, always engaging in more or less shady business deals.

Somehow he became acquainted with Major Henry and, on learning he belonged to the Second Bureau, went out of his way to be friendly with the dull and plodding fellow, inviting him to dinner, introducing him to his friends (such as the anti-Semitic editor, Drumont), and doing other favors for him, including translating certain foreign documents that came into the Second Bureau. Henry, scorned by his fellow General Staff officers, was flattered and dazzled by the attention of this tall, lean count with wolflike visage and great yellow mustaches. At last he had achieved social recognition!

Esterhazy's motives in cultivating Henry, who must have bored him exceedingly, were quite obvious. He wanted to become a member of the General Staff and, unaware of the contempt with which Henry was regarded by his fellow officers, believed the major would help him. He also hoped to pick up some information from Henry about the activities of the Second Bureau— information that might help pay his debts.

On July 20, 1894, four months before the arrest of Dreyfus, Esterhazy paid a call on Colonel von Schwarzkoppen at the German Embassy, saying he was a good friend of the head of the French Second Bureau and in a position to render valuable services to Germany. Von Schwarzkoppen was so shocked at this brazen offer of a French officer to betray his country that he ordered him out, but as a matter of routine he reported the visit to his superiors in Berlin. Orders came back immediately for him to negotiate with the French officer. When the count showed up two days later, the German Military Attaché took him into his office. Tentatively he was put on the German payroll but was dropped a few months later, since the information he turned over proved useless. But before this happened, Esterhazy had left the *bordereau* in the German attaché's mail box.

Several times in the course of the Dreyfus affair, Von Schwarzkoppen was asked whether Dreyfus was a spy, and invariably he said he was not. The full account of his relations with Esterhazy was not produced until the publication of Von Schwarzkoppen's memoirs, after his death.

In due time, as the result of the charge of Mathieu Dreyfus, an investigation of Esterhazy was set in motion. General de Pellieux, who was in charge of it, called on Mathieu to present his proof. Mathieu had only the *bordereau* and Esterhazy's letters to the stockbroker, Castro. The general ruled that the *bordereau* could not be used as evidence, since to do so would mean to re-open the Dreyfus case, which was closed!

The general next summoned Senator Scheurer, demanding if he had any pertinent documents. Scheurer told him he did not, but suggested he talk to the lawyer, Louis Leblois. On the witness stand, Leblois felt he could keep his secret no longer. He named Georges Picquart as the source of his information about Esterhazy.

By so doing, he succeeded only in getting Picquart in trouble. In his final report on the investigation, General de Pellieux announced there was no real evidence against Major Esterhazy—but that Picquart had committed a grave fault by disclosing confidential material to his lawyer. The investigation was ended. At this point, Esterhazy, made bold by the general's verdict, did a stupid thing. Declaring that his honor had been injured, he insisted on a public trial to vindicate himself.

Shortly before this new trial, a widow named Madame de Boulancy turned over to her lawyer some letters she had received from Esterhazy, telling him to do with them as he saw fit. The lawyer gave them to Senator

Scheurer. They provided damning evidence of Major Esterhazy's disloyalty to the country he was engaged to serve.

"I would not harm a puppy, but I would kill ten thousand Frenchmen with pleasure," Esterhazy had written. "These people aren't worth the cartridges it would take to kill them." There were other passages in the same vindictive vein.

Scheurer made sure General de Pellieux had these letters in time for the Esterhazy trial, but Major Henry insisted they must be forgeries and they were not used as evidence. Georges Picquart was summoned back from North Africa as a witness for the prosecution, but his testimony was given behind closed doors. The verdict of the judges was unanimous for Esterhazy's exoneration. The next morning Picquart was arrested, charged with betraying his post, and taken to the fortress of Mont Valerien.

Although so far in this long fight, injustice had triumphed regularly over justice, the Dreyfus affair had become headline news everywhere. Dreyfus supporters, who called themselves *Dreyfusards*, were increasing by the hundreds and thousands. Dreyfus had become the symbol of the oppressed all over the world. Everywhere people heard with sorrow of the release of Esterhazy and of Picquart's imprisonment. In France, a minority group of intellectuals dared speak out.

Senator Scheurer was one of them. Another was the French deputy and historian, Joseph Reinach, a veteran of many battles in defense of the Jewish people. There was also Georges Clemenceau, who was later to become France's Prime Minister.

"Every man has two countries, his own and France,"

Clemenceau wrote in his newspaper, *L'Aurore*. "A country is made up not only of its soil, its rocks, its waters, forests and fields . . . but also of the ideas that knit the soils together. . . . When it will be perceived that right and justice in our country are words deprived of significance . . . we may still sit on French soil. But we shall have ceased to be the France our fathers desired to create and left to us to make a reality." In all, Clemenceau wrote some eight hundred articles demanding the release of Alfred Dreyfus.

It remained for one man to crystallize public sympathy. This was Emile Zola, the great French novelist. "What a poignant drama, what superb characters," Zola wrote of the Dreyfus affair on November 25, 1895. Little by little he found himself becoming deeply involved. Toward the end of the Esterhazy trial, he shut himself in his study and worked "in a fever of anger and inspiration."

The result of Zola's labors was an open letter of appeal to Félix Faure, President of the French Republic, published in Clemenceau's *L'Aurore* on January 13, 1898, and called *J'Accuse* (*I Accuse*). It has long since taken its place among the greatest political documents of all times.

"Mr. President," he began, "Permit me, I beg you, in return for the gracious favors you once accorded me, to be concerned with regard to your just glory and to tell you that your record, so fair and fortunate thus far, is now threatened with the most shameful, the most ineffaceable blot. . . .

"A court-martial had but recently, by order, dared to acquit one Esterhazy—a supreme slap at all truth, all justice! And it is done; France has this brand upon her visage; history will relate that it was during your administration that such a social crime could be committed.

"Since they have dared, I too shall dare. I shall tell the truth because I pledged myself to tell it if justice, regularly empowered, did not do so, fully, unmitigatedly. My duty is to speak; I have no wish to be an accomplice. My nights would be haunted by the specter of the innocent being, expiating, under the most frightful torture, a crime he never committed. . . .

"The truth, first, on the trial and condemnation of Dreyfus. One pernicious individual arranged, planned, concocted everything—Lieutenant Colonel du Paty de Clam, then only Major. He is the whole Dreyfus Affair; we shall only understand it after an honest inquiry shall have definitely established all his acts and responsibilities. . . . I declare simply that Major du Paty de Clam, designated as prosecuting officer, is the one who is first and most of all guilty of the fearful miscarriage of justice.

"The *bordereau* had been for some time previously in the hands of the late Colonel Sandherr, head of the Secret Service. 'Leaks' had been discovered, papers had disappeared, as they still do today: when a perfectly arbitrary guess suggested that the author of the document could only be an artillery officer, attached to the General Staff; manifestly a double error, which reveals in what a superficial manner the *bordereau* had been studied, for a reasonable examination shows that it could only have emanated from a line officer.

"A search was made then; handwritings were examined, at home; it was all a family affair; a traitor was to be found right under their noses, and to be expelled. . . . And Major du Paty de Clam enters as the first suspicion falls on Dreyfus. . . . There is also the Minister of War, General Mercier, at work, whose intellect seems but mediocre; there is also the chief of staff, General Boisdeffre, who seems to yield to his clerical passions; and there is the under-chief of the General Staff, General Gonse, whose conscience adjusts itself readily to many things. But at bottom, there is at first no one so busily involved as Major du Paty de Clam, who leads them all, who hypnotizes them, for he is also interested in spiritism, occultism, he talks with spirits. The experiments to which he had the unfortunate Dreyfus submitted, the traps he laid, seem incredible; the mad investigations, the monstrous hoax, a whole harrowing dementia.

"Ah, that first affair is a nightmare for whoever knows it in its true details! . . .

"But here is Dreyfus before that court-martial. The most rigorous secrecy is preserved. A traitor might have opened the frontier to the enemy and led the German emperor clear to the Notre Dame cathedral and no more extreme measures of silence and mystery would have been taken. The nation is horror-stricken, the most terrible details are whispered of monstrous treasons that make all history cry out; obviously, the whole nation bows to the court. No punishment is severe enough for the criminal; the country will applaud the public degradation, she will want the guilty man to stay eternally on his rock of infamy, devoured by remorse. Is there any truth in those whispered unmentionable things, capable of setting all Europe aflame, that they must needs be buried in the deep secrecy of star-chamber proceedings? No. . . .

"Ah! the inanity of that accusation! That a man could have been condemned on such a charge is a prodigy of iniquity. I challenge honest people to read it and not be overcome with indignation, and not cry out their revulsion at the superhuman expiation of the man on Devil's Island.

"Dreyfus, it is shown, knows several languages: crime; he works hard: crime; no compromising papers are found in his home: crime; he goes occasionally to the country of his origin: crime; he endeavors to learn everything: crime; he is not easily worried: crime; he is worried: crime. . . ."

Zola continued, giving the details of Picquart's discovery of Esterhazy's authorship of the *bordereau*, of Picquart's subsequent exile, of the treatment given Scheurer-Kestner.

"Dreyfus cannot be vindicted unless the whole General Staff is indicted," he prophesied. "How pitiful that this truth, this justice we have so passionately desired, seems now more mutilated, punished, cast off than ever before!"

And then Zola's conclusion:

"I accuse Colonel du Paty de Clam of having been the diabolical agent of the judicial error. . . .

"I accuse General Mercier of having made himself an accomplice in one of the greatest crimes in history, probably through weak-mindedness. . . ."

He accused other officers, including Generals de Boisdeffre, Gonse, and de Pellieux, as well as three handwriting experts for "having made lying and fraudulent reports, unless a medical examination will certify them to be deficient in sight and judgment."

Next: "I accuse the War Office of having led a vile campaign in the press . . . in order to misdirect public opinion and cover up its sins."

Finally: "I accuse, lastly, the first court-martial of having violated all human rights in condemning a prisoner on testimony kept secret from him, and I accuse the second court-martial of having covered up this illegality by order, committing in turn the judicial crime of acquitting a guilty man [Esterhazy] with full knowledge of his guilt.

"In making these accusations I am aware that I render myself liable to articles 30 and 31 of Libel Laws of July 29, 1881, which punish acts of defamation. I expose myself voluntarily. . . .

"I have one passion only, for light, in the name of humanity which has borne so much and has a right to happiness. My burning protest is only the cry of my soul. . . .

"I am waiting."

The day *J'Accuse* was published, *L'Aurore* sold out an edition of 300,000. Thirty thousand letters and telegrams flooded the newspaper offices. Up until now, the villains of the Dreyfus drama had been nebulous. But Zola had named names—missing only Major Henry, whose role no one as yet suspected—and most of those he had named were high-ranking French officers. As he had expected, he was indicted for libel.

The trial of Emile Zola opened on February 7, 1898, four years and eight months after the arrest of Dreyfus. It was held in the Palace of Justice jury room and was as crowded with spectators as a first-night opera. Zola, bearded and serene, had the look of an unworldly professor. His attorney was Fernand Labori, a younger version of the good Edgar Demange, and known as "Lungs of Steel" because of his thundering voice.

Zola had given Labori instructions to defend Dreyfus

rather than himself. It was not he and not Dreyfus who were on trial, Zola told the jury in his eloquent plea, but France. The question to be decided was whether France was still true to her character as the guardian of justice and humanity. "Dreyfus is innocent, I swear," he concluded. "By my forty years of work, by the respect earned by the work of my life, I swear that Dreyfus is innocent."

For the prosecution, General de Pellieux took the stand. The army had been subject to a base attack, he said, his commanding personality overflowing with honest indignation. He mentioned a letter that gave absolute proof of the guilt of Dreyfus—one that had not come to public attention before—and quoted a part of it from memory. But neither then nor later was this letter produced, and for good reason.

Lieutenant Colonel Georges Picquart had been brought from Mont Valerien to testify. The army was giving him a chance to redeem himself. But Picquart, who had wavered so long between conflicting loyalties, had now made up his mind. Poised and tranquil, he answered all questions truthfully. He said that he too would like to comment on the document of which General de Pellieux had spoken: "That document is a forgery."

There was dead silence in the court. Major Henry, responsible for this forgery as for others, must have writhed uncomfortably.

The trial continued for fifteen days. It was the talk of Paris, better than the theater, more exciting than anything found in books. In the end, Emile Zola was pronounced guilty and sentenced to a year in prison. Lieutenant Colonel Picquart was returned to Mont Valerien.

Zola's lawyer and Clemenceau persuaded the novelist he

would be of more use if he did not go to jail. On their insistence, he left reluctantly for London. He was out of the country when Major Esterhazy was arrested, not as a traitor, but for "moral conduct unbecoming an officer." A new Minister of War had been appointed, Godefroy Cavaignac, an avowed critic of the government's awkward handling of the Dreyfus case. Cavaignac assigned a Captain Cuignet to examine the Dreyfus file and all the secret documents that allegedly substantiated his guilt. Cuignet was studying this material when he noticed a letter with lines at the top of the page of a different shade from those of the lower part. He held it up to the light. There was no doubt about it—two sheets had been glued together. He showed the letter to Cavaignac who summoned Generals de Boisdeffre and Gonse and demanded an explanation. They knew at once whom to blame.

Major Hubert Henry was called in and accused of having taken an innocent missive and inserting incriminating statements about Dreyfus into it. Henry first denied the accusation, but after an hour of questioning, he admitted it was true. He was taken to the Mont Valerien fortress. The next day he committed suicide.

Other forgeries for which Major Henry was responsible came to light. Henry's accomplice in forgery, Lemercier-Picard, was found hanged in his room. General de Pellieux offered his resignation, on the grounds that, because of Major Henry, he had been put in the position of giving false evidence at Zola's trial. Major Esterhazy heard about Henry's suicide and confession and promptly fled to England, where he spent the rest of his life.

On October 27, 1898, the High Court of Appeal considered the petition of Mathieu Dreyfus for a revision of the Dreyfus verdict. In their investigation they studied some 373 documents from the "secret Dreyfus file." About fifty of these were obvious forgeries. The rest had nothing to do with Dreyfus. Eventually the High Court of Appeal reached a decision. The sentence of Dreyfus was null and void and he should be tried anew. In June, 1899, a telegram was dispatched to Devil's Island to return the prisoner to France.

Zola came back to Paris after eleven months' exile in England, elated at the good news. Georges Picquart, after 324 days in prison, was released. A reunion was held of the Dreyfusards. Only the aging Senator Scheurer was missing. He was near death and would not live to see the triumph of justice. In the streets of Paris a hundred thousand workers, artisans, and students paraded, singing the *Marseillaise* in a celebration that was still premature.

The new trial, held at Rennes, Brittany, opened on August 7, 1899. The central character of the case that had shaken the world was brought in by a sergeant. The spectators gasped in sympathy. At the age of thirty-nine, Alfred Dreyfus was an emaciated old man, blinking incredulously at the crowds through his glasses, his hair thin and white, his yellow skin drawn tautly over his cheekbones. But he had not forgotten his military training. He wore his uniform and held himself stiffly at attention. Once or twice he fumbled and asked to have a question repeated. Otherwise his memory did not fail him and he was specific in all his answers.

Both his own lawyer, Demange, and Zola's lawyer, Labori, served as defense attorneys. The conservatism of the older man complimented Labori's fiery defense. A week after the trial started, Labori was shot in the back. A passerby, who knelt by him supposedly to give his assistance, fled with his briefcase and papers. Fortunately, the wound was not serious and Labori could return to the trial the next week.

The dominant figure at the trial was the thin-lipped General Mercier, who had lived with the Dreyfus case for five years. Neither the forgeries of Major Henry nor the proof of Esterhazy's guilt had changed his opinion about Dreyfus. He had become "hallucinated" on the subject, people said. The trouble was that he was able to "hallucinate" others.

Demange finished his summing up of the retrial at noon of September 9. The seven judges retired, returning with their verdict shortly before five in the afternoon. By a majority of five to two, they again found that Alfred Dreyfus was guilty of treason. Labori and Demange wept. Demange could not bear to face the prisoner, waiting in an adjoining room, and it was Labori who told him the terrible news. "Console my wife," Dreyfus said gently.

In view of "extenuating circumstances," his prison sentence was reduced from life to ten years. No one explained what "extenuating circumstances" might be in a case of treason.

The decision of the Rennes trial swept the world like an evil tidal wave. Mass meetings, held as far away as Chicago and Washington, urged a boycott of everything French. Dreyfus received thousands of letters and telegrams of support. Largely to appease world public opinion, on September 19, 1899, came a formal announcement that Dreyfus was pardoned. At long last he was free.

On September 20, a carriage took him to a small railroad station outside of Rennes; unobserved, he boarded a train to Carpentras in the south of France, where his married sister, Henriette, lived. Mathieu met him at Nantes, and the evening of his arrival at his sister's he was joined by Lucie. She had come direct from Paris to avoid publicity.

Except for their brief meetings in the Rennes prison, this was their first reunion since Alfred Dreyfus had left his home so unsuspectingly that morning of October 15, 1894. The next day, his wife's family arrived with his children, Pierre and Jeanne. Dreyfus had been worried lest they be afraid of him, but they threw themselves in his arms and embraced him affectionately.

The next summer, on the advice of his physician, Dreyfus went to Switzerland with his family. They stayed in a villa looking out on Lake Geneva and the lovely snow-covered mountains of the Jura. Health came back to Dreyfus and his mind cleared, but one torment remained.

He had accepted a pardon only after making it clear that this was not enough. Why should a man be pardoned for a crime he had not committed? So asked all those who had given their time and their fortunes and their talent, and, in the case of Picquart, liberty itself, that justice might be done. The fight went on for six more years.

At last, on July 12, 1906, the Rennes sentence was set aside. Dreyfus was proclaimed innocent of the charge against him. Ten days later a military parade took place in the courtyard of the Ecole Militaire. George Picquart watched from one window and Lucie Dreyfus from another. Dreyfus, in full-dress uniform, was brought in by a captain. He was trembling. The ceremony brought back all too vividly the shameful one of his degradation. As he was led in front of Brigadier General Gillain, a trumpet blew four calls.

"In the name of the President of the Republic . . . Commander Dreyfus, I make you a Knight of the Legion of Honor," the general said. He touched his sword thrice to the shoulders of the man before him, pinned a cross on him, and kissed him on both cheeks. Pierre, Dreyfus's son, ran up and embraced him too.

As he left the parade grounds with his brother Mathieu, they were surrounded by a crowd of several hundred thousand, this time without hostility.

"Long live Dreyfus!" they called out. "Long live justice!"

After twelve long years, the Dreyfus Affair was finally closed.

THE NUREMBERG
TRIAL

"The trial which is now about to begin is unique in the history of the jurisprudence of the world and it is of supreme importance to millions of people all over the globe."

With these words Lord Justice Geoffrey Lawrence of Great Britain opened the First International Military Tribunal, on November 21, 1945, in the brightly neon-lighted courtroom of the Palace of Justice, Nuremberg, Germany. In Europe, World War II had been over just six and a half months.

Lord Justice Lawrence was both president of the tribunal and tribunal member representing Great Britain. He was one of eight men, clad in judges' robes, seated along the high bench of the courtroom: Francis Biddle for the United States, Henri Donnedieu de Vabres for France, Major General I. T. Nitikcheno for the Soviet

Union, and four alternate judges, one from each country. Behind them hung the flags of their nations.

At the tables below them were the tribunal personnel, prosecuting attorneys, court reporters, translators. In the prisoners' dock, with a row of solemn-faced young American soldiers in white helmets behind them, sat the defendants, twenty-one men who had once occupied high positions in the government of Nazi Germany.

This international court, the first in history, was trying them as major criminals. The proceedings would last 216 days, with testimony amounting to seventeen thousand pages.

That leaders of nations engaging in unjustified warfare should be brought to justice like other criminals was not a new idea. After the First World War, the Allies had turned over to the new German Weimar Republic a list of some nine hundred German war criminals. Only twelve of these were ever brought to trial, of whom six were pronounced guilty, given light sentences, and soon freed—several to fight for Adolf Hitler, the instigator of World War II. In 1943, in the midst of the fighting, the Allies had sent a warning to Germany that this time their leaders would not escape so easily, that they would be tried for their crimes not by their own country, but by the countries against which they had waged war.

Beginning on June 22, 1945, one month and fifteen days after Germany's surrender, representatives from the United States, England, France, and the Soviet Union held a series of meetings in London to complete plans for an International Military Tribunal. Its charter, signed on August 8, represented the joint efforts of these four major powers, with the approval of seventeen smaller nations.

No trial in history had ever required such extensive preparations as the International Military Tribunal.

Nuremberg was chosen as site of the tribunal, in part because this ancient city had once been the setting for enormous Nazi rallies and it seemed fitting that the true nature of the Nazis should be exposed here. Allied representatives arrived on July 21 to make preliminary arrangements. They found the city in almost total ruin as a result of Allied bombardments. A good part of the population was living in shanties built from rubble. No street cars were running and there was no electricity or potable water. Consumer goods were scarce and expensive and the only stores were wooden shacks.

A mighty rebuilding project was undertaken, with German civilians and prisoners-of-war employed for the construction work. The Grand Hotel and the Guest House, Nuremberg's two leading hostelries, which had both suffered direct bomb hits, were among the first buildings to be made habitable. The tribunal's working personnel were lodged mainly in the Guest House. The Grand Hotel was retained for official visitors from Europe and the United States.

The Courthouse, where the trial was to be held, and the adjoining Palace of Justice, which housed the tribunal's many offices, had both been severely damaged by bombs and needed extensive alterations. For this work, from July to December, 1945, 1357 soldiers put in 83,396 man-hours and German civilians gave 143,000 man-hours; 717 German prisoners-of-war were employed on an average day. Repainting the buildings took 5,200 gallons of paint. More than a million feet of wire and cable were needed to install electricity and modern electrical equipment. In a city bereft of everything, all materials had to be imported, many of them flown from the United States.

The courtroom was remodeled completely. To provide room for the 250 seats for the press, a back wall was torn out. A gallery to accommodate some one hundred visitors was built by cutting an opening into the attic. A glass booth was specially constructed for photographers, and on one side of the room was a large screen on which films could be shown.

Even water was a problem. Army Lister bags served as a substitute for drinking fountains. These water canteens held some fifteen gallons; the water was purified by dropping halazone tablets in the bag and letting it stand for thirty minutes.

Everyone present at the sessions was provided with headsets, a unique feature of the trial. Each set had a small dial, like that on a telephone, that enabled the wearer to listen to verbatim proceedings in English, Russian, French, or German. Some 550 of these earphones were purchased, mostly from the United States.

Three batteries of interpreters of twelve members each provided the translations. Each group worked from one to two hours and was then relieved by another group. The Allies pooled their interpreting personnel before the trial. They were of many nationalities and backgrounds and included college instructors, radio broadcasters, lawyers, professional interpreters, a French medical student, and one French newspaperwoman.

Whereas Socrates had only Plato to write down his defense—and that, long after the event—the trial at Nuremberg was the most carefully recorded of all time. Expert court reporters, stenotypists, and stenographers took careful notes. In addition, all proceedings were re-

corded on disks and film. In case these methods failed,
wire recordings could be made. Two sets of records
were kept, one as a permanent official record and the
other for use in checking the accuracy of the translations.

The prosecution counsel for the four participating
countries was composed of a total of fifty-two leading
jurists. Twenty-four of these were Americans, with Justice Robert H. Jackson as chief of counsel. Great Britain
had seven, headed by Sir Hartley Shawcross, chief prosecutor. General R. A. Rudenko was chief prosecutor
for the Soviet Union, which had a staff of nine prosecuting attorneys in all. The chief prosecutor for France was
François de Menthon, a former member of the French
Resistance; France had a total of twelve prosecuting attorneys.

The prosecution called a minimum of witnesses to the
stand. The reason was that, although such witnesses
would add drama, their testimony might always be subject to doubt on the grounds of bias or faulty memory.

Many witnesses, however, both Nazis and victims of
Nazi persecutions, were interviewed in private interrogations. Some nine hundred of these interrogations were
made, mostly before the trials started. They took place
in eight separate rooms of the palace, sometimes as many
as twelve interrogators working at a time. Each interrogation was attended by a court reporter, an interpreter,
and one or more attorneys and technical assistants. The
interrogator, court reporter, and interpreter were under
oath, and made a triple check of the transcript to prevent
errors. These interrogations gave valuable background
data for the prosecution.

The main foundation for the case of the prosecution

was not the interrogations or the individual witnesses but Nazi documents captured after the war—confidential archives of the German government and its branches, private diaries, secret meetings, conference reports and correspondence, even transcripts of telephone conversations of the Nazi leaders tapped by a special office set up by defendant Herman Goering. In the search for evidence, nearly three thousand tons of these documents were reviewed. Never had a nation supplied its conquerors with such a complete account of its activities.

From this mountain of material, tribunal researchers culled pertinent documents or parts of documents, to be translated and mimeographed. Before they had finished, the mimeographed translations mounted to around half a million, requiring five million sheets of paper. In addition, ninety thousand original documents were photostated. Of these, some four thousand were exhibited at the trial.

Nazi documents were supplemented by Nazi photographers. Heinrich Hoffman, Hitler's ex-photographer, was employed to classify five hundred thousand captured German negatives. Hoffman was chosen because of his intimate knowledge of pictures taken during Hitler's rule, and he was closely guarded. When defendant Herman Goering learned of Hoffman's assignment, he said, "The swine made a million marks on my pictures and now he's sorting photographs to hang me."

One of the photographic exhibits was a Nazi report called "The Warsaw Ghetto is No More," which told in pictures and text the tragic story of the ghetto's resistance. According to the report, the ghetto housed four hundred thousand Jews when it was established in November, 1940. Prior to its destruction, some 316,000 had been deported. One photograph was of a small boy, his face contorted with fear, his hands held high in surrender. A burly Nazi soldier was pointing his rifle at him. Another photographic masterpiece showed a man in mid-air as he leaped from the upper story of a blazing building set on fire by the Nazis. "Masses of them—entire families—" read the text, "were already aflame and jumped from the windows or endeavored to let themselves down by means of sheets tied together or the like. Steps have been taken so that these Jews, as well as the remaining ones, were liquidated at once."

These examples, among countless others, indicate why the prosecution was able to base its case almost entirely on evidence of the defendants' own making.

As in any trial, the defendants were allowed their own counsel. They employed forty-nine in all, forty of their own choosing and the remaining nine appointed by the court. Every facility the defense counsel needed was placed at their disposal. They had their own room in the palace and their own document library. They conferred with their clients through a screened partition. A small slot on the left side of the petition enabled them to pass papers back and forth, after they had been inspected by a guard. All the defense counsel were searched before they entered the conference room by a guard. In the course of the trial the defendants and their lawyers called a total of sixty-one witnesses and used interrogatories answered by 143 witnesses.

An essential part of the tribunal was news coverage. This was a public trial. It was not enough to bring the defendants to justice—in any case, they could never be punished to match in any measure the suffering they had caused others. What was even more important was that everyone should know the extent of their crimes, so that the world would never again allow such crimes to be repeated.

Allied correspondents from twenty-three nations attended the sessions, as many as two hundred and fifty at a time. They provided information to major networks, press associations, newsreels, newspapers, and magazines. Some wrote books about the trial. News staffs for the United States, Great Britain, France, and Russia covered the proceedings for licensed German newspapers in their various zones, to give German citizens the truth of how their country had been brought to disaster.

The castle of Baron Faber, "the pencil king," was requisitioned for the press lodgings. Some seven miles from Nuremberg, it was set in a vast park "where bronze lions slept" and was replete with marble stairways, crystal chandeliers, and impressive, if mediocre, nineteenth-century paintings. Meals were served in the grand ballroom by liberated German concentration camp inmates, and American Army officers acted as hosts.

Elaborate facilities for the press were set up. Correspondents could listen to the trial proceedings either in reserved seats in the courtroom or over loudspeakers in a separate room. Telephone and wire facilities were adjacent to working pressrooms, so stories could be filed in a minimum of time. In the trial's first week, 1,224,895 words were transmitted. Radio commentators broadcast from five soundproof booths equipped with earphones, also carrying the court proceedings.

All pictures taken in the courtroom by commercial photographers were placed in a common pool and made available to wire services and newspapers. In the courtroom special lighting made the use of flash bulbs unnecessary. As documents were introduced into the evidence, former German war prisoners carried mimeographed copies to the newsmen in the pressrooms.

Only television coverage was lacking. That would have to wait until the trial of Adolf Eichmann some fifteen years later.

While the trial lasted—more than ten months—there was no busier place in Europe. Nearly three thousand persons, including some four hundred visitors, passed through the portals of the Palace of Justice on a normal day. A six-position switchboard, manned by GI's, was installed to take care of the vast number of phone calls. On busy days, the GI's handled as many as six hundred long-distance calls.

Since this was a trial of German nationals by Germany's conquerors and held in Germany, the fullest safety precautions were warranted. No one could enter the Palace of Justice or the courthouse without the blue pass issued through the security office, bearing the photograph of the person who carried it. There was regular inspection of handbags and parcels of the five-hundred-odd German civilians employed in the buildings, and no women visitors were allowed to carry handbags.

The surrounding area was one of the most heavily defended in the occupied zone. While the court was in session, five Sherman tanks armed with 76mm. guns, all equipped with radios tuned to the main security office, guarded the two buildings. A roadblock could have been set up in a matter of minutes. In February, 1946, sandbag barricades were built in key spots around the courthouse and soldiers armed with machine guns were stationed behind them. In the jail an air-raid siren was installed. Nine guards armed with clubs guarded the prisoners while they sat in the dock. When a defendant was on the stand, twelve guards were on duty. Guards were a minimum height of five feet, ten inches, and were always taller than the man they guarded.

Perhaps because of these precautions, or perhaps because the German people no longer cared about what happened to their former bosses, no attempt was made to engineer an escape.

Beginning in August, 1945, the defendants were lodged in individual cells in the Nuremberg jail, near the courthouse. The cell block was three tiers high. As a security measure, eight thousand feet of wire mesh were fastened along the tiers. After defendant Robert Ley committed suicide, guards were stationed outside each cell, night and day.

Defendants were permitted to walk in the dreary jail yard forty minutes daily. Only defendant Rudolf Hess insisted on goose-stepping in the Nazi manner. A covered passageway was built the short distance from the jail to the courthouse basement. Each day of the trial the prisoners were escorted along this passageway by guards, then brought up to the courtroom in the elevator, two at a time.

The prison cells had a minimum of furniture and none of it was allowed within four feet of the window wall. The cot was fastened to the floor. At night the single chair was removed. Meals, plain but adequate, were served from GI mess kits and had to be eaten with a spoon, since knives and forks were forbidden. Prisoners could write their families one letter and two cards each week. They were permitted to have books and a few personal belongings.

The twenty-one defendants were not spoiled; neither

were they mistreated as the Nazis had mistreated their own countless prisoners. Who were the defendants, and why had the International Military Tribunal decided they should be held responsible and brought to trial for the crimes of a nation? Before proceeding further with the story of their trial, it is time to stop and briefly identify them.

HERMAN GOERING. Former President of the Reichstag (the German parliament); minister for air forces, commander in chief of the air force, president of the council of ministers for the defense of the Reich (the German Government); field marshal and general in the SS (Hitler's elite guard, known as "Blackshirts"). In the heyday of his power, Goering had strutted grandly, a stout, bellicose figure in his splendid uniform decorated with the medals of his rank. Since his arrest he had lost weight. His moon-shaped face was wrinkled, there were pouches under his eyes, and his uniform, shorn of insignia, hung on him loosely. His gestures were still regal and his expression was as mocking and cynical as ever. "Corrupt and a drug addict," Hitler had called Goering when he turned against him the last days of the war.

JOACHIM VON RIBBENTROP. He had been Reich Minister of Foreign Affairs, member of the secret cabinet council and of Hitler's political staff, and general in the SS, but at Nuremberg he seemed a frightened and weary man. His sparse gray hair crowned a thin drawn face, with narrow lips, sharp nose, and receding chin. His co-defendant, Von Schirach, dubbed him a "social upstart"; since Ribbentrop was not of noble birth, Von

Schirach pointed out, he had no right to use "von" as part of his name.

WILHELM KEITEL.   Between 1938 and 1945, he had been chief of the high command of the German armed forces, a field marshal, member of the secret cabinet council and the council of ministers for the defense of the Reich. Like Goering, he still wore his uniform, without insignia. This former rigid German militarist, now that his authority was gone, gave the impression of an obsequious, cringing character.

ERNST KALTENBRUNNER.   Under Hitler, he had been chief of the security police and head of the RSHA (Reich central security office), which included the Gestapo, the SD (security service) and the *Einsatzgruppen* (the task forces assigned to follow the army and murder civilians). He was a gaunt man with a lantern jaw and a flat, expressionless face. The scar across his cheek was the result of a saber duel in his youth. Perhaps more than any of the others, he looked the part of a villain.

ARTHUR ROSENBERG.   He had joined the Nazi party at its inception in 1920, and supervised Nazi secret agents sent to all parts of the world. Hitler had rewarded him by making him Reich leader for ideology and foreign policy, head of the Nazi Foreign Political Office, Reich Minister for Eastern Occupied Territories. As editor of the Nazi newspaper *Völkischer Beobachter*, he spouted a muddled philosophy designed to justify anti-Semitism. This "philosopher of the Nazis" was ponderous, boring, and vicious.

HANS FRANK. As "Hitler's lawyer," he was given the titles of Reich commissar for the coordination of justice; president of the International Chamber of Law and Academy of German Law; Reich Minister Without Portfolio, and eventually, Governor General of the Occupied Polish Territories. A reporter at the trial summed him up as a "dark, dapper, bouncy fellow."

WILHELM FRICK. At the trial he wore a loud sports jacket of brown and green. His hair was cropped short and there was a childlike smirk on his aging features. Like Hans Frank, he was a lawyer and his titles under Hitler included general in the SS, Reich minister of the interior, Reich director of elections, general plenipotentiary for the administration of the Reich; head of the central office for the reunification of Austria and the German Reich, and director of the central office for the incorporation of Sudetenland, Memel, and Danzig.

JULIUS STREICHER. For more than twenty-five years, Streicher spoke, wrote, and preached hatred of the Jews. His weekly paper, *Der Stuermer*, thrived on lurid tales of alleged Jewish crimes and his obscenity revolted even his Nazi comades. When Hitler was in power, Streicher was a member of the Reichstag and a general of the SA (Hitler's storm troopers or "Brownshirts"), and rarely appeared in public without a whip in his hand or in his belt. He liked to boast about how many times he had used it on "Jewish infidels." At the trial, the court at Nuremberg saw only a bald, withered old man who muttered insanely and inanely that the judges were all Jews.

FRITZ SAUCKEL.   Former general in the SS and the SA, and, as plenipotentiary general for the allocation of labor, in charge of the vast Nazi program of importing forced labor from occupied countries. A sneering little man with round pig-eyes and tiny mustache whom Goering, not noted for loyalty to his codefendants, called "the dullest of the dull." The testimony of the court would bring forth a more apropos designation: "most evil of the evil."

ALFRED JODL.   Once he had been chief of operations for the High Command of the German armed forces, and chief of staff under Keitel. A native of Bavaria, with an apoplectic complexion and receding hairline, he still had more of the air of a Prussian officer than his superior, Keitel.

ARTHUR SEYSS-INQUART.   This former Viennese lawyer had been a secret Nazi party member before the outbreak of the war, when he was serving in the cabinet of the Austrian Chancellor, Schuschnigg. His intrigues against his own countrymen won him the dubious honor of being "the first Quisling." (Quisling was the Norwegian Nazi who betrayed his country). Hitler rewarded him by making him Nazi Chancellor of Austria after Austria capitulated. Later, as Reich Commissioner for Occupied Netherlands, he became better known as "the butcher Governor of Holland." During the trial he chewed gum incessantly; otherwise his manners were impeccable.

RUDOLPH HESS.   Hess was one of Hitler's first supporters, an active member of the Nazi party from 1921 to

1941, personal deputy to Hitler, Reich Minister Without Portfolio, general in the SS and the SA. In May, 1941, without authorization, he set off alone for Scotland in a fighter plane, under the delusion that he could arrange a peace settlement with England on Hitler's terms through the Duke of Hamilton, whom he had met at the Olympic Games. During most of his trial he claimed amnesia (loss of memory). Obviously mentally disturbed, he was frightening in appearance, with grayish skin drawn taut, sunken cheeks, and wide eyes staring out beneath his bushy black eyebrows.

WALTER FUNK.   This fat, bald, shifty-eyed man was the financial genius who negotiated a deal between the Nazis and the leading German industrialists that brought millions into the Nazi party coffers. Hitler appointed him his economic adviser and press chief of the Reich government. Funk's ruthless treatment of Russian prisoners-of-war made him a special target for the Soviet representatives at Nuremberg.

ERIC RAEDER.   From 1928 to 1945 he was commander in chief of the German navy. His other titles included general-admiral, grand admiral, admiral inspector of the German navy, and secret cabinet council member. He was a swashbuckling figure at one time, never without his ornate gold-handled dagger and a heavily padded uniform with wide lapels that made him look like a broad-shouldered athlete. The slight, mild-mannered man in the dark blue suit sitting in the prisoners' dock at Nuremberg would have looked more comfortable behind the counter of a country grocery store.

ALBERT SPEER.   A former architect, he had served Hitler as Reich minister for armament and munitions and commander in chief of labor organization. Together with defendant Fritz Sauckel, in defiance of international law he had enlisted prisoner-of-war and slave labor in the millions to work in armament plants. A dark-haired, powerfully built man, six feet, three inches tall, whose haughty bearing had survived the humiliation of prison.

BALDUR VON SCHIRACH.   This blond-haired blue-eyed Teuton, whose voice was gently persuasive, had, as Reich Youth leader, the job of warping with race hatred the minds of some ten million German children. As Reich Governor and Gauleiter of Vienna, he authorized the deportation of Viennese Jews to the wretched ghettos of Eastern Europe. At thirty-eight, Von Schirach was the youngest of the defendants.

CONSTANTIN VON NEURATH.   The aristocratic Baron von Neurath, now a white-haired old man, had been Ambassador in London at the time of Queen Mary and George V. He claimed to despise the Nazis, but he had given his diplomatic skills to the New Germany and served Hitler as general in the SS, Reich Minister of Foreign Affairs, president of the secret cabinet council, and Reich Protector for Bohemia and Moravia.

KARL DOENITZ.   "Kill and keep on killing," the thin-lipped Doenitz had told his submarine commanders back in the days when he was commander in chief of the U-boat arm of the German navy. "Remember, no survivors. Humanity is a weakness." Hitler thought so highly of Doenitz' lack of "humanity" that he made him his successor—just a few days before Germany's collapse. In his cheap store suit, without uniform or medals, he appeared a very ordinary figure, as unimpressive as his former commander in chief, Eric Raeder.

HJALMAR VON SCHACHT. The former Reich Minister of Economics and president of the German Reichsbank was a tall man, stiff as a plank. His considerable contribution to Nazi Germany was a financing system known as "Mefo bills," by which huge sums were raised to pay for the secret rearming of Nazi Germany. Several years later he turned against Hitler; for his part in a conspiracy to overthrow him, he was confined in the concentration camp of Dachau.

FRANZ VON PAPEN. This fastidious German nobleman had preceded Hitler as Chancellor of Germany and served under him first as Vice Chancellor and later as Ambassador to Turkey and Austria. No one was more expert at diplomatic intrigue than he; at seventy, he gave the impression of a wily old fox.

HANS FRITSCHE. He had headed the radio division of the Propaganda Ministry under Josef Goebbels, with the title of Plenipotentiary of the Political Organization of the Great German Radio. This youngish broadcaster of Nazi propaganda was generally regarded the least important of the major Nazi war criminals.

All twenty-one of these men had known high position and honors in an evil state with a twisted morality and under a fanatical leader. Now they would be tried for crimes so hideous they surpassed human understanding. Rather to the surprise of many of the trial's spectators, who knew of their deeds but not of the men who had done them, they did not look like monsters. No more did they look like members of what Adolf Hitler liked to call the "master race." As time went on, they seemed to shrink in stature and take on a similar aspect, as though all had been molded from the same gray clay.

There were some Nazis whose rank and responsibility in Nazi Germany would warrant their presence at the trial, but who were missing. Their leader, Adolf Hitler, according to very substantial evidence, had shot himself on April 30, 1945, as Berlin was being surrounded. So had Josef Goebbels, his sinister Minister of Propaganda. Heinrich Himmler, chief of the Reich political police, was captured by the British at the end of the war but had escaped being brought to trial by swallowing a vial of potassium cyanide, said to have been hidden in his gums. Reinhard Heydrich, deputy chief of the Gestapo, whom the people of Czechoslovakia had named "Hangman Heydrich," was assassinated by two Czechs on May 29, 1942.

Another absentee, frequently mentioned in the trial's testimony, was Adolf Eichmann, chief of the Jewish Office of the Gestapo, who once boasted of sending five million Jews to their death. He escaped from an American internment camp and fled to Argentina. It would be fifteen years before he, too, would be tried—and condemned to death—in Israel, the new country of the people he had persecuted so mercilessly.

Twenty-three defendants had been named in the original indictment, two more than were brought to trial. Robert Ley, who, as chief of the German Labor Front, had reduced German workers to the status of medieval serfs, had been arrested and taken to Nuremberg but, like Himmler, had found a way out. A month before the trial's opening he hanged himself in his cell with an army towel torn in strips. Also indicted was Martin Bormann, Hitler's personal secretary. He was thought to have been killed by Russian fire the last days of the war and was tried *in absentia*. There is some doubt about Bormann's fate. He is still being sought as these pages are written.

The trial that had taken such long and thorough planning, the First International Military Tribunal for major Nazi war criminals, opened on November 20, 1945, with an address by Lord Justice Lawrence, the tribunal president. The defendants were charged on four counts:

1. Conspiracy to seize power, establish a totalitarian regime, and prepare and wage a war of aggression.

2. Crimes against peace—the actual waging of aggressive wars.

3. Violation of the laws of war—of international conventions, internal penal laws, and of general principles of criminal law.

4. Crimes against humanity, including imprisonment in concentration camps, use of torture, deliberate extermination of noncombatants.

The formal indictment of the defendants, a long document of more than twenty-eight thousand words, was read aloud. To clarify the nature of the "four counts," it traced the "Nazi conspiracy" from its inception. The defendants stirred restlessly during the reading. The indictment had been served on them in their cells before they came to trial and they were familiar with its contents. The rise of a nobody to the position of dictator in his own country and a threat to the well-being of the world was an old and boring story to them. Others could not take so lightly this strange and terrible drama.

It was in Munich, on July 29, 1921, that Austrian-born and unemployed Adolf Hitler became chairman of a shabby group of misfits who called themselves the National Socialist German Workers Party, *Nationalsozialistische Deutsche Arbeiterpartei*, abbreviated to *Nazi*. Hitler, a frustrated artist, designed their flag—red with a white disk, a black swastika in the center. Allegedly to keep hecklers away but in reality to terrorize other political parties, the Nazis recruited a gang of tough ex-servicemen, who were outfitted in brown uniforms and called the SA, or storm troopers.

In 1923, the Nazis risked an abortive insurrection, known as the "Beer Hall *Putsch*," since it started in a beer hall. Goering, Hess, Streicher, Frank, and Rosenberg were with Hitler in this ill-planned attempt to seize power. Hitler was subsequently tried for treason and sentenced to five years at Landsberg fortress, of which he served only five months.

During his imprisonment Hitler dictated *Mein Kampf* to his fellow prisoner, Rudolf Hess. The book, a blueprint of Hitler's plan for world conquest, was widely read but few took its warning seriously.

The Nazi party quickly recuperated from its setback, due largely to Hitler's driving ambition. In 1925, he created the SS known as "Blackshirts" because of their black uniforms, an elite guard that soon rivaled the storm troopers in acts of violence. By 1928 the Nazis succeeded in electing twelve deputies to the Reichstag and polled two per cent of the total vote. In 1932, they elected 196 deputies and had 33½ per cent of the vote.

On January 30, 1933, through a series of shrewd intrigues, Hitler became German Chancellor. He selected Von Papen as Vice Chancellor and a cabinet that included Von Neurath, Goering, and Wilhelm Frick. The Nazi party still did not have a majority vote.

Less than a month later, on February 27, a fire broke out in the Reichstag (the German parliament). The Nazis falsely blamed the Communists, and Hitler used the fire as an excuse to suspend the basic civil rights granted by the constitution and to throw Communist deputies in prison. The Reichstag was shorn of its powers by an "emergency" edict of March 15; henceforth its member deputies had little to say in Hitler's government. The next day Schacht was appointed president of the National Bank (*Reichsbank*).

New edicts followed in rapid succession. A death penalty was evoked for "crimes against public security." A boycott against Jewish doctors, lawyers, and business houses was the first step toward sweeping anti-Semitic laws that eventually deprived Jewish citizens of their right to existence. Christian leaders who criticized Nazi brutality were thrown in prison. Trade unions were banished and, with them, all rights of organized labor. Books not in agreement with Nazi ideology were publicly burned. Hitler appointed Hess as deputy leader of the party.

Under Goering, the first concentration camps were built to hold the increasing masses of prisoners—Jews, Communists, Christians, men and women denounced as "enemies of the State," and even those suspected of *harboring unfavorable thoughts* toward the state. Heinrich Himmler, a plump-faced, monocled former chicken

farmer, was made chief of the Prussian Gestapo and began to build up a Nazi secret police empire.

The weak had no place in the New Germany. Mentally ill persons were taken from sanitariums, escorted
to specified centers, and killed by injections. This was
Hitler's first experiment in mass murder.

When the aged German President, Paul von Hinden-
burg, died on July 25, 1933, Hitler declared himself head
of the German State. Henceforth he was absolute dictator. He alone made the laws that ruled Germany.

To formulate and carry out his edicts and plans Hitler
enlisted his own staff—masters of propaganda like Rosenberg, Streicher, and Fritsche; the lawyers Frank and
Frick; financiers such as Schacht and Funk; military
men: Keitel, Jodl, Doenitz, and Raeder; experts on foreign intrigue: Ribbentrop, Von Neurath, Von Papen;
others . . .

In a Germany impoverished by World War I, Hitler
won popular support by preaching rearmament. On
March 9, 1935, the government announced the existence
of its Luftwaffe (Air Force) in violation of the Versailles Treaty, which marked Germany's surrender at the
end of World War I in 1918. In 1936 German troops
marched into the demilitarized Rhineland, in defiance of
the Locarno Pact. In April, 1937, the Luftwaffe, fighting
for Franco in the Spanish Civil War, destroyed the un-
defended Spanish town of Guernica, slaughtering thousands of civilians. Spain was a testing ground for German might. Brazenly, rearmament continued. In October, the Italian-German Axis Pact was announced.

In March of 1938, Germany took over Austria. "Case
Otto" was the code name given to the Austrian con-

quest. On October 1, troops entered the Sudeten terri-
tory, ceded to Germany by the Munich Pact, an agreement made with the Italian leader, Mussolini, England's
Chamberlain, and France's Daladier. Germans occupied
Czechoslovakia (Case Green) in March of 1939. In August, a Soviet-German Non-Aggression Pact was signed
by the Russian foreign minister Molotov and German
foreign minister Von Ribbentrop, an uneasy agreement
of brief duration. On September 1, the Nazis crossed the
Polish border (Case White). Warsaw, Poland's capital,
fell into German hands eleven days later.

Germans invaded Norway and Denmark in April of
1940. ("Weser Exercise" was the Nazi code name for
these two conquests.) Holland capitulated on May 14.
Two weeks later, King Leopold of Belgium surrendered
the Belgian army. ("Case Yellow" covered the invasion of the Netherlands, Belgium, and little Luxembourg.) Paris fell on June 14, and when, six days later
Germany and France signed an armistice at Compiègne,
Adolf Hitler danced a jig of triumph. Britain was next
on the list, but after heavy air losses, the Nazi decided to
postpone an invasion attempt.

In September, Germany, Italy, and Japan signed a
three-power agreement known as the Tripartite Pact.
On October 6, German troops entered Rumania. Hitler's
wars of aggression continued in 1941, with an invasion
of Yugoslavia and Greece (Case Marita) on April 6,
and an invasion of the Soviet Union (Case Barbarossa)
on June 22, in breach of the Soviet-German pact. On
December 7, Japanese planes attacked Pearl Harbor and
Japan was at war with the United States and Great
Britain. Four days later, Germany and Italy declared
war on the United States.

The small group that only twenty years before had named itself the Nazis and taken the swastika as its symbol had set half the world on fire. But they never invaded England. Nor did they reach Moscow, stopped by winter snows and the fortitude they did not expect of the Soviet armies. And the United States, like a slow-to-anger lion, rallied its forces and charged into the fight so that mankind could be free again. The bombs stopped falling at midnight May 8, 1945. At a little red schoolhouse at Reims, France, General Jodl had, the previous day, signed Germany's surrender.

The Nazi had violated all existing treaties, the rules of the Hague Convention, and international law. Their barbarities, which had commenced with dissenters and those of Jewish heritage among their own people, had extended to all the countries they had captured. Public and private property had been plundered on a mass scale. Occupied countries had been forced to pay exorbitantly for their own enemy occupation. They had been stripped of food, coal, raw materials, art treasures, people. The Nazis had committed piracy at sea and wanton devastations of cities, towns, and villages.

The indictment listed instances of these barbarities, dryly and factually.

Regarding treatment of prisoners-of-war:

"Frequently prisoners captured in the Western Front were obliged to march until they completely collapsed. . . . Many ill-treatments were submitted without motives . . . stabbing with bayonets, striking with rifle butts, and whipping; in Stalag XXB the sick themselves were beaten many times by sentries. . . . In May, 1942, one loaf of bread only was distributed in Rava-Rusha to each group of 35 men. . . ." American prisoners were starved, beaten and otherwise mistreated in numerous Stalags in Germany and in the occupied countries . . . in 1943, 1944, 1945 . . . Soviet prisoners were murdered *en masse*. . . .

About treatment of civilians and inmates in the three hundred-odd concentration camps:

"Out of a convoy of 230 French women deported from Compiègne to Auschwitz in January 1943, 180 died of exhaustion by the end of four months . . . 143 Frenchmen died of exhaustion between 23 March and 6 May 1943 in Block 8 at Dachau . . . 22,761 deportees died of exhaustion at Buchenwald between 1 January 1943 and 15 April 1945 . . . 780 priests died of exhaustion at Mauthausen . . . of 228,000 French political and racial deportees in concentration camps only 28,000 survived . . ."

A new word sprang up in the 1940's—"genocide," meaning the deliberate killing of nationalities or ethnic groups. The Nazis made this word a reality:

"About 1,500,000 persons were exterminated in Maidanek and about 4,000,000 in Auschwitz . . . In the Lwow region, the Germans exterminated about 700,000 Soviet people, including 70 persons in the fields of the arts, science, and technology, and also citizens of the United States of America, Great Britain, Czechoslovakia, Yugoslavia, and Holland, brought to the region from other concentration camps.

". . . in the Ganov camp 200,000 peaceful citizens were exterminated. The most refined methods of cruelty were employed in this extermination, such as disemboweling and freezing of human beings in tubs of water. Mass shootings took place to the accompaniment of the music of an orchestra recruited from the persons interned. . . . They brought many persons to those camps from typhus hospitals intentionally, for the purpose of infecting the other persons interred. . . . In the Latvian SSR, 577,000 persons were murdered. . . . In the Leningrad region there were shot and tortured over 172,000 persons. . . . After the Germans were expelled from Stalingrad more than a thousand mutilated bodies of local inhabitants were found with marks of torture. . . . In the Crimea over 144,000 peaceful citizens were gathered on barges, taken out to the sea and drowned. . . . In Babi Yar, near Kiev, they shot over 100,000 men, women, children and old people. . . ."

The indictment, with its fearful statistics, continued. . . .

On November 21, the second day of the trial, Otto Stahmer, lawyer to defendant Goering, rose to carry through the formality of contesting the legality of a trial of war crimes and asked that the tribunal be declared incompetent. Lord Justice Lawrence ruled that the conclusions of the defense were contrary to the tribunal charter and that the court reject them.

All the defendants pleaded "not guilty" or "not guilty in the sense of the indictment."

Justice Robert Jackson, chief counsel for the United States, opened the Anglo-American part of the prosecution:

"May it please Your Honors," he began, "The privilege of opening the first trial in history for crimes against the peace of the world imposes a grave responsibility. The wrongs which we seek to condemn and punish have been so calculated, so malignant and so devastating, that civilization cannot tolerate their being ignored because it cannot survive their being repeated. That four great nations, flushed with victory and stung with injury, stay the hand of vengeance and voluntarily submit their captive enemies to the judgment of the law is one of the most significant tributes that Power ever had paid to Reason. . . ."

On November 22, the American counsel Colonel G. Storey began the case of the prosecution by describing how the Nazi documents on which the trial was based were traced down—some found in a salt mine, some hidden behind a false wall in a Bavarian castle. Counsel Frank R. Wallis, reviewing the growth of the Nazi party, quoted Hitler as saying in a secret cabinet meeting, "We can suppress the Communists and eliminate the Reichstag," just three days before the Reichstag fire, used as an excuse to accomplish both aims. A secret order to send all German Communists to concentration camps was signed by defendants Von Papen, Von Neurath, Frick, Goering, and Frank, a first step toward eliminating all opposition. Another order read by Wallis was signed by absent defendant Martin Bormann: "The Nazi party can be assured of absolute control of Germany only if the people are separated from the Church. . . . If the young are raised in complete ignorance of Christianity it will disappear of itself."

Day after day the prosecution built up its massive case involving each defendant in turn. For instance, on November 23, United States prosecutor Thomas Dodd described defendant Schacht's intensive efforts to raise money for Hitler's war and Counsel Wallis elaborated on how Von Shirach, leader of German youth, supported the dismissal of all professors who did not follow the Nazi line. On November 27, United States Counsel Sidney Alderman read from a secret book published in 1937, *The German Fight against the Treaty of Versailles*, which described the resurrection of the German navy under defendant Raeder.

On November 29, the prosecution introduced a unique type of evidence—a transcript of actual telephone calls made by defendant Goering to various personages in Vienna on March 11, 1938. In these calls, made from two o'clock in the afternoon until ten at night, Goering arranged the resignation of Austrian Chancellor Schuschnigg (later deported to Dachau) and appointed defendant Seyss-Inquart, the Austrian Quisling, in his place, with an all-Nazi cabinet—all before the German army marched triumphantly into Austria. (Austria was really conquered by telephone, it was said later.)

In the prisoners' dock, Goering, Ribbentrop, and Hess found the show extremely amusing. Their smiles and smirks stopped when American Commander Donovan presented a documentary film on Nazi concentration camps, as they were found by American troops: piles of dead in a slave labor camp . . . a Buchenwald crematorium . . . Dachau . . . men in striped suits more like skeletons than human beings . . . a female doctor describing the agonizing "medical" experiments on female prisoners at Belsen . . . women's corpses being thrown into a pit. . . .

During the showing of the atrocity film, Herman Goering covered his eyes with both hands. Keitel played with his earphone cord and turned away several times. Doenitz clenched his fists, looking at the picture only occasionally. Von Papen would not look at all. Sauckel kept shaking his head. Funk broke down and cried. Rosenberg fidgeted continually. Fritsche became tense and pale. Only Streicher and Von Neurath watched, seemingly without emotion.

The first witness for the prosecution was questioned on November 30. He was General Erwin Lahousen, ranking surviving member of Abwehr (counterintelligence), who had been part of an underground movement against Hitler led by Admiral Canaris. Lahousen testified that defendants Goering, Keitel, and Jodl worked closely with Hitler in planning the bombardment of Warsaw, and that, after Poland was invaded on a trivial excuse, they ordered the extermination of Polish Jews as well as of Polish nobility, clergy, and intelligentsia. ("Poland shall be treated as a colony," wrote defendant Frank, as Governor General of Occupied Poland. "The Poles shall be the slaves of the Greater German World Empire.")

On November 30, defendant Hess rose and made the dramatic announcement that his memory had returned, adding that he had simulated amnesia as a strategy, even deceiving his own lawyer. Within a few minutes radio broadcasters had his statement on the air all over the world. Psychiatrists were dubious of his claim to mental clarity.

The hearing of December 3 was devoted to the five defendants, Goering, Keitel, Raeder, Jodl, and Ribbentrop and the part each had played in Nazi aggression against Czechoslovakia. This marked the end of the strictly American part of the prosecution proceedings.

The next day, British Counsel Sir Harley Shawcross opened the English prosecution with a speech on the criminal nature of aggressive war as the Nazis had waged it. On December 5, British Counsel Sir David Maxwell-Fyfe listed violations by the Reich of international law and of existing treaties between 1933 and 1941, and Counsel G. D. Roberts, also a Britisher, produced evidence to show that defendant Keitel had ordered the invasions of Belgium, Holland, and Luxembourg. On December 11, a captured Nazi film showed some of the defendants in their days of glory. One of the scenes in this film was the Luftwaffe bombardment of the fjord of Oslo.

Later, Counsel Wallis read from a remarkable diary written by defendant Frank: "That we sentence 1,200,-000 Jews to die of hunger should be noted only marginally. It is a matter of course that should the Jews not starve to death it would, we hope, result in a speeding up of anti-Jewish measures." And from a Polish document describing the gassing of Jews at Treblinka and Auschwitz: "All victims had to strip off their clothes and shoes, which were collected afterwards, whereupon all victims, women and children first, were driven into the death chambers. . . . Small children were simply thrown in."

To Captain Gilbert, the prison psychiatrist, defendant Sauckel said later, wringing his hands: "I want to tell you that I know absolutely nothing of these things, and I certainly had absolutely nothing to do with them!" His protest of ignorance and innocence was a clue to the defense of all the defendants.

The next days unfolded the tragic story of the importation of foreign workers who, while technically not prisoners, were in fact slaves. In January, 1945, these foreign workers in Germany totaled 6,500,000, including 2,500,000 Russians; over 1,500,000 French; 150,000 from Belgium; 431,000 from Holland. It was shown that the men largely responsible for the "continuance and upkeep" of the supply of human beings were defendants Sauckel and Speer, and that Ley, Frank, Goering, Rosenberg, Seyss-Inquart, and Keitel had a share in this assignment. From Heinrich Himmler: "Whether ten thousand females fall down from exhaustion while digging an anti-tank ditch or not interests me only insofar as the anti-tank ditch for Germany is finished."

The two "prime materials" of occupied countries were "agricultural products and human labor," wrote Sauckel—who throughout the trial insisted he knew nothing of concentration camp exterminations—in a letter to defendant Rosenberg. Also quoted was a missive from Rosenberg to Sauckel, dated December 12, 1942; "We are now in the grotesque situation of having to recruit millions of workers from occupied Russia after war prisoners have died like flies, in order to fill the gaps that have formed within Germany."

A secret report enclosed with Rosenberg's letter described how forced labor was "recruited": "In order to secure the required number for the labor transport, men and women, including youngsters from fifteen years on up, are taken from the street, from the market place and village festivals . . . inhabitants hide themselves in fear. . . . After public beatings . . . came the burning down of homesteads and of whole villages as retributions for failure to comply with the demand for the appropriation of labor forces. . . ."

A German doctor's report portrayed all too vividly the conditions under which the foreign workers lived: "In some camps there were twice as many people in barracks as health conditions permitted. . . . The diet prescribed for eastern workers was altogether insuffi-

cient. . . . Sanitary conditions were exceedingly bad.
. . . Tuberculosis was widespread. . . . As a result of
the filthy conditions nearly all eastern workers were af-
flicted with skin disease. . . . With the onset of heavy
air raids in March, 1943, conditions greatly deteriorated.
. . . At times the water supply was completely shut off
for periods of eight to fourteen days . . ."

On December 14, documents were presented to show
the horrors of the concentration camp of Flessenburg.
It was there that on Christmas of 1944, the camp commanders devised the ingenious cruelty of hanging prisoners from lighted Christmas trees. The entire camp was
summoned to witness the spectacle.

The prosecution on this day presented the most ma-
cabre exhibit of the trial: a shrunken human head and a
piece of tattooed human skin. They were souvenirs of
Buchenwald, though these indignities were practiced at
other camps as well. "It is dangerous to have a good skin
at Dachau," inmates there claimed. Franz Blaha, a Czech
physician imprisoned at Dachau, later testified that he
had been forced to remove skin from the dead, and that
this skin was used for women's handbags, lampshades,
and other gruesome mementos.

On December 17, Colonel Storey, showing how the
Nazi party had tried to suppress Christianity, quoted a
secret decree of Martin Bormann: "National Socialist
and Christian concepts are irreconcilable"—a statement
with which millions would agree. During the next days,
Storey gave concrete evidence of the persecution of the
Catholic Church. He also described the Nazi pillage of
great art treasures of occupied Europe, giving staggering statistics of this pillage and naming Rosenberg, Kei-

tel, Frank, and Goering as responsible for a mass robbery that could not in any way be excused as a "military
necessity."

The tribunal was adjourned for the Christmas recess.
The defendants spent the holidays in their cells. The
correspondents, most of them, took off for brief vaca-
tions to Nice or Cannes or some other festive resort.
The American soldiers stationed in Nuremberg gave a
party for children from the nearby displaced persons
camp—for some of them the first party they had ever
celebrated. A Mickey Mouse film was shown, refresh-
ments were served. The children devoured the sand-
wiches but many stared in bewilderment at the ice cream
and cake.

On January 3, the prosecution resumed, still basing its
charges on Nazi documents. Colonel Storey named defendant Kaltenbrunner as author of an inhuman order to
annihilate certain concentration camps before the Allies
arrived. . . . Witness Otto Ohlendorf, Hitler police chief,
testified he had personally ordered the massacre of ninety
thousand Russian Jews. When asked if he had scruples,
he said that, being only a subordinate, he had to obey.
. . . Next, factual evidence was produced of the murder of prisoners-of-war, including British parachutists.
. . . Frank's terrible diary was quoted again: "I have not
hesitated to announce that for each German killed, we
will shoot a hundred Poles." It was Frank who, in
August, 1942, when forty per cent of the Polish population was sick as a result of malnutrition, ordered that
their rations must be cut in half so that more food could
be sent to Germany. . . . British prosecutor Colonel
Griffith-Jones quoted defendant Streicher, after he had

beaten the Jewish Professor Steinruch in his cell until the blood flowed: "Now I feel better."

The French prosecution began on January 17 with an opening address by François de Menthon:

"France, who was systematically plundered and ruined; France, so many of whose sons were tortured and murdered in the jails of the Gestapo or in their concentration camps; France, who was subjected to the still more horrible grip of demoralization and return to barbarism diabolically imposed by Nazi Germany, asks you, above all in the name of the heroic martyrs of the Resistance, who are among the greatest heroes of our legend, that justice be done . . ."

Heroes of the Resistance, of whom M. de Menthon was one, had sprung up in all the occupied countries, men and women who risked their own lives and those of their loved ones to carry on an underground war against the Nazi invaders. When captured, as many of them were, the Gestapo had almost invariably tortured them to force them to reveal the names of their leaders and comrades.

Gestapo "third degree" methods were endorsed officially by Heydrich, not only for members of resistance groups but for "Communists, Marxists, Jehovah's Witnesses, saboteurs, terrorists . . . parachute agents, asocial elements, Polish or Soviet Russian loafers, or tramps." "Third degree can, according to the circumstances," continued this same endorsement, "consist among other methods of: very simple diet (bread and water); hard bunk; dark cell; deprivation of sleep; exhaustive drilling; also in flogging (for more than twenty strokes a doctor must be consulted)." The "other methods" included hanging up the victims by the hands until their shoulders were dislocated, cutting soles of their feet with razor blades and then making them walk on salt; forcing victims to watch torture of husband or wife; squeezing their heads with an iron band.

Justice Robert Jackson, examining a former Gestapo official: "I am asking you as to the crimes committed by the Gestapo . . . if it included the torturing of thousands of persons?"

The witness: "Yes."

The French prosecution included Counsel Charles Gerthofer's account of the German economic exploitation of France that had brought financial ruin to the country and near-starvation to its people. It ended with a condemnation by Pierre Mounier of defendant Rosenberg, who justified the stealing of art treasures from the Rothschild family on the grounds that the Rothschilds were Jewish.

The Soviet Union prosecution began on February 8. General Rudenko, in his opening address, described in all its horrors the Nazis' massive devastation of the eastern countries:

"When entire regions of flourishing countryside were turned into desert areas, and the soil was drenched with the blood of those executed, it was the work of their hands, of their organization, their instigation, their leadership. And just because the masses of the German people were made to participate in these outrages, because . . . the defendants for years had poisoned the conscience and the mind of an entire generation of Germans by developing in them the conceit of 'the chosen,' the morals of cannibals and the greed of burglars, can it be said that the guilt of the Hitlerite conspirators is any less great or grave? . . . The populations of . . . Slav countries first of all, were subjected to merciless persecutions and mass extermination. Russians, Ukranians, Belo-Russians, Poles, Czechs, Serbians, Slovenes suffered more than others. . . .

"In the name of the sacred memory of millions of innocent victims of the fascist terror," he concluded, "for the sake of the consolidation of peace throughout the world, for the sake of the future security of nations, we are presenting the defendants a just and complete bill that must be paid. This is a bill on behalf of all mankind, a bill backed by the will and the conscience of all freedom-loving nations. May justice be done."

For ten days the Russians, who had lost twenty-five million lives in the holocaust, hammered out the Nazi crimes. On February 19 they presented their atrocity film, a document of mass murder even more frightful than the American film: acres of corpses of Russian prisoners-of-war murdered or left to starve in the fields where they had been captured . . . guillotines and instruments of torture . . . bodies hanging from lampposts as they were found when their towns were recaptured . . . baskets of human heads . . . children who had been beaten to death . . . women weeping over their dead . . . bales of women's hair, taken from the living and the dead alike . . . the ruins of Lidice. This Czechoslovakian town was razed to the ground in reprisal for the assassination of Reinhard "Hangman" Heydrich; its male population executed; its women sent to concentration camps and its children transported to Germany to be brought up in the Nazi manner. The name of Lidice has become synonymous with horror throughout the world.

The defendants were unaffected. Throughout the film, the paunchy Goering pretended to read a book, yawned in boredom, and occasionally turned to make a sarcastic remark to Hess or Von Ribbentrop.

The Soviet documentation of Nazi crimes proceeded relentlessly. A surviving Jewish resident of the Russian town of Vilna described the slaying of all but six hundred of the town's eighty thousand Jewish population. A woman survivor of Auschwitz testified she had seen Jewish children thrown alive into the crematorium furnaces. Russian prosecutor Colonel Smirnov read a Nazi document authorizing the wholesale murder of the sick at concentration camps.

At this point in the testimony, Herman Goering removed his earphones.

The counsels for the prosecution from four nations— Great Britain, United States, France, and the Soviet Union—had now spent more than three months presenting their case against the Nazi war criminals. They had gone into great detail, of which there has been space in these pages to give only a few examples, and they could, from the material at hand, have gone on endlessly. It would only have been more of the same—mass murder, torture, robbery, slavery, the breaking of treaties, and the cynical disregard of international law. There had to be a halt to this nightmare. On March 7, 1946, the case of the prosecution was completed. On March 8, the defense of the defendants began.

Herman Goering, former President of the Reichstag and commander in chief of the Nazi air force, was the first of them given the opportunity, in accordance with legal practice, to proclaim his innocence or deny the charges against him.

He called as one of his witnesses his former adjutant, Bodenschatz, who testified that Goering was a good-hearted man, since he had secured the release of his personal friends from concentration camps. On March 13, Goering took the witness stand himself. His hands trembled and his face twitched, and with little of his usual bravado, he gave his version of the growth of the Nazi party, minimizing his own part in it.

Justice Robert Jackson began the cross-examining of Goering on March 20. As specific accusations of specific crimes bombarded him, Goering repeated over and over that his intentions had been good, that it was his duty to be loyal to Adolf Hitler, no matter what that loyalty involved. But he could not deny that he had more influence on Hitler than any other man up until 1943, that he had supported the anti-Semitic decrees within Germany, including the levying of a fine of a billion marks on the Jewish population, and that he had said to Reinhard Heydrich, after the pogroms of November 9 and 10, 1938, "I wish you had killed two hundred Jews and not destroyed such valuable property." He had made this statement, Goering contended, in "spontaneous excitement."

Sir David Maxwell-Fyfe took over Goering's cross-examination on March 21, facing him with proof of the murder of imprisoned British RAF officers who had tried to escape, and with handing Russian prisoners-of-war over to the Gestapo. Goering denied all responsibility.

In the course of the cross-examination, Goering became increasingly arrogant. "That is irrelevant," he said on several occasions, and, "Do not distort my words." When Lord Justice Lawrence stepped in to cross-examine him, Goering went too far. "I did everything to avoid this war," he declared piously. "But after it had started it was my duty to do everything to win it."

"We have heard you say that before and we do not wish to hear it again," Lawrence snapped at him.

Goering's testimony, the longest of any of the defendants, lasted until March 22, on which day General Rudenko made a brief cross-examination for the Soviet Union, and the French prosecutor stated there was nothing to add.

"Well, I didn't cut a *petty* figure, did I?" Goering boasted to Captain Gilbert, the prison psychiatrist, when it was over.

The defense of Rudolf Hess, Hitler's close comrade for more than twenty years, came next. Hess did not take the stand himself. His excuse was another spell of amnesia; he was afraid of embarrassment in case he could not remember the answers to the questions of the prosecution. Two witnesses called to testify in his favor did him little good. His defense was concluded within three days.

He was followed by Joachim von Ribbentrop, the tired old man who had once been Hitler's powerful foreign minister. He testified with the air of believing what he said, that he and Hitler did not like war, that they had broken pacts only with the greatest regret, and that he had lost two nights' sleep when the Low Countries were invaded. Like all the other defendants, he insisted he knew nothing of Nazi atrocities.

Sir David Maxwell-Fyfe cross-examined him:

Q. Are you saying that you did not know that concentration camps were being conducted on an enormous scale?

A.   No, I knew nothing of that . . . I can say that I had heard of only two concentration camps before I came here—no, it was three, Dachau, Oranienburg, and Theresienstadt.

Q.   Are you telling the tribunal that . . . you never heard of the camp at Mauthausen, where a hundred thousand people were shut up?

A.   That was entirely unknown to me, and I can produce dozens of witnesses who can testify to that.

Q.   I do not care how many witnesses you produce. . . . Are you telling the tribunal that anyone could be a responsible minister in that country where hundreds of concentration camps existed and not know anything about them but two?

A.   It may be amazing but it is absolutely true.

Q.   Did you know that at Auschwitz alone . . .

A.   I heard the name Auschwitz here for the first time.

Q.   The German official at Auschwitz has sworn in an affidavit that four million people were put to death in the camp. Are you telling the tribunal that happened without your knowing anything about it?

A.   That was entirely unknown to me. I can state that here on my oath.

Of all the defendants, only one, Hans Frank, author of the diary that served again and again to prove Nazi callousness toward human life, made a partial confession. He was asked if he had participated in the destruction of the Jews.

"I say yes. . . . We have fought against Jewry; we have fought against them for years. . . . A thousand years will pass and the guilt of Germany will not be erased."

As for the others, they knew nothing, had seen nothing, had done nothing but follow the orders of their superiors. Keitel said he had only done his duty as a soldier. Arthur Rosenberg, the "philosopher of the Nazis," claimed he had always been in favor of "a chivalrous solution of the Jewish problem." The filthy old man, Julius Streicher, described himself as an "apostle of anti-Semitism," but blandly denied all knowledge of atrocities against the Jews. Hjalmar von Schacht, the former Reich Minister of Economics, claimed he had supported Hitler in the beginning only because his program had not sounded so bad, emphasizing that later he had plotted to overthrow him, which was true. (Cross-examination forced his admission that in spite of his alleged disapproval of Nazism he had assumed control for Hitler of Austrian and Czechoslovakian banks, and that he had made speeches glorifying the "Fuehrer.")

Eric Raeder, former grand admiral and commander in chief of the German navy, insisted he believed Hitler had peaceful intentions and had attacked Czechoslovakia and Poland only for "security reasons." Baldur von Schirach described his Hitler Youth as a mild Boy Scout-type of organization, interested mainly in sports. Alfred Jodl spoke of himself as a professional soldier, not interested in politics. The wily Franz von Papen said he had been astounded when he heard of the outbreak of war in 1939. ("You were prepared to serve these murderers as long as your dignity was put right!" Sir David Maxwell-Fyfe pointed out.)

Albert Speer admitted that he had employed some prisoners-of-war in his armament factories but denied knowledge that this was against the rules of the Hague Convention. He contended he had been against bringing forced labor into Germany, and ended his testimony with an anguished lament against Hitler for "betraying" him.

Karl Doenitz, the U-Boat commander, also said he had never heard of concentration camps, and in cowardly fashion blamed his subordinates for all the crimes of his command. He grew flustered, however, when asked for an explanation of his order: "Do not pick up survivors and take them with you. . . . We must be harsh in war."

Walter Funk, the little banker, knew nothing at all about his verified agreement with Heinrich Himmler to store in the state banks or send to pawn shops the personal belongings of concentration camp victims, a weird loot that included coins, bank notes, jewels, watches, and even gold from eyeglasses and gold fillings from teeth.

All the defendants lied. With one exception, all revealed under cross-examination that they were far more deeply involved than they wanted to admit. The exception was defendant Ernst Kaltenbrunner, Nazi chief of the security police, who proved the most blatant perjurer of them all. According to his testimony, during his two years in office he never signed a "protective custody order" or a death sentence. He established no concentration camps, or so he said. He was confronted with a sworn and detailed statement by former Mauthausen prisoners that they had seen him there and that he had witnessed executions and visited the crematorium. "I can refute this document in every point," he announced. His signature on various significant orders did not faze him. He simply denied the signature was his.

By the third of July the prisoners had completed their

defense and their lawyers began their summations.

Dr. Stahmer made his plea for Goering, spending most of his allotted time analyzing his client as "psychologically interesting." (A dodge to hide Goering's lack of moral sense, Speer said to his fellow prisoners.) Dr. Horn, speaking for Ribbentrop, explained that it was Hitler who determined foreign policy, not his client. Dr. Nelte, Keitel's lawyer, based his defense on the *Fuehrerprinzip*, the "leader principle"; that is, he held that Keitel should be exonerated because he was only a soldier, obliged to obey orders.

Dr. Marx, Streicher's lawyer, characterized his client as a fanatic anti-Semite who had never been taken seriously by either Hitler or the German people, thus ironically dealing a severe blow to Streicher's vanity. Dr. Sauter, for Von Schirach, pleaded leniency on the ground that the former Hitler Youth leader had repented and denounced Nazism and anti-Semitism.

The lawyers for the other defendants continued their summations along similar lines.

Justice Robert Jackson gave the summation speech for the American prosecution on July 26. There had been a great deal of eloquence in this long trial, but nothing that had been said was more moving or more damning to the defendants than when Jackson pointed to each in turn, summing up the charges against him.

". . . we have now before us the tested evidences of criminality and have heard the flimsy excuses and paltry evasions of the defendants. The suspended judgment with which we opened this case is no longer appropriate. The time has come for final judgment and if the case I present seems hard and uncompromising, it is because the evidence makes it so. . . .

"The large and varied role of GOERING was half militarist and half gangster. He stuck a pudgy finger in every pie. . . . He used his SA musclemen to help bring the gang into power. In order to entrench that power he contrived to have the Reichstag burned, established the Gestapo, and created the concentration camps. . . . He built up the Luftwaffe and hurled it at his defenseless neighbors. He was among the foremost in harrying the Jews out of the land. By mobilizing the total economic resources of Germany he made possible the waging of the war which he had taken a large part in planning. He was, next to Hitler, the man who tied the activities of all the defendants together in a common effort. . . .

"The zealot HESS, before succumbing to wanderlust, was the engineer tending the party machinery, passing orders and propaganda down to the leadership corps, supervising every aspect of party activities, and maintaining the organization as a loyal and ready instrument of power. When apprehensions abroad threatened the success of the Nazi scheme for conquest, it was the duplicitous RIBBENTROP, the salesman of deception, who was detailed to pour wine on the troubled waters of suspicion by preaching the gospel of limited and peaceful intentions. KEITEL, weak and willing tool, delivered the armed forces, the instrument of aggression, over to the party and directed them in executing its felonious designs.

"KALTENBRUNNER, the grand inquisitor, took up the bloody mantle of Heydrich to stifle opposition and terrorize compliance, and buttressed the power of National Socialism on a foundation of guiltless corpses. It was ROSENBERG, the intellectual high priest of the 'master race,' who provided the doctrine of hatred which gave the impetus for the annihilation of Jewry, and who put his infidel theories into practice against the eastern occupied territories. His woolly philosophy also added boredom to the long list of Nazi atrocities. The fanatical FRANK, who solidified Nazi control by establishing the new order of authority without law, so that the will of the party was the only test of legality, proceeded to export his lawlessness to Poland, which he governed with the lash of Caesar and whose population he reduced to sorrowing remnants. FRICK, the ruthless organizer, helped the party to seize power, supervised the police agencies to insure that it stayed in power, and chained the economy of Bohemia and Moravia to the German war machine.

"STREICHER, the venomous vulgarian, manufactured and distributed obscene racial libels which incited the populace to accept and assist the progressively suave operations of 'race purification.' As Minister of Economics FUNK accelerated the pace of rearmament, and as Reichsbank president banked for the SS the gold teeth fillings of concentration camp victims—probably the most ghoulish collateral in banking history. It was SCHACHT, the façade of starched respectability, who in the early days provided the window-dressing, the bait for the hesitant, and whose wizardry later made it possible for Hitler to finance the colossal rearmament program, and to do it secretly.

"DOENITZ, Hitler's legatee of defeat, promoted the success of the Nazi aggressions by instructing his pack of submarine killers to conduct warfare at sea with the illegal ferocity of the jungle. RAEDER, the political admiral, stealthily built up the German navy in defiance of the Versailles Treaty, and then put it to use in a series of aggressions which he had taken a large part in planning. VON SCHIRACH, poisoner of a generation, initiated the German youth in Nazi doctrine, trained them in legions for service in the SS and Wehrmacht, and delivered them up to the party as fanatic, unquestioning executors of its will.

"SAUCKEL, the greatest and cruelest slaver since the Pharaohs of Egypt, produced desperately needed manpower by driving foreign peoples into the land of bondage on a scale unknown even in the ancient days of tyranny in the kingdom of the Nile. JODL, betrayer of the traditions of his profession, led the Wehrmacht in violating its own code of military honor in order to carry out the barbarous aims of Nazi policy. VON PAPEN, pious agent of an infidel regime, held the stirrup while Hitler vaulted into the saddle, lubricated the Austrian annexation, and devoted his diplomatic cunning to the service of Nazi objectives abroad.

"SEYSS-INQUART, spearhead of the Austrian fifth column, took over the government of his own country only to make a present of it to Hitler, and then, moving north, brought terror and oppression to the Netherlands and pillaged its economy for the benefit of the German juggernaut. VON NEURATH, the old-school diplomat, who cast the pearls of his experience before Nazis, guided Nazi diplomacy in the early years, soothed the fears of prospective victims, and as Reich Protector of Bohemia and Moravia, strengthened the German position for the coming attack on Poland. SPEER, as Minister of Armaments and War Production, joined in planning and executing the program to dragoon prisoners of war and foreign workers into German war industries, which waxed in output while the laborers waned in starvation.

FRITSCHE, radio propaganda chief, by manipulation of the truth goaded German public opinion into frenzied support of the regime and anesthetized the independent judgment of the population so that they did without question their master's bidding."

Jackson had a word to say too of the twenty-second defendant, Martin Bormann, whose crimes were no less because he had died, or vanished, before they came to light: "And BORMANN, who has not accepted our invitation to this reunion, sat at the throttle of the vast and powerful engine of the party, guiding it in the ruthless execution of Nazi policies, from the scourging of the Christian church to the lynching of captive Allied airmen. . . .

"In opening this case I ventured to predict that there would be no serious denial that the crimes charged were committed, and that the issue would concern the responsibility of particular defendants. The defendants have fulfilled that prophecy. Generally, they do not deny that these things happened, but it is contended that they 'just happened,' and that they were not the result of a common plan or conspiracy. . . .

"These men in this dock, on the face of the record, were not strangers to this program of crime, nor was their connection with it remote or obscure. We find them in the very heart of it. The positions they held show that we have chosen defendants of self-evident responsibility. They are the very top surviving authorities in their respective fields and in the Nazi state. No one lives who, at least until the very last moments of the war, outranked Goering in position, power, and influence. No soldier stood above Keitel and Jodl, and no sailor above Raeder and Doenitz. Who can be responsible for the duplicitous diplomacy if not the Foreign Ministers, Von Neurath and Ribbentrop, and the diplomatic handyman, Von Papen? Who should be answerable for the oppressive administration of occupied countries if Gauleiters, Protectors, Governors, and Commissars such as Frank, Seyss-Inquart, Frick, Von Schirach, Von Neurath, and Rosenberg are not? Where shall we look for those who mobilized the economy for total war if we overlook Schacht, and Speer, and Funk? Who was the master of the great slaving enterprise if it was not Sauckel? Where shall we find the hand that ran the concentration camps if it is not the hand of Kaltenbrunner? And who whipped up the hates and fears of the public, and manipulated the party organizations to incite these crimes, if not Hess, Von Schirach, Fritzsche, Bormann, and the unspeakable Julius Streicher? The list of defendants is made up of men who played indispensable and reciprocal parts in this tragedy. The photographs and the films show them again and again together on important occasions. The documents show them agreed on policies and on methods, and all working aggressively for the expansion of Germany by force of arms.

"Each of these men made a real contribution to the Nazi plan. Every man had a key part. . . .

"It is against such a background that these defendants now ask this tribunal to say that they are not guilty of planning, executing, or conspiring to commit this long list of crimes and wrongs," Jackson concluded. ". . . If you were to say of these men that they are not guilty, it would be as true to say there has been no war, there are no slain, there has been no crime."

The First International Military Tribunal continued another month for the purpose of passing judgment on

a number of Nazi organizations that had been indicted.
Four of these, the Leadership Corps of the Nazi party,
the Gestapo, the SD, and the SS were all judged criminal
in nature. On September 30 and October 1 the tribunal
rendered its verdict on the defendants. Eleven were sentenced to death by hanging. Three were given imprisonment for life. Four were sentenced to terms of ten to
twenty years, and three were acquitted on the grounds
that there was a reasonable doubt as to their guilt:

	VERDICT	SENTENCE
GOERING	GUILTY on counts 1, 2, 3, 4	Death by hanging
HESS	GUILTY on counts 1, 2	Life imprisonment
RIBBENTROP	GUILTY on counts 1, 2, 3, 4	Death by hanging
KEITEL	GUILTY on counts 1, 2, 3, 4	Death by hanging
KALTENBRUNNER	GUILTY on counts 3, 4	Death by hanging
ROSENBERG	GUILTY on counts 1, 2, 3, 4	Death by hanging
FRANK	GUILTY on counts 3, 4	Death by hanging
FRICK	GUILTY on counts 2, 3, 4	Death by hanging
STREICHER	GUILTY on count 4	Death by hanging
FUNK	GUILTY on counts 2, 3, 4	Life imprisonment
SCHACHT	NOT GUILTY	
DOENITZ	GUILTY on counts 2, 3	10 years imprisonment
RAEDER	GUILTY on counts 1, 2, 3	Life imprisonment
VON SCHIRACH	GUILTY on count 4	20 years imprisonment

SAUCKEL	GUILTY on counts 3, 4	Death by hanging
JODL	GUILTY on counts 1, 2, 3, 4	Death by hanging
VON PAPEN	NOT GUILTY	
SEYSS-INQUART	GUILTY on counts 2, 3, 4	Death by hanging
SPEER	GUILTY on counts 3, 4	20 years imprisonment
VON NEURATH	GUILTY on counts 1, 2, 3, 4	15 years imprisonment
FRITSCHE	NOT GUILTY	

Martin Bormann, who was tried *in absentia*, was also found guilty and sentenced to hanging.

On October 15, the night before the executions were scheduled, Goering asked the prison chaplain for the Lord's Supper and the blessing of the Lutheran Church. The chaplain refused, saying that Goering had never shown any sign of repentance. Sometime that night or early morning Goering chewed a capsule of cyanide of potassium, said to have been passed to him by his wife. No doubt he died gloating that he had played a final trick on his captors. Ribbentrop was the first of the remaining condemned to be hanged in the grimy, barnlike gymnasium inside one of the prison yards of the Nuremberg jail. The executions took just one and a half hours.

Two months later, in December, 1945, the Allied Control Council established military tribunals in each of the four zones into which Germany had been divided, for the purpose of trying lesser Nazi criminals. Between 1947 and 1949, the United States tribunal conducted twelve individual trials, all at Nuremberg.

The Nuremberg "Medical Trial" charged twenty-four defendants, of whom twenty were physicians, with responsibility for dangerous, painful, and usually fatal experiments on some hundreds of thousands of human subjects, prisoners, allegedly for science. The "Justice Case" charged sixteen defendants with committing war crimes and crimes against humanity through abuse of the judicial process. The "Pohl Case" tried Oswald Pohl and seventeen other heads of concentration camps and slave labor camps. The "I. G. Farben Case" charged twenty-four defendants, officers of this international chemical company, with spoliation of property in invaded countries and participation in the Nazi slave labor program. The "Krupp Case" charged twelve defendants, including high executives of the Krupp industrial empire, with similar crimes. The "Einsatzgruppen Case" charged twenty-three officers of the SS Elite Guard and heads of extermination squads for murder of some two million persons.

In these twelve trials, 185 Nazi war criminals were indicted, of whom more than half received prison terms, while twenty-four were sentenced to hanging.

The Nuremberg Trial also served as a precedent for the "Tokyo War Crimes Trial" in which certain Japanese political and military leaders were charged with engaging in criminal acts against the laws of nations.

From beginning to end, the various military tribunals were the subject of debate and discussion. Some said it would have been better to shoot the war criminals and have it over with. Certain jurists questioned their legality. Could an international tribunal be a true court of law, since there was no world state in existence? Their legal aspect has been analyzed in innumerable articles and books. That many defendants were released or given light sentences, for lack of sufficient evidence, has caused bitterness and some disillusionment.

Whatever their failings, the First International Tribunal at Nuremberg and the trials that followed marked a milestone in legal history. Said Lieutenant Commander Whitney Harris, one of the United States prosecution counsel, "The most significant thing about Nuremberg is that it happened."

The trials set a pattern for punishment of makers of aggressive wars for future generations to follow or modify. In so doing, they have provided a powerful weapon against such wars. Just as significant, they created a fully documented account of the rise of Nazism and Fascism, with their wake of suppression of human rights, war, lawlessness, robberies, tortures, and murders. No informed person could ever say that perhaps their crimes and atrocities had been exaggerated. They are all on the record for anyone to read.

BIBLIOGRAPHY

SOCRATES

Couch, H. N. *Greece*. New York: Prentice Hall, 1951.

Durant, Will. *The Life of Greece*. New York: Simon & Schuster, 1939.

Montgomery, John, Editor. *The State Versus Socrates*. Boston: Beacon Press, 1954.

Plato. *Dialogues of Plato*. Selections from the Translation of Benjamin Jowett, Edited by William Chase Green. New York: Liveright Publishing Corp., 1927.

Plutarch. *Plutarch's Lives*. Edited by Eduard C. Lindeman. New York: New American Library, 1950.

Winspear, Alban D. and Silverberg, Tom. *Who Was Socrates?* The Gordon Company, 1939.

JOAN OF ARC

Michelet, Jules. *The Life of Joan of Arc*. The Spencer Press, 1937.

Scott, W. S. *The Trial of Joan of Arc*. Westport, Conn. Associated Booksellers, 1956.

Shaw, Bernard. *Saint Joan, Major Barbara, Androcles and the Lion*.* New York: The Modern Library, Random House, 1956.

Stolpe, Sven. *The Maid of Orleans*. New York: Pantheon Press, 1956.

GALILEO

Clason, Clyde B. *Men, Planets and Stars*. New York: G. P. Putnam's Sons, 1959.

* While Shaw's great play is fictionalized and takes liberties with the sequence of events, the long Preface to *Saint Joan* gives an excellent account of the times she lived in and an original interpretation of her character.

De Harsanyi, Zsolt. *The Star-Gazer*. New York: G. P. Putnam's Sons 1939. (A Novel)

De Santillana, Giorgio. *The Crime of Galileo*. Chicago: University of Chicago Press, 1955.

Fermi, Laura and Bernardini, Gilberto. *Galileo and the Scientific Revolution*. New York: Basic Books, 1961.

Galileo. *Discoveries and Opinions of Galileo*. Edited by Stillman Drake. Garden City, New York: Anchor Books, Doubleday & Company, 1957.

PETER ZENGER

Buranelli, Vincent. *The Trial of Peter Zenger*. New York: New York University Press, 1957.

Brown, James Wright. *Life and Times of John Peter Zenger*. New York: *Editor and Publisher*. March 14 through April 11, 1953.

Goodwin, Maud Wilder. *Dutch and English on the Hudson*. New Haven, Conn., 1919.

Konkle, Burton Alva. *Life of Andrew Hamilton*. Philadelphia: National Publishing Co., 1941.

Rutherford, Livingston. *John Peter Zenger*. New York: Dodd, Mead & Company, 1904.

ROBERT EMMET

Emmet, Thomas Addis, M.D., LL.D. *Memoir of Thomas Addis and Robert Emmet*. Two Volumes. New York: The Emmet Press, 1915.

Landreth, Helen. *The Pursuit of Robert Emmet*. New York: Whittlesey House, 1948.

Madden, R. R. *The Life and Times of Robert Emmet*. New York: Excelsior Publishing House, 1901.

Postgate, R. W. *Dear Robert Emmet*. New York: Vanguard Press, 1932.

ALFRED DREYFUS

Chapman, Guy. *The Dreyfus Case*. New York: Reynal & Company, 1955.

Dreyfus, Pierre. *The Dreyfus Case*. New Haven, Conn.: Yale University Press, 1937.

Halasz, Nicholas. *Captain Dreyfus*. New York: Simon & Schuster, 1955.

Josephson, Matthew. *Zola and His Time*. Garden City, New York: Garden City, New York.

THE NUREMBERG TRIAL

Bernstein, Victor H. *Final Judgment*. New York: Boni & Gaer, 1947.

Crouquet, Roger. *Le Procès de Nuremberg*. Paris: Editions Dupuis-Charleroi, 1946.

Fishman, Jack. *The Seven Men of Spandau*. New York: Rinehart & Company, 1954.

Gibb, Andrew Dewar. *Perjury Unlimited*. Edinburgh: W. Green & Son, Ltd., 1954.

Gilbert, G. M. *Nuremberg Diary*. New York: Farrar, Straus and Cudahy, 1947.

Harris, Whitney R. *Tyranny on Trial*. Dallas, Texas: Southern Methodist University Press, 1954.

Jackson, Robert H. *The Nürnberg Case*. New York: Alfred A. Knopf, 1947.

Keeshan, Anne (text) and Alexander, Charles W. (photographs). *Justice at Nuernberg*. Marvel Press, 1946.

Reitlinger, Gerald. *The SS—Alibi of a Nation*. New York: The Viking Press, 1957.

Shirer, William L. *The Rise and Fall of the Third Reich*. New York: Simon and Schuster, 1960.